POLITICAL GOVERNANCE

POLITICAL GOVERNANCE

(In 3 Volumes)

(Public Policy and Administration)
Volume 3

Editor
J.C. Chatturvedi

ISHA

ISHA BOOKS
Delhi-110033

Political Governance
(Public Policy and Administration)

Rs. 2500 (Set)
Rs. 835 (Each Volume)

ISBN : 81-8205-208-4 (Set)
ISBN : 81-8205-318-8 (Vol. 3)

Published in 2005 in India by
Isha Books
D-43, Prithviraj Road,
Adarsh Nagar, Delhi - 110033
e-mail : ishabooks@hotmail.com

Laser Typesetting at : Global Printers, New Delhi
Printed at :
Rajdhani Printers, Ph. : 011-23215190

Contents

Preface

It is generally acknowledged that development is impossible in the absence of true democracy, respect for human rights, peace and good governance. Governance is the complex ensemble of mechanisms, processes, and institutions through which citizens and social groupings manage their interests and conflicts. It manages a society's internal functions as well as its relationship with the outside world and thus guarantees its stability and adaptability.

The term 'political governance' is defined as the manner in which power is exercised in the management of a country's economic and social resources for development. The role of good political governance is critical for it determines human societies' ability to equip themselves with systems of representation, institutions, rules, procedures, measuring tools, processes and social agents that are capable of managing interdependencies in a peaceful manner.

This work in three volumes is designed for students and scholars in a wide range of disciplines, including political science, history, legal studies, etc. It provides important insights into theoretical and practical aspects of political governance in detail. The first volume *Political Theory* provides an effective and sophisticated analysis of various political theories. Undertaking a conceptual approach, the second volume, *Comparative Politics* provides a comprehensive introduction to the field. The third volume, *Public Policy and Administration* provides a detailed description of the salient theories, issues, and concepts within the broad fields of public policy and public administration.

Editor

1

Introduction

Public administration is, broadly speaking, the implementation of policy within a state framework. The adjective 'public' denotes 'government'. It is different from private administration. A good working definition is, "taking care of the state's, and international organizations', business by civil servants within the executive branch of government, other than public policy."

Like law or medicine, but unlike economics and political science/politics, public administration is the term both for the subject matter and for the academic study of the same.It is used to denote the activity/art of administration as well. The more specific term public management refers to ordinary, routine or typical management concerns, but in the context of achieving public good with public infrastructure. There is necessarily some overlap between the terms.

According to Thomas A. Birkland's book *An Introduction to the Policy Process*, there is a "lack of a consensus definition of public policy. Thomas Dye argues that this search for a definition of public policy can degenerate into a word game." That said, here is a starting point.. Public policy is the study of policy making by governments. A government's public policy is the set of policies (laws, plans, actions, behaviors) that it chooses.

Since governments claim authority and responsibility (to varying degrees) over a large group of individuals, they see fit to establish plans and methods of action that will govern that society.

Birkland offers these common traits of all definitions of public policy:

— The policy is made in the "public's" name.

— Policy is generally made or initiated by government.

— Policy is interpreted and implemented by public and private actors.

— Policy is what the government intends to do.

— Policy is what the government chooses not to do.

The field of public policy involves the study of specific policy problems and governmental responses to them. Political scientists involved in the study of public policy attempt to devise solutions for problems of public concern. Public policy, of course, overlaps with many other subject areas. Other related areas include political science, government, philosophy, economics, law, social welfare, public administration, public health, and statistics.

People of different political persuasions have varying ideas about the proper purpose of government. One way to evaluate the success of public policy is to examine the extent to which it increases the well-being of its citizens. But how is well-being defined? Should governments strive for equality of condition, i.e. to eliminate poverty and hunger? Or should governments strive for equality of opportunity, i.e. that all people have access to the tools they need to shape their own future? An interesting way to illustrate differences in public policy approaches is to consider the tradeoff between equality and efficiency:

Equality

A government policy that seeks to increase equality (of

condition) usually does so by redistributive means, i.e. taxing the rich and channeling the funds to help low-income people.

To some, such redistribution seems unfair. For example, consider a rich person who feels that he has earned every penny of his income. He would ask, "why should my income be taxed away and given to the poor, who did not work for it?" His argument has two key underlying points. First, the government's philosophy of giving money to the poor is wrong, because it will not encourage the poor to work harder. Second, the government's taxation process is relatively inefficient and therefore money is wasted as it passes through layers of government bureaucracy.

To others, redistribution is the humane thing to do. Government should provide a safety net to keep society running smoothly. There are empathetic as well as practical reasons for this. One, these believers in social welfare argue that not all poor people are lazy. Everyone has rough times and needs some help from time to time; one cannot always rely on private charity, so it makes sense for the government to step in. Two, a civil society tends to have less crime and allows stronger economic growth. Three, do wealthy people really deserve to keep 100% of their profits? Does not the government provide roads, national defense, stability, and a good climate for economic activity? How could anyone become wealthy if there was no rule of law? Proponents of redistribution would say that paying taxes is a simple matter of reimbursing government for the services that it provides.

Efficiency

A government policy that seeks to increase efficiency usually does so by market-based means, i.e. making policies that allow free markets to function smoothly.

It is generally recognized that a free market leads to significant disparities in wealth. Economists often say that the rich and powerful deserve the money they earn by working long and hard hours. Moreover, such hard work leads to innovations. These innovations spill over and help propel society forward. Therefore, all of society gains. In this way, "a rising tide lifts all boats."

Critics say that the rich and powerful have got that way due to an uneven playing field. Sure, many are intelligent and do create good innovations. What concerns the social minded critics is that the richer keep getting richer while the poor get poorer. This gap in wealth tends to lead to a dysfunctional society. Should not all people be guaranteed certain things, such as a quality education and decent wages?

A Not-so-idealistic View of Public Policy

In a democracy, an idealist would like to see policies created to serve the public interest. There is a less mainstream way to view the policy-making process; skeptics would argue that the real goal of public policy is to increase the wealth and power of the rulers and wealthy. Hopefully, along the way, the health and well-being of the general society is improved as well, but that cannot be guaranteed.

Freedom of the Press

According to the United States Constitutional notions of freedom of the press, journalists should be free to report about anything at all. (The Constitution does offer some limitations on these freedoms, however.) Market forces will drive journalists to communicate to masses of people about major problems. Some of these problems may be domestic social issues and some may be foreign policy issues. In time, new policies may lessen these problems. While this frequently annoys the wealthy and powerful, they also benefit from the improved society. (A rioting, unstable society is no good for business, after all.)

Republican Government

The basic political structure of a group should be controlled in some fashion by people with ordinary amounts of wealth and no power. If this group does not have control, it will create rebels and organize, especially if modern communication methods are available. While this definitely annoys the wealthy and powerful, it also is the only known method of creating a stable government. Since social stability is essential to the creation and maintenance of wealth and power, it directly benefits wise members of wealthy and powerful groups.

Since government administration can be a real specialty, the most long lasting governments generally assign it to specialists, and yet give ordinary citizens some say in the decisions and selection of the specialists. This is called a republic.

A Government of Law, not People

The government should be subject to law, in such a way that it can be predicted and controlled. Again, this is a two-edged sword that both hampers and benefits the wealthy and powerful. The advantage to the poor and weak is that they can form common cause and use legal means to redress major social wrongs. In general, the government's deliberations, laws and budget should be published. Without this, the above safeguards may fail.

A Free Market

A free market creates extremes of both wealth and poverty. However, some say that it is so much more efficient than other systems that it should be encouraged to be the primary means to distribute wealth. The government generally adjudicates contracts and regulates fair weights and measures. More recently, governments have regulated industrial wastes. One of the more successful programs has issued permits for a fixed tonnage of a pollutant, and established a market in permits. Private groups are permitted to purchase and retire pollution permits.

As well, polluters then have an incentive to invest in technology to reduce pollutants and sell their permits. Still, the market is less efficient in fields that would be regarded at "market failures," even in basic economic terms: Natural monopolies, public goods, and imperfect information, for example, prevent consumers from making efficient decisions because they cannot judge the quality and price of different suppliers. In health care, brain scans vary from $1,000 to $10,000, and competition is almost nonexistent because consumers have few ways to compare prices the way they do with the latest cell phone.

Others argue, however, that the "free market" as a whole is in fact a misnomer, since it actually requires a large number of regulations supporting private property, e.g., patents and anti-trespassing laws. In the end, it requires as many laws as a "non-free" market, just of a different sort.

Adoption of Positive Economies of Scale

Some networks and services have positive economies of scale. That is, as they are more widely used, they become more valuable. The classic examples are money, weights and measures, roads, a common language, public education, and an agreed public ethical system. With industrialization, a large number of other situations have developed positive economies of scale: screw profiles, a thousand types of industrial linkages and methods, networks to provide credit, water, electric power, gas, sewage, telephone and data, computer operating systems, computer languages, and media.

The most advantageous regulation seems to be for the government to wait for a standard to predominate in the market, then require use of the prominent standard, and suppress the rest. This can be done benignly by simply having the government refuse to purchase other standards. This method was used from antiquity until the European religious wars of the 1700s trained western society to value freedom.

The classic method seems to retain all of its ancient advantages for industrial standards, even though it arguably fails for religion and ethics. The classic method succeeded for measures and, eventually, even for a calendar. A universal money, gold, was once available. One of the most valuable, peculiar and complex networks is a network for credit. Traditionally, this was centered on a national bank that certified subscribers. A credit network allows money to flow anywhere in the countries that subscribe. The advantage is that regional economies have access to more credit when they need to borrow to plant crops or improve structures (both are seasonal in many areas). In the past, in such situations, regional banks would often lend all their money, and then stop lending because no more money was available. This limits production, as well as limiting recovery from natural disasters.

Military Defense

Successful governments develop means to perform a military defense of their regions. The wealthy and powerful limit the power of these groups by inculcating (and perhaps believing) propaganda about civic duties. Many long-term republics supplement this with a civil militia, and political and military structures that are not centralized, and therefore not easy to conquer or subvert.

Health and Safety

Successful governments develop regulations to preserve health and safety. The more notable successes are public sanitation, drinking-water, health-education, vaccination and quarantine programs, and building codes. Successful governments develop means to provide some minimal care for paupers and during emergencies. The level of care can be extremely crude, as long as it is not life-threatening. The classic, relatively successful programs are social security, with private investment, unemployment insurance paid for by workers, and some sort of civil defense or emergency program. The emergency and civil defense programs can be far more effective if made part of education and building codes.

Progressive Taxation

It is known that certain types of taxation are very difficult for poor people. Many poor people are poor not because they do not work hard. For these people, assembling large amounts of cash money on a fixed date can be nearly impossible. Therefore, poll taxes and franchise taxes are traditionally thought evil.

Science Policy

Some scientific research costs little compared to the pain, suffering, and expense that new techniques can prevent. At the same time, much basic research may not produce products that can be sold, and thus might never be supported by business. A progressive science policy that combines both utilitarian science, and inexpensive basic science and technology development can thus help people quite a bit.

When public policy and large financial or other stakes are in the balance, vested interests will often resort to "junk science" to support their positions. But few among the general public can judge whether science is junk or not. Many people choose simply to disregard the results of any research that was not conducted and paid for by disinterested parties, a tactic that often excludes most or all of the scientific evidence that exists on an issue.

Consider the following example. A company is releasing a chemical into a stream. Environmentalists offer "scientific evidence" that the chemical is harmful in the amounts being released. The company offers "scientific evidence" that the release is harmless. Unable to evaluate the science, the public is liable to weigh the evidence according to their prejudices—for example, that companies or that environmentalists are never to be trusted. In the face of such disputes, the government may call for an independent scientific assessment. But this is not so tidy a solution as it looks. A dispute may then erupt regarding the composition of the assessment committee, whether about the independence of particular scientists or about the balance between committee members who tend toward one side or the other.

2

Public Policy on Social Development

Social development has come to acquire a very important and new salience in the literature and practice of development. Development is now perceived and defined in a very different way than it was during the first three decades after the Second World War. Development was identified with economic development and social development was brought in only as thin icing on the economic cake. In more specific terms, it was seen as promoting social welfare and providing social services. The crucial role of the activities in the social sector in promoting development remained unrecognised for several years. Concepts such as meeting the basic needs of the people, changing the social structure and participation in the process of development were articulated only towards the end of the 60s and the early 70s. Even then they did not make much of an impression on mainstream thinking.

Recently Prof. Amartya Sen has brought about a veritable revolution in development thinking by defining development as "expansion of opportunities", or "freedoms" that individuals in society enjoy. Opportunities can be of an intrinsic importance and therefore worth pursuing as a goal by itself or having the instrumental value of promoting development. Prof. Sen's deeper insight into the development process has now come to be almost universally accepted and has become the basis for policy formulation by the governments of almost all developing countries. Developed countries are also trying to promote this concept of development through the leverage they have by virtue of their aid programmes and trade policy; international organisations like the World Bank, UNDP, United Nations and its specialised agencies have been trying to reorient their normsetting and theoretical work as well as their development cooperation programmes on the basis of this broader definition of development.

To expand the "opportunities" and "freedoms" of the individual, it is necessary to enhance her or his capabilities. Enhancement of capabilities, therefore, is now widely recognised as the objective of development. The World Development Report (1999-2000) defines the goal of development policy as the creation of "sustainable improvements in the quality of life for all people". Improvement in the quality of life is implicit in Amartya Sen's concept of development as the expansion of choice or opportunities or freedom. What the World Development Report definition adds is the concept of sustainability and equity by using the words "sustainable" and "for all people".

Sustainable development for all people means, in addition to raising per capita income, improving peoples' health and educational opportunities, giving every one the chance to participate in public life and helping to ensure a clean environment. Accumulation of human capital has proved to be a key factor in accelerating development in several countries, particularly the East and South East Asian countries. Provisioning of education, health and nutrition play a very important role in the accumulation of human capital. Thus human development is the key to the formation of human capital. But as Prof. Amartya Sen has stated, 'human development' goes beyond that. It makes a direct contribution to the expansion of human capabilities and the quality of life. The annual release by the UNDP of its Human Development Reports since 1990 has been the most important factor popularising the concept of human development.

The W.D.R. brings in the concept of social capital, defined as "the network and relationship that both encourage trust and reciprocity and shape the quality and quantity of the society's social interactions". Social capital thus defined has a significant impact on a range of development processes. To illustrate, the Report says that empirical evidence has shown that in education, teachers are more committed, students achieve higher test scores and school facilities are better utilised in communities where parents and citizens take an active interest in children's educational well-being. In health services, doctors and nurses are more likely to show up for work and perform their duties more attentively where their actions are supported and monitored by citizen groups. In rural development, villages with higher social capital seek greater use of credit.

Social capital serves as an insurance mechanism for the poor who are unable to access market-based alternatives. The role of human development in bringing about social and economic restructuring has been brought out very succinctly in Professor Amartya Sen's Asia and Pacific lecture. A special feature of the East and South East Asian development process has been an emphasis on basic education as a prime mover for change and wide dissemination of basic economic entitlement through education and training, through land reform and through availability of credit. Professor Sen argues that there is sufficient evidence that even with relatively low income, a population that guarantees basic social services can improve length and quality of life.

Because of this factor, China already had quite a high life expectancy at birth even in the pre-reform era i.e. prior to 1979. Since basic education and health are also exceptionally labour-intensive activities, they are much cheaper in poorer countries than in the richer ones. Thus human development contributes to the quality of life even in the absence of its impact on economic and industrial expansion. Secondly, it greatly facilitates such expansion. Thirdly, it improves the efficiency and widens the reach of the market economy. For example, literacy contributes to economic development through quality control and production to specification. Empirical studies show that whereas there is a weak relationship between economic development and rates of improvements in vital measures of development like education, life expectancy, child mortality and gender equality, there is a strong positive relationship between key social characteristics and the attainment of development defined in the broader sense of the term.

Government'S Role in Social Development

At the beginning of the drive for reforms in developing countries, there was a deliberate effort to exaggerate the adverse implications of government's role in development and to suggest the withdrawal of the government from the development process. This swing of the pendulum has more or less been arrested and a more balanced view is taken of the role of the government. That the government has to play a crucial role in the development process is no longer an issue. The issue basically is the extent, nature and direction of government interventions. The areas in which the government's role is regarded as most conducive to development are provisioning of social services and social and physical infrastructure building. There is an emerging consensus that the government can play its role best in partnership with other agents of development, particularly the private sector, the NGOs and civil society organisations.

There is also a great deal of emphasis today on good governance, free from corruption and embodying transparent and participatory processes. In his Asia and Pacific Lecture, Prof.Amartya Sen underlines that a deliberate combination of State action and the use of the market economy was one of the special features of the East and South East Asian development process. The WDR makes the same point when it states that the governments in the East and South East Asian countries intervened in trade to regulate exports and to regulate financial markets. They directed investments in particular areas, encouraged savings and lower interest rates and increased profitability.

Sen states that the overall achievement of the market are deeply contingent on political and social arrangements. The market mechanism has achieved great successes under conditions in which opportunities offered by it have been reasonably shared. Provision of basic education and health and widely shared command over elementary resources like land have been conducive to ensuring the success of the development process. But these demands call for appropriate public policies and "carefully and determined public action going well beyond the simple fostering of markets". The role of institutions in a dispensation where the State occupies pride of place has come to be recognised as a crucial factor in the development process. The W.D.R. (1999-2000) states, "a strong network of effective organisations and enabling institutions is central to holistic development".

Countries with stable governments, predictable method of changing laws, secure property rights and a strong judiciary saw higher investment and growth than those lacking these institutions. Even the outcome of privatisation is heavily dependent on government's structure, macroeconomic and structural factors, competitiveness of markets, social sustainability, regulatory regimes and corporate and commercial law. Today "people" are regarded as the means and the end of development. Even with the best will in the world, a government is unlikely to meet collective needs efficiently if it does not know what these needs are. It can know this only if it comes closer to the people. This means bringing popular voices into policy making; and opening up ways for individual users, the private sector organisations and other groups in the civil society. It can also mean greater decentralisation of government power and resources. Increasing opportunities for participation of the people can enhance State's capabilities in the following ways:

a. When citizens can express their opinions and press their demands publicly within the framework of the law, States acquire some of the credibility that they need to govern well. Broad-based discussions of policy goals can also reduce the risks implicit in a powerful minority monopolising the direction of government. The States that achieve credibility in this fashion have more flexibility in policy implementation and have an easier time engaging citizens in the pursuit of collective goals.

b. Where markets are absent, as in the case of most public goods, popular voice can reduce information problem and lower transaction costs. The emergence of private and NGO alternatives for the provisioning of public goods and services can help meet gaps in the supply of such goods and services. NGOs can both be partners and competitors in the delivery of public services. When backed by the citizens' voice, they can exert useful pressure on government to improve the delivery and quality of public services.

c. In the management of common property resources, the provision of basic infrastructure and the delivery of essential services, there is considerable scope for involving the public directly.

Economic Reforms

Prof. Sen puts the reforms-social development dilemma in the correct perspective when he says that whereas on the one hand, the opportunities offered by a well functioning market may be difficult to use when a person is handicapped by, say, illiteracy or ill health, on the other hand, a person with some education and fine health may still not be able to use his or her capabilities because of the limitations of economic opportunities, arising from absence of markets, or overzealous bureaucratic control or lack of finance. Social opportunities are, thus, influenced by a variety of factors which include both a properly functioning market as well as a deliberate provisioning of social services. Taking the case of India, Prof. Sen states that the blame for independent India's past failures is often put on the insufficient development of market incentives. While there is considerable truth in that diagnosis, it is quite inadequate as an analysis of what has gone wrong in the country. There are many failures, particularly in the development of public educational facilities, health care provisions, social security arrangements, local democracy, environmental protection, and so on, and the stifling of market incentives is only one part of that larger picture.

Prof. Sen, therefore, suggests that we should get the "debate on contemporary India's political economy beyond the familiar battle-lines around the issues of economic reforms, liberalisation and de-regulations". The main problem in focussing on that question is the resulting neglect of other public policy matters, dealing in particular with education, health and social security. "If the central challenge of economic development in India is understood in terms of need to expand social opportunities, then liberalisation must be seen as occupying only one part of that large stage."

The United Nations Charter reflects a more balanced development thinking than that prevalent in the three decades after the promulgation of the Charter. Both in the Preamble as well as in Article 55 of the Charter under the heading International Economic and Social Cooperation, social and economic progress has been accorded equal importance. In the Preamble, one of the objectives of the United Nations is "to promote social progress and better standard of life in larger freedom." Under Article 55, the United Nations has undertaken to promote "higher standards of life, full employment and conditions of economic and social progress and development". The Organisation is also committed to seek solutions to "international economic, social, health and related problems" and to promote "international cultural and educational cooperation".

Moreover, both the Preamble and Article 55 give equal primacy to "universal respect for, and observance of, human rights and fundamental freedoms", which are now seen as closely related to social development. Soon after its establishment, the United Nations institutionalised its activities in the field of social development by establishing a Commission on Social

Development as well as a Division in the Secretariat to undertake research on and provide advisory services in the field of social development. This Division, apart from discharging its function of back-stopping the work of the Commission, undertook projects of its own in this area, financed by UNDP, and made suggestions for the inclusion of social development elements in national development plans and in UNDP projects. It may be noted here that the founder of the Council for Social Development (C.S.D.) and its first Executive Chairperson-cum-Director, Dr. (Ms.) Durgabai Deshmukh, had used the services of the experts of this Division for suggesting elements of social development to be built into the development planning process in India.

In spite of the above-cited Charter provisions and institutional arrangements made in the Secretariat, development activities under the U.N. systems of organisations were influenced by the then dominant thinking on development, reflected in the Harrod-Domar model and Roster's concepts of stages of growth and take-off. Social development remained a peripheral aspect of the over-all development activities of the United Nations even though United Nations organisations were the only ones which devoted resources and attention to social development. Social development was a minor aspect of the research work undertaken by the U.N. for the analysis of the trends in the world economy and international economic relations, as embodied in the successive World Economic Surveys. This trend continued till almost the beginning of the 1970s.

A striking example of this was the manner in which the International Development Strategy for the 1970s relegated issues of social development to the margins of the Strategy. Apart from the influence of the dominant thinking on development, there were some other reasons, mostly of a political nature, which resulted in relegating social development to the background in the discussion on and formulation and adoption of policy measures for development at the international level. These were:

a. Developing countries regarded social development as an underlying assumption behind all their development activities, but they did not articulate problems of social development in any detail because they believed that social development could be best promoted by faster economic growth.

b. They thought that social development fell in the realm of their national responsibility. Therefore, international cooperation did not have any significant role to play in this area.

c. They thought that if social development was discussed in international fora it would become a device for interference in their domestic affairs.

d. Foreign assistance was mainly seen in the form of foreign exchange designed to augment the import capacity of developing countries or bridging the import-export gap. It was intended to supplement domestic resources by meeting a part of the foreign exchange component of development. Domestic resources were not regarded as much of a constraint. This left very little scope for discussing social aspects of development in international fora.

Another important development starting from the late 1970s and continuing until now is the demonstrated incapability of developing countries to raise resources of their own for adequately financing development, and the emergence of fiscal imbalances in their economies.

We now witness the allpervading phenomenon of paucity of domestic resources to meet basic needs, finance local currency components of foreign assisted projects and invest in social and physical infrastructures. This has emerged as a major factor why the commitment of the governments of developing countries to social development are no longer taken as axiomatic as was the case during the 50s and the early part of the 60s. From the 1970s onwards, there has been an increasing emphasis on foreign assistance for local cost financing, and donor countries and agencies redirecting their assistance for meeting basic human needs and for human development.

Foreign assistance is now being given mostly as a substitute for domestic resources and not necessarily as a supplement to them. This has enabled the donor countries and international agencies increasingly to use commitment and attention to social objectives as conditionalities for assistance. Recipient countries have increasingly started accepting these conditionalities. A significant development during the last decade or so has been attaching non-economic conditionalities to aid and trade concessions, designed to promote social goals. These include good governance and human rights conditionalities. The recipient countries have increasingly come to accept these conditionalities also.

By the late 1980s and the early 1990s, the entire orientation of the economic bodies and the organisations of the U.N. System underwent a drastic change, shifting emphasis towards social development. The U.N. system of organisation became increasingly concerned with socio-economic developments within the economies of developing countries and less and less with adjustments and changes in the policies of governments at the international level, let alone with the harmonisation of such policies. Discussions of and policy formulation on hard core economic issues were transferred to the World Bank, I.M.F. and the W.T.O. and the time and energy of the United Nations and its specialised agencies was directed mainly to the discussion of social and humanitarian issues. This led to a division of labour between the World Bank, IMF and WTO on the one hand and the U.N. and its Specialised Agencies on the other, which was not envisaged in the Charter.

This development has led some critics to comment that the United Nations today has become primarily a forum for prescribing self-help kits for developing countries. A similar shift also took place during this period in the development plans and policies of developing countries. Social Development Summit. It was in this background that the World Summit for Social Development was held under the aegis of the United Nations in Copenhagen in March 1995. The Summit was most timely. It was a recognition at the highest political level of the fait accompli of the changes in development thinking towards greater emphasis on social development. It thus gave a seal of approval to these changes. It brought together different trends of thought evident in the field, tried to put them into an interdisciplinary and coherent framework and developed global consensus as a guide for future national and international actions.

The government leaders assembled at the Summit undertook commitments in major areas of social development and set goals and agreed on a Plan of Actions in each area. Since they could not have covered all sectors and issues of social development, they concentrated on three i.e. poverty, unemployment and social exclusion. These are all cross-cutting themes straddling a number of sectors and areas and covering several disciplines. The Summit adopted a Declaration and a Programme of Action on Social Development. This was subsequently endorsed by the General Assembly of the United Nations. At the Summit, the participants launched "a global drive for social programmes and development", embodying commitments taken in ten areas. These were:

a. Creating an enabling environment for social development.

b. Eradicating poverty

c. Promoting full employment.

d. Promoting social integration.

e. Achieving gender equality.

f. Identifying and deploying the means for tackling the problems of social development.

g. Addressing the special problem of Africa and the least developed countries in the field of social development.

h. Bringing World Bank/IMF sponsored structural adjustment programmes in harmony with the goals for social development.

i. Increasing the resources allotted to social development.

j. Achieving cooperation for social development at the sub- regional, regional and international levels.

In the Declaration, the Heads of State and Government recognised "the significance of social development.... for all and decided to give highest priority to the goals set out in the Declaration". They addressed the underlying and structural causes of the problems of social development and their distressing consequences. They launched "a new commitment to social development" in each of their countries and "a new era of international cooperation" in this field. They saw an intrinsic relationship between social development and peace. The Declaration states: "Social development and social justice are indispensable for the achievement and maintenance of peace and security within and among our nations. In turn peace and security and respect for all human rights and fundamental freedoms are necessary for attaining social development and social justice."

They also emphasised the link between economic development, social development and environmental protection. They stated that these are "interdependent and mutually reinforcing components of sustainable development". They recognized, in particular, that broad-based and sustained economic growth is necessary to sustain social development. Moreover, "equitable social development that recognized empowering the poor to utilize environmental resources sustainable is a necessary foundation for social development". In the document adopted by the Summit, an attempt has been made to present a brief review of the current social situation. Progress in some areas of social and economic development has been noted. These include:

a. Global wealth of nations multiplied seven-fold during the 50 years before the Conference. International trade grew even more dramatically.

b. Life expectancy, literacy and primary education and access to basic health care increased in the majority of the countries. Average infant mortality came down considerably even in developing countries.

c. Democratic pluralism, democratic institutions and fundamental civil liberties expanded.

d. At the global level, one of the principal objectives of

the United Nations, that is, decolonisation was substantially realised and dramatic progress was made towards the elimination of apartheid.

In spite of the progress, the social situation in most of the countries remained a matter of great concern. The following major nagging problems of social development were identified by the Summit.

a. The income gap increased both within and among nations.

b. One billion people were living in abject poverty. Most of them went hungry. A large proportion of them had limited access to income, resources, education, health care and nutrition.

c. Unsustainable pattern of consumption and production remained the major cause of the continued deterioration of the environment and the aggravation of poverty and imbalance.

d. 120 million people worldwide were unemployed and many more were under-employed.

e. More women than men lived in absolute poverty. Women carried a disproportionate share of the burden of poverty, social exclusion, unemployment, environmental degradation and effects of war.

f. Health services remained meagre and serious health problems arose because of the incidents of communicable diseases. These are hindrance to social development and causes of poverty and social exclusion.

g. Millions of people were reduced to the position of refugees or were internally displaced.

h. The problems of disability and old age were also matters of concern.

i. Transnational problems like drug trafficking, organised crime, arms trafficking, terrorism, armed conflicts, intolerance and xenophobia, and incitement of racial, ethnic and religious hatred, remained the major challenges for the international community.

A special session of the U.N.General Assembly was held in Geneva in June/July, 2002, to assess the achievements of and obstacles to social development and to decide on further initiatives for accelerating it. The participants in the Conference reaffirmed their will and commitment to implement the Copenhagen Declaration and Programme of Action, which "will remain the basic framework for social development for years to come." The document adopted in the Geneva Conference reviewed the progress in attaining the quantitative targets adopted at the Copenhagen summit in 13 areas of basic social services, including the flow of official development assistance. It concluded that progress in most of these areas remained meagre or unsatisfactory.

The Copenhagen Summit had pronounced its judgement on the implications of globalisation for social development. It stated that globalisation, while opening new opportunities for sustained economic growth and permitting countries to share experiences and learn from each other's experience with greater facility and speed, has been accompanied by intensified poverty, unemployment and social disintegration. Threats to human beings, such as environmental risks, have also been globalised. The challenge, therefore, is how to manage these processes and threats so as to enhance their benefits and mitigate their negative effects. At the Geneva Conference, the implications of globalisation for social development were more sharply brought out. The document adopted at the Conference mentions that "current patterns of globalisation have contributed to a sense of insecurity as some countries, particularly developing countries, have been marginalised from the global economy".

Moreover, "the growing interdependence of nations which has caused economic shocks to be transmitted across national borders, as well as increased inequality, highlight weaknesses in current national and international institutional arrangements, and economic and social policies." The Copenhagen Summit committed itself to "a political, economic, ethical and spiritual vision for social development that is based on human dignity, human rights, equity, respect, peace, democracy, multilateral responsibility and cooperation". The summit leaders adopted the following goals in the social field:

a. Placing people at the centre of development; and directing their economies to meet human needs.

b. Ensuring inter-generational equality by protecting the integrity and sustainable use of the environment.

c. Integrating economic, social and cultural policies.

d. Promoting democracy, human dignity, social justice and solidarity; and ensuring tolerance, non-violence, pluralism and non-discrimination.

e. Promoting equitable distribution of income.

f. Ensuring the inclusion of disadvantaged and vulnerable persons and groups in the process of social development.

g. Promoting universal respect for and observance and protection of all human rights and fundamental freedoms.

h. Protecting the rights of children and youth.

i. Empowering people - full participation of people in the formulation, implementation and evaluation of decisions determining the functioning and well being of societies.

j. Facilitating access to advanced technologies, particularly information technology, which can play a very important role in fulfilling social development goals.

k. Strengthening policies and programmes that improve, ensure and broaden the participation of women in all spheres of life, as equal partners.

Environment for Social Development.

One of the Commitments adopted at the Summit was to create an economic, political, social, cultural and legal environment that will enable people to achieve social development. To this end, the Summit adopted the following goals

a. To provide a stable legal framework which includes equality between men and women, respect for human rights, rule of law, access to justice, transparent and accountable governance and elimination of all forms of discrimination.

b. To provide more equitable access to income, resources and social services.

c. To promote participatory development through association of NGOs and civil society organisations and through decentralisation; and

d. To reinforce peace by promoting tolerance, non-violence and respect for diversity.

In the Plan of Action under this Commitment, it is stated that "social progress will not be realised simply through the free interaction of market forces. Public policies are necessary to correct market failures, to complement market mechanism, to maintain social stability and to create a national and international environment that promotes sustainable growth on a global scale". Detailed recommendations have been made in the Plan of Action regarding the actions to be taken for creating an enabling environment for social development. These include: equitable and non-discriminatory distribution of the benefits of growth; interaction of market forces conducive to efficiency and social development; public policies that seek to overcome disparities and respect pluralism and diversity; strengthened role of the family; expanded access to education, health care services, information, knowledge and technology; increased solidarity, partnership and cooperation; policies for empowering people; and protection and conservation of the environment.

In the Geneva conference, the crucial role of the government in advancing people-centred sustainable development through actions to ensure increased equality and equity, and ensuring that markets function efficiently, were emphasised. The Conference also renewed commitment to efficient, transparent and accountable government and to decmocratic institutions.

Eradication of Poverty

Poverty has generally been associated with paucity of income to meet basic needs. Most of the measures of poverty have used per capita income to identify people above and below the poverty line. However, mainly due to the thinking of Prof. Amartya Sen, poverty has come to be increasingly seen as deprivation of capability rather than merely lowness of income. However, income is clearly one of the major causes of poverty, since lack of income can be a principal reason for a person's capability deprivation. Prof. Amartya Sen brings out the advantages of capability approach to poverty. These are:

a. Poverty as capability deprivation concentrates on deprivations that are intrinsically important and not only instrumentally important. It brings out factors other than lowness of income which influence capability deprivation.

b. Real poverty, i.e. poverty in terms of capability deprivation, may be in a significant sense more intense than what appears in the income space. This can be of crucial concern in assessing what public action is needed to target some particular groups or individuals.

c. The capability deprivation approach to poverty enhances the understanding and causes of poverty by shifting primary attention away from means to ends.

d. Distribution within the family raises further complications with the income approach to poverty. If the family income is used disproportionately in the interest of some family members and not others (for example, because of systematic boy preference) then the extent of deprivation of the neglected members (for example, the girls) may not be adequately reflected in terms of family income. The deprivation of girls is more readily checked by looking at capability deprivation (in terms of greater mortality, morbidity, under nourishment, medical neglect etc.,) than can be found in the income analysis.

The instrumental relations between low income and low capability is variable between different communities and even between different families and different individuals. The relationship between income and capability is strongly affected by the age of the person, by gender and social roles, by location, by insecurity and by other variations over which a person may have no or only limited control. In the context of the definition of poverty as capability deprivation, Prof. Sen tries to link poverty with inequality. He states that inequality can have a negative effect on capability. Severe inequalities are not socially attractive. The sense of inequality may also erode cohesion and some types of inequalities can make it difficult to achieve even efficiency.

Prof. Sen argues that relative deprivation in terms of incomes can yield absolute deprivation in terms of capabilities. Being relatively poor in a rich country can be a great capability handicap even when one's absolute income is high in terms of world standards. Prof. Sen concludes by observing that poverty debates have been distorted by an over-emphasis on income poverty and income inequality to the neglect of deprivations that relate to other variables, such as unemployment, ill health, lack of education and social exclusion.

The U.N.D.P. Human Development Report, 1997, devoted to the theme of poverty, focuses on the same dimensions of poverty as brought out by Prof. Sen in his definition of poverty as capability deprivation. However, in the HDR, 1997, the idea is sought to be linked to human development. It is stated that from the human development angle, poverty means denial of choices and opportunity for a tolerable life. It can mean more than what is necessary for material well being. It can also mean the denial and choices most basic to human development - to lead a healthy and productive life and to enjoy a decent standard of living, freedom, dignity, self-esteem and respect of others.

The Human Development Report, 1997, reports progress in reducing poverty over the 20th century. In the past 50 years, poverty has fallen more than in the previous 500 years and it has been reduced in some respects in almost all countries. Since 1960, in little more than a generation, child death rates in developing countries have been more than halved. Malnutrition rates have declined by almost a third. The proportion of children out of primary schools has fallen from more than half to less than a quarter. And the share of rural families without access to safe water has fallen from 9/10th to about a quarter. By the end of the 20th century, some 3 to 4 billions of the world's people will have experienced substantial improvements in their standards of living and about 4 to 5 billion will have access to basic health and education. China and East and South East Asian countries have made the most spectacular progress in reducing poverty. China reduced its poverty from 33 per cent to 7 per cent between 1978-1994, Malaysia from 60 to 14 per cent between 1970-1993, Indonesia from 60 to 15 per cent between 1970-1990 and the Republic of Korea from 23 to 5 per cent during the same period. Between 1970 and 1995, the largest reductions in the adult illiteracy rate took place in the Republic of Korea (from 12% to 2%), Thailand (21% to 6%), the Phillippines (17% to 5%), Indonesia (46% to 16%) and Cuba (13% to 4%).

However, the advances made have been uneven and marked by setbacks. Poverty still remains pervasive. Nearly a billion people were illiterate at the time of the writing of the Report, well over a billion lacked access to safe water, some 840 million went hungry or faced food insecurity. The U.N.D.P. Human Development Report, 1997, introduced a Human Poverty Index (HPI). Instead of measuring poverty by income, it uses indicators of the most basic dimensions of deprivation i.e. short life, lack of basic education and lack of access to public and private resources. The finding of the Report was that more than a quarter of the developing world's people still lived in poverty as measured by this index. About a third lived on incomes of less than 1 dollar a day. Sub-Saharan Africa had the highest proportion of people in human poverty. Among these broad groups, the children, women and aged suffered most. Some 160 million children were moderately or severely malnourished. Some 100 million were out of school.

A comparison of the HPI with income measurement of poverty based on 1 dollar a day poverty line, revealed the following interesting contrasts:-

a. Sub-Saharan Africa and South Asia had the highest incidents of both income and human poverty.

b. Most of the Arab States had made remarkable progress in reducing income poverty, at that time a mere 4 per cent; but faced a large backlog of human poverty (32 per cent).

c. 'Many countries in Latin America and the Caribbean had reduced human poverty, which was 15 per cent; but income poverty was still 24 per cent.

The U.N.D.P. Human Development Report, 1997 puts emphasis more or less on the same measures. However, it attaches much greater importance to the empowerment of people and to institutional factors, like political commitment to promote and protect the rights of the poor people and policy reforms to enable them to gain access to assets and security of tenure. Like other reports, this HDR also regards gender equality as absolutely essential for eradicating poverty. This would involve focussing clearly on ending discrimination against girls in all aspects of health, education and upbringing; empowering women by ensuring equal rights and access to land, credit and job opportunities; and taking action to end violence against women.

Globalisation, according to the HDR, offers great opportunities for reducing poverty but only if it is managed more carefully and with greater concern for global equity. Globalisation has seen a widening gap between winners and losers in both developed and developing countries. Therefore, better management of globalisation both nationally and internationally, in terms, amongst others, of improved access of the poor and weak countries to the markets of the developed countries, is called for.

Among international measures for reducing poverty, the Report attaches priority to debt relief, larger flow of resources, and the opening up of the markets of developed countries for products of developing countries. Preparatory to the Geneva Conference, the U.N.D.P. prepared a Poverty Report, 2000 under the title Overcoming Human Poverty. The Report was designed to contribute to U.N. General Assembly's review of the progress in the implementation of the Commitments of the Social Summit and to help accelerate the collective campaign against poverty in the next five years. A brief summary of the progress made, the implications of measures that have been taken and can be taken, and measures recommended in the Report are given below:

a. Commitment to reduce poverty. Some progress was made in estimating poverty but there was little progress in setting targets.
b. Integrating poverty reduction programmes into national development plans. The Summit made this recommendation because it is an evidence of the

national commitment to eradicate poverty and also an evidence of explicit location of resources to this task as well as of the determination to mobilise additional resources. Only a few governments took measures in pursuit of this recommendation.

c. Linking poverty to international policies. Such a link is seen mainly in terms of tackling the problem of external debt, harnessing trade for poverty reduction and making aid work for the poor. The record on all these counts was not very encouraging.

d. Governance as a missing link. When governments are unaccountable or corrupt, poverty reduction programmes have little success in targetting the poor. Corruption deprives the poor of an equitable share of society's resources and indirectly reduces the opportunities for poverty reduction by dampening economic growth. Having regular and free and fair elections can boost accountability. But government officials must be made accountable also between elections. For this, people have to organise themselves.

e. Organising the poor.

   1. The foundation of poverty reduction is for the poor to organise themselves. This will enable them to influence the local government and hold it accountable. Through their organisation the poor can form coalitions with other social forces and build broader organisations to influence regional and national policy making. What the poor need most are resources to build their organisational capacity.

   2. Civil societies can play a very important role in this. The most common use of civil society is to entrust them with the delivery of goods and services where local governments cannot do it

effectively. But this may not be advisable over the long term. For, the capacity of the government to deliver goods and services must be built up. In fact, the civil society organisations can perform a better function by representing the poor and in their advocacy role when national and local governments are unresponsive, rather than by serving as a channel for delivering goods and services. They should engage national policy makers on poverty issues. The strategic goal should be to forge an alliance between the State and civil society for poverty reduction.

f. Formulating and implementing pro-poor poverty programmes. Pro-poor poverty programmes should not have a separate existence of their own. They should be integrated with the micro-economic policies of the government. In the ultimate analysis, the focussing of resources on the poor can be achieved best by empowering the poor and for this the poor have to be organised. However, parallel macro-economic policies should be so framed as to confer direct benefits on the poor. This could be done, for example, by:

1. Focusing on geographical areas where the poor are dominant. The deficiency of this approach is that it may include many non-poor households, which could lead to a significant leakage of benefits.

2. Targetting households or communities. This is a very labourious process and to achieve this an active collaboration of the poor is needed. Besides, the latest thinking on human poverty shifts emphasis from the household to the individual - to identify deprivation among, say, women and children. There is also a shift of emphasis to specific interventions to address specific deprivations.

3. Reaching disadvantaged social groups.
4. Targetting by type of intervention, that is, to concentrate on projects which can have the direct effect of benefiting the poor, like providing schools for elementary education, child clinics, micro-finance etc. However, these interventions have not always proved successful in reaching the poor. They have also overlooked such measures as economic policy making or institution building.
5. Access to basic social services. An enhanced supply of services does not necessarily ensure that it will go to the poor. Poverty programme should, therefore, focus not merely on providing services meant for the poor but also on ensuring that the poor are able to take advantage of them.
6. Micro-finance. Micro-finance no doubt contributes to community empowerment but it can be captured by local political elites. Moreover, the hard core poor, having few assets, are reluctant to take on the risk of credit. For example, in Bangladesh, which is a pioneer in micro-finance, only a fourth of micro-finance clients are hard core poor.
7. Supplying physical infrastructures in poor regions, like rural roads, irrigation works, drinking water systems etc. China's anti-poverty programme is very much distinguished by an emphasis on developing infrastructure in the poor regions. However, in this approach, those better off and closer to towns and existing roads, usually benefit more than the poor.
8. Much of the success of infrastructure projects depends on whether communities are involved in selecting them. The advantage of this approach is

that unlike micro-credit, wage employment carries little risk and, therefore, in many regions only hard core poor gravitate to the construction jobs in infrastructure projects.

g. Integrated approach to poverty programme. A general weakness of most poverty programmes has been lack of integration. The problem is particularly severe with regard to integration with gender and environmental issues. There are also weak links between protecting health and reducing poverty. Gender equality does not figure prominently as a source of poverty in most poverty programmes. Nor do gender programmes focus on poverty. Combating gender inequality is not regarded as the same as combating poverty.

h. Monitoring poverty programmes. Not much progress has been made in this area. Most of the developing countries still need a workable poverty monitoring system to assess progress towards the target of eradicating extreme poverty and reducing over-all poverty. For this, participatory poverty assessment is particularly useful. Besides, most poverty monitoring systems continue to rely on income poverty measures. This needs to be broadened.

The Geneva Conference regarded poverty eradication as "an ethical, social and economic imperative of humankind". A target was set for reducing the proportion of people living in extreme poverty by one half by the year 2015. This was basically the reiteration of the target agreed in the Millenium Session of the U.N. General Assembly. The Genevá Conference reiterated most of the measures recommended by the Summit. However, it put emphasis on those measures which can have direct impact on the amelioration of the conditions of the poor. These included: using employment policies to reduce poverty, improving productivity in the informal sector, increasing and facilitating the development of cooperatives among the poor, encouraging sustainable rural development, especially in areas like agricultural production, encouraging the growth of small and medium size enterprises by formulating a consistent long term policy to support them, promoting small business and self-employment for rural workers in view of increasing rural poverty, landlessness and urban rural migration.

Most of these measures would seem to fly against the face of the reforms recommended under the structural adjustment programmes of the World Bank and I.M.F. The consensus arrived at the Geneva Conference, with the participation of governments and NGOs, is a truer reflection of the perception of the vast majority of the countries in the world on what needs to be done for eradicating poverty than that recommended under the Washington Consensus. This also reflects the strong urge in these countries to protect the small farmers and enterprises and informal sectors against the onslaught of globalisation. The Geneva Conference also put considerable emphasis on institutional factors for combating poverty. It emphasised the role of the N.G.Os and civil society organisations in ensuring community participation in the formulation and implementation of poverty reduction strategies and programmes. It recommended that institutional mechanism that ensured a multi-sectoral approach to poverty eradication should be established and strengthened.

On the role of gender equality for reducing poverty, it recommended that the potential role of women in poverty eradication should be kept in mind and appropriate measures should be taken to counter the "feminisation of poverty." The World Development

Report, 2000-2001, recognises that poverty is "the result of economic, political and social processes that interact with each other and frequently reinforce each other in ways that exacerbate the deprivation in which poor people live". Meagre assets, inaccessible markets and scarce job opportunities lock people in material poverty. That is why, the Report says, promoting opportunity by stimulating economic growth, making markets work better for the poor people and building up their assets is key to reducing poverty.

Security is not defined in the narrow sense of providing social security net for those who are rendered unemployed or otherwise marginalised during the reform process, but includes the security of millions of those suffering under structural poverty. Recommendations made in the Report under the headings of the three elements are set in the broader context of the new definition of poverty. Among measures for enhancing security are included micro-insurance and micro-finance and not reducing expenditure in the social sector during the period of adjustment or crisis management. The heading 'social empowerment' includes transparency in governance, sound legal system, decentralisation, gender equality, removal of social exclusion and combating corruption.

The World Development Report, 1990, devoted to the poverty issue, proposed a two-part strategy: promoting labour-intensive growth through economic openness and investment in infrastructure, and providing basic services to the poor people in health and education. In the 1990s, governance and institutions moved centre stage, as did the issues of vulnerability at the local and national levels.

Gender Equality

Gender equality has emerged as a key variant for ensuring the desired outcome through activities in the field of social development, particularly in the areas of education, health and nutrition and for dealing with the problems of poverty and unemployment. The present almost universal recognition of the importance of gender equality in social development represents a veritable revolution. Prof. Amartya Sen is a strong believer in the importance of women's empowerment for bringing about social change. He states that women are no longer the passive recipient of social welfare; they are increasingly seen as an active agent of change: the dynamic promoters of social transformation that can alter the life of both women and men. Professor Sen draws from empirical studies to demonstrate the connection between women's empowerment on the one hand and child's survival and fertility on the other hand. He states that it is striking that demographically backward regions of India, where mortality and morbidity are high, tend to be those where gender relations are highly unequal.

Conversely, States which have experienced rapid progress in improving health and reducing mortality and fertility are often those where women have played far more an active role in society. Given the gender division of labour that prevails in most of India, nutrition, child health, and related matters typically depend primarily on women's decisions and actions. It is, therefore, hardly surprising that social achievements in this domain are more impressive where women are better educated, more resourceful, more valued, more influential and generally more equal agents within the household and in society.

There is considerable evidence to show that the fertility rate tends to come down with greater empowerment of women and that women's education and literacy tend to reduce the mortality rates of children. It works through the importance that mothers typically attach to the welfare of the children and the opportunities that the mothers have, when they are respected and empowered, to influence family decisions in that direction. Female literacy is found to have an unambiguous statistically significant reducing aspect on under-5 mortality. High levels of female literacy and labour force participation by women are strongly associated with lower level of family disadvantage in child survival.

By contrast, variables that relate to the general level of development and modernisation either turn out to have no statistically significant effect or suggest that modernisation can even strengthen, rather than weaken, the general bias in child survival. Statistics also show that male literacy or general poverty reduction have comparatively ineffective roles to play as instruments of child mortality reduction. Thus the same variables relating to women's empowerment, in this case their literacy, plays a much more important role in promoting social well-being than variables relating to the general level of populace in societies. Women's empowerment improves not only their condition but also the condition of everyone in the family.

Prof. Sen brings this out very convincingly by analysing how a change in the arrangement in sharing within the family in favour of women can enhance the welfare of all the members of the family. The arrangement for sharing within the family is to a great extent done by established conventions, but they are at the same time influenced by such factors as the economic role and empowerment of women and the value system of the community at large. In the evolution of value systems and conventions within the family, an important role can be played by female education, female employment and ultimately ownership rights and thus social features can be very crucial for the economic fortunes of all members of the family.

Distributional problems within the family are particularly crucial in determining the general undernourishment and hunger of different members of the family in situations of persistent poverty. It is the continued inequality in the division of food - and perhaps even more so in that of health care - that gender inequality manifests itself most blatantly and persistently in poor societies with a strong anti-female bias. On the other hand, there is considerable evidence to show that when women can and do earn income outside the household, they stand to enhance their relative position even in the distribution within the household. Thus the freedom to seek outside jobs can contribute to the reduction of women's relative and absolute deprivation. Freedom in one area seems to help foster freedom in others.

Prof. Sen draws a distinction between what he calls the "agency" aspect of women's movements and its "well-being" aspect. By "agency" he means the combination of all factors which make women the agent of social transformation. He brings out the inter-relationship between these two aspects. He states that agency aspect plays a very important role in removing the inequities that depress the well being of women. Empirical studies have brought out how the relative respect and regard for women's well-being is strongly influenced by such variables as women's ability to earn an independent income, to find employment outside the home, to have ownership rights, to have literacy, and be educated participants in decisions within and outside the family.

Gender inequality does not decline automatically

with the progress of economic growth. In fact, in some cases there is an inverse relationship between the two. Secondly, gender inequality is not only a social failure in itself, but also it leads to other social failures. An innovation in the U.N.D.P. Human Development Report, 1995, was the inclusion in it of a Gender-related Development Index (GDI) reflecting gender disparity in basic human capabilities. The variables taken into account for developing the GDI were women's empowerment, literacy rates among women vis-a-vis men, combined enrolment for females, life expectancy and women's earned income. The Report reveals the following facts

a. Poverty has a woman's face - of the 1.3 billion people in poverty, 70 per cent were women. The increasing poverty among women is linked to their nequal situation in labour market, their treatment under social welfare systems and their status and power in the family.

b. Women's labour force participation has risen by only 4 percentage points in 20 years i.e. from 36 per cent in 1970 to 40 per cent in 1990.

c. Women receive a disproportionately small share of credit from formal banking institutions.

d. Women normally receive a much lower average wage than men.

e. All regions recorded a higher level of unemployment among women than men.

In addition to the GDI, the 1995 HDR introduced another concept called Gender Empowerment Measure (GEM), which looks at women's representation in parliaments, women's share of positions classified as managerial and professional, women's participation in the active labour force and their share of national income. The Report also points out that a major index of neglect of women is that many of women's economic contributions are grossly undervalued or not valued at all. The contributions not valued may very well be in the order of 11 trillion dollars a year. Finally it brings out that the most painful devaluation of women is the physical and psychological violence that stalks them from cradle to grave. One of the Commitments undertaken at the Copenhagen Social Development Summit was on "gender equality".

.The Geneva Conference underlined that participation in leadership role of women in all spheres should be recognised and enhanced. The Copenhagen Summit recommended the integration of the gender perspective in the design and implementation of all policies of development The Geneva Conference embraced the same idea but put it somewhat differently i.e. the need for "mainstreaming of gender considerations in all levels of policy making". As a follow up of the Millennium Session of the General Assembly, the Geneva conference reiterated the targets set at that session, i.e.

a. Ensuring free, compulsory and universal primary education for both boys and girls by 2015.

b. Achieving 50 per cent improvement in the level of adult literacy by 2015; and

c. Closing the gender gap in primary and secondary education by 2005.

The Geneva Conference set the objective of promoting the full enjoyment of all human rights and fundamental freedoms by all women and girls. Governments should ensure that human rights of women and girls are respected and promoted. Another additional commitment undertaken at the Geneva conference was to increase the participation of women and bring about a balanced representation of men and women in all sectors and occupations in the labour market and close the gender gap in earnings.

The U.N.D.P. Human Development Report, 1995 identified a 5-point strategy for accelerating progress towards achieving gender equality:

a. National and international efforts must be mobilised to win legal quality within a definite period, say the next ten years;

b. Many economic and institutional arrangements may need revamping to extend more chances to women than men in the work place;

c. A threshold limit must be fixed as minimum share of women in decisionmaking at the national level (this could be, say, 30 per cent);

d. Key programmes should embrace universal family education,

e. National and international efforts should target programmes that enable women to gain greater access to economic and political opportunities through basic social services and through credit for the poor.

Human Rights

Recently human rights have emerged as a very important under-pinning of the objectives of human development. Human rights have acquired a truly universal character in that they flow from the dignity that is attached to human being. This essentially modernistic concept has deep religious roots. Rabindra Nath Tagore in his book *Religion of Man* has observed that what is most striking is the divinity of the human being and the humanity of the divine. This is what lends dignity to human being and makes for the unity of humankind. Looked at from this angle, human rights cannot be culture-specific as has been claimed by some Asian intellectuals and political leaders. They have invoked the distinctive nature of the Asian values as a justification for not accepting human rights as a universal value.

In this connection, they have particularly referred to the Confucian culture where the focus is on discipline rather than on rights, on loyalty rather than on entitlement. Prof. Amartya Sen does not agree with this "cultural critique" of human rights. He says that generalisations about Asia are not easy, given its size. There are no quintessential values that apply to the immensely large Asian population, which separates them out from people in the rest of the world. Besides, Confucianism is not the only tradition in Asia. In the last couple of decades, we have witnessed the expanding horizon of human rights. Traditionally, human rights concentrated on the right of the individual. Subsequently, it expanded to cover the rights of communities, ethnic groups, and distinctly marginalised and neglected groups like women, children and the aged. Traditionally human rights were more or less identical with political rights; now they have been extended to cover social and economic rights.

In his criticism of the "coherence critique" and the "legitimacy critique" of human rights, Prof. Sen has widened the horizon of human rights still further. According to the "legitimacy critiques", there are no inborn human rights and they have to be acquired through legislation. Prof. Sen finds this thesis as militating "in a rather fundamental way against the basic idea of universal human rights". According to him, human rights can be effectively invoked in the context even where their legal enforcement would appear to be most inappropriate. For example, the moral right of a wife to participate fully as an equal in serious family decisions may be acknowledged by many who nevertheless want this right not to be legalised or imposed. Prof. Sen argues that it is best to see human rights as a "set of ethical claims", which must not be identified with legal rights.

According to the "coherence critique", one cannot talk about human rights without specifying whose duty it is to guarantee the fulfillment of the rights. In this view, rights can be sensibly formulated only in combination with corelated duties. Prof. Sen dismisses this critique on the ground that human rights can be addressed to any one who can help, even though no particular person or agency can be charged to bring about the fulfillment of the rights involved. He says, "it is surely possible for us to make a distinction between a right that a person has which has not been fulfilled and the right that a person does not have." Thus human rights can be seen as an entitlement, power, or immunity that benefits all who have them, even though they may not be legally guaranteed or it may not be possible to assign responsibilities on individuals or agents for guaranteeing them.

The very fact of the articulation of these rights can result in the widening of freedom and can help to mobilise support from a great many people. Social development or human development on the one hand and human rights on the other share a common vision and a common purpose - that is, to ensure the freedom, well-being and dignity of all people everywhere. They are both about securing basic freedoms which may include:

a. Freedom from discrimination by gender, race,

ethnicity, national origin or religion;

b. Freedom from want - to enjoy a decent standard of living;

c. Freedom to develop and realise one's human potential;

d. Freedom from fear - from physical violence, from threats to personal security, from torture, from arbitrary arrest and other violent act;

e. Freedom from injustice and violation of the rules of law;

f. Freedom of thought and speech and to participate in decision making and to form associations.

g. Freedom for decent work without exploitation.

If human development focuses on the enhancement of the capabilities and freedoms that the members of the community want to enjoy, human rights represent the claims that individuals have on the conduct of other individuals and collective agents and on the design of social arrangements to facilitate or secure these capabilities and freedoms. Human rights can add value to the agenda of human development. These rights direct legal tools as a means to secure freedom and human development. The rights also lend moral legitimacy and the principle of social justice to the objective of human development. The rights perspectives help shift the priority to the most deprived and excluded, especially to deprivation because of discrimination. It also directs attention to the need for information and a political voice for all people.

The human rights approach may offer an additional and more useful perspective for the analysis of human development. This approach links the human development approach to the idea that others have duties to facilitate and enhance human development. For example, when we assert right to education we are not only saying that all are entitled to a free elementary education but we are also saying that there must be some culpability somewhere in the social system. Thus the focus on locating accountability for failures within a social system can be a powerful tool for seeking remedies. Concern with duties enhances the ways of judging the nature and demands of programmes. Since the process of human development often involves great struggle, the empowerment involved in the language of rights can be of great practical importance. Human rights analysis thus involves an assessment of the extent to which institutions and social norms that provide security to human development achievements within a society are in place.

The concepts and tools of human development provide a systematic assessment of the economic and institutional constraints to the realisation of rights. Human development thus contributes to building a long term strategy for the realisation of rights. Gains in human development are not always attended by gains in human rights fulfillment and, therefore, human development accounting may fail to pick up on the vulnerability of individuals and groups within a society. For example, the instability of the market combined with inadequate social security provisions exposed the insecurity of East Asia's human devẽlopment gains.

By attending to the process of human development, an idea can be gained as to how far it is feasible to achieve human rights given the resources and the institutional constraints that prevail within a society. All rights cannot be fulfilled simultaneously even though they are all valid and sacrosanct. The fulfillment of several rights depends upon structural changes and on programmes for social and economic transformation to which human developments contributes a great deal. The idea of human development involves change. Its concern is with progress. The insistence on a dynamic view can be particularly useful in considering human rights over time. For example, when a country is poor it cannot fulfil all its human rights obligations. In this way, there may be some human rights that receive priority even though all human rights ultimately have value and importance.

By adding the perspective of change and progress for conceptual and practical reasoning about human rights, human development can help to deepen the understanding and broaden the usefulness of the human rights approach. It is already recognised that some rights must be only progressively realised, and not overnight. This underlines the need for establishing priorities among human rights. The Human Development Report, 2000, of the UNDP is devoted to human rights and human development. It analyses the relationship between human rights and human development, traces the evolution of human rights since the adoption in 1948 of the Universal Declaration of Human Rights and outlines the challenges of and recommends measures for achieving the universal realisation of human rights in the 21st century.

Promotion of Social Integration

The promotion of social integration was one of the principal themes of the Copenhagen Social Summit. This was also the theme of one of the Commitments undertaken at the Summit. The aim of social integration under this Commitment is to create " a society for all" in which every individual, each with rights and responsibilities, has an active role to play. Such an inclusive society must be based on respect for all human rights and fundamental freedoms, cultural and religious diversity, social justice, democratic participation and rule of law. The positive factors for integration identified in this part of the Summit document are: decolonisation; elimination of apartheid; spread of democracy; wider recognition of the need to respect human dignity, all human rights and cultural diversity; unacceptability of discrimination; extended opportunities in health, education and economic development; globalisation of communications; and greater possibilities of social mobility, choice and autonomy of action.

The negative factors identified are: social polarisation and fragmentation; widening disparities and inequalities; uncontrolled urban development; degradation of the environment; marginalisation of people, families, social groups, communities, and entire countries; strains on individuals, families, communities and institutions as a result of the rapid pace of social change; economic transformation; migration and major dislocations of population. Total social breakdown, organised crime, drug trafficking, arms smuggling, trafficking in women and children, ethnic and religious conflicts, civil war, terrorism and xenophobia and genocide are identified as factors presenting fundamental threats to societies and the global social order. Following are some of the major goals for achieving social integration:

a. Promoting respect for democracy, the rule of law, pluralism, diversity, tolerance, non-violence and solidarity.

b. Eliminating discrimination and fostering respect for human dignity.

c. Ensuring equality and non-discrimination.

d. Ensuring respect for rights and promoting access to

education, information and technology.

e. Addressing the problems of crime, violence and drug trafficking as factors of social disintegration.

Among the means suggested are inter-generational dialogue and strengthening institutions that enhance social integration. Here a very important role is assigned to the family. In the light of the developments during the five years after the Copenhagen Summit, the Geneva Conference adds some new measures in its recommendations for securing social integration:-

a. Encouraging sustained investment in social institutions and social capital and enhancing social network.

b. Ensuring an enabling environment for civil society organisations.

c. Promoting the contribution that volunteerism can make to the creation of caring societies.

d. Encouraging the media to contribute to the promotion of social integration and use of the internet and other forms of information technology for this purpose.

e. Identifying and taking measures to counter the increasing dissemination of child pornography and other obscene materials, intolerance, hatred, racism, xenophobia, incitement to violence, discrimination based on sex, through the media and information technology.

Promote Full Employment

Full and adequately remunerative employment is an effective method of eliminating poverty and promoting social integration. If poverty is defined as capability deprivation, then unemployment is a major factor for such deprivation. Prof. Amartya Sen argues that if income loss were all that were involved in unemployment, then that loss could to a great extent be erased by income support. If, however, unemployment has other serious effects on the lives of the individuals, causing deprivation of other kinds, then the amelioration through income support would be to that extent limited. There is plenty of evidence to show that unemployment has many harmful effects other than loss of income, including psychological harm, loss of work motivation, skill and self-confidence, increase in ailment and morbidity, disruption of family relations and social life, hardening of social exclusion, accentuation of racial discrimination and gender asymmetries.

Following are the goals for promoting full employment:-

a. Putting employment at the centre of development strategy.

b. Developing policies to expand work opportunities, particularly through economic growth, investment in human resource development, promotion of employment-generating technologies and encouragement of selfemployment.

c. Improving access to land, credit and other assets.

d. Putting special emphasis on education and training and promoting workers' rights.

The Plan of Action spells out detailed measures under each of the above headings. Among workers' rights, emphasis is laid on human rights, healthy and safe working environment, removal of exploitation, abolition of child labour, and full participation of women in the labour market place. Separate recommendations have been made on enhancing employment opportunities for groups with special needs, particularly the disadvantaged ones like women, children, disabled, indigenous people, displaced persons and migrant workers. There is also emphasis on the importance of acknowledging the important contribution of UN-remunerated work to the well being of the society and bringing respect, dignity and value to such work and people who do it. For this purpose, it is important to develop more comprehensive knowledge of such work through research.

Importance of small and medium size enterprises and of the informal sector is emphasised as a source of growth in employment in developing countries. This leads to the recommendation that obstacles to the operation of such enterprises be removed and support be provided for their establishment. In the Geneva Conference, special emphasis is laid on the prohibition of child labour. Governments are urged to support and participate in the global campaign for the immediate elimination of the worst forms of child labour.

Means for Tackling

The participants in the Copenhagen Summit Conference undertook a separate Commitment on the means for dealing with the problems of social development. Among the means identified are education, health, removing inequalities, respect for culture, and people-centred sustainable development. The governments participating at the Summit have committed themselves to promoting and attaining the goals of universal and equitable access to quality education; the highest attainable standards of physical and mental health; access of all to primary health care; making particular efforts to rectify inequalities relating to social conditions and without distinction as to race, national origin, gender, age or disability; respecting and promoting common and particular cultures; striving to strengthen the role of culture in development; preserving the essential basis of people-centred sustainable development; and contributing to the full development of human resources. An integrated approach is suggested for achieving these goals. In this regard, special emphasis has been put on partnership, empowerment, international solidarity and recognition of diversity.

The Geneva Conference, under this Commitment, deals primarily with health and education. Having been held after the dust settled following discussions on the role of the State in the development process, the Conference recognises the primary responsibility of governments for providing and ensuring access to basic social services for all; and developing sustainable pro-poor health and education systems by promoting community participation in planning and managing basic social services. It states that there is inter-dependence between health on the one hand and employment, education, environment, transport, nutrition, and food security on the other. Reference is made to the Dakar Framework of Action for Education for All adopted at the World Education Forum in April 2000. It is recalled that the fulfillment of the goals of the Dakar Framework of Action would call for the mobilisation of additional resources amounting to 8 billion dollars per annum.

The document summarises the main goals of the Framework which include providing access to free and compulsory primary education of good quality to all children by 2015; improving early childhood care and education; achieving 50 per cent improvement in levels of adult literacy; improving the quality of education; and removing gender disparity. The Geneva Conference document, under this Commitment, deals with the problem of protecting intellectual property rights and at the same time providing access to essential drugs. The document is somewhat ambivalent on this issue. On the one hand it emphasises the "critical importance of access - - - at affordable prices" and for members States to "freely exercise - —in an unrestricted manner, the options available to them under international agreements to protect and advance access to life-saving essential drugs". But on the other hand, it also recognises the contributions of intellectual property rights to promoting research, development and distribution of drugs; and qualifies member State's freedom to ensure access to essential drugs by the phrase "consistent with national laws and international agreements acceded to."

Instrumentalities for Promoting Social Development

Institutions play a very important role in promoting social development. We have already dealt with the role of institutions at the national level i.e. governments, NGOs and civil society organisations. In addition, the Copenhagen Summit Conference adopted separate Commitments under the headings "Structural Adjustment Programmes", "Financial Resources for Social Development" and "Improved and Strengthened Framework for International, Regional and Sub-regional Cooperation for Social Development".

Structural Adjustment Programmes

The Conference recommended that structural adjustment programmes should incorporate social development goals. They should promote basic social programmes, in particular those affecting the poor and the vulnerable, and protect them from budget reductions. The Geneva Conference recommended that structural adjustment programmes addressed to economic crisis, including those negotiated between national governments and IMF, should strive to ensure that they do not lead to a sharp drop in economic activity or sharp cuts in social spending. It was further recommended that governments and international financial institutions should be encouraged to improve the on-going dialogue on the design, implementation and role of structural adjustment programmes so as to ensure the full integration of social and economic components, and the protection of social policies and programmes. The Geneva Conference has also recommended that national policies should be so designed as to take into account the concerns of people living in poverty. This can be done by incorporating social development goals in the formulation of structural adjustment programmes, including poverty reduction, in consultation with civil society.

Financial Resources

Non-availability of adequate resources constitutes an important constraint to the realisation of the goals of social development. The various estimates made for the requirement of additional resources to achieve the multiplicity of goals in the field of social development add to an astronomical sum. The bulk of these resources are expected to come from the efforts of the developing countries themselves, through the moblisation of additional resources. Since the main focus of attention till recently has been on economic development, a reprioritisation of development goals in order to shift the emphasis to social development would involve a commensurate shift of resources from economic development to social development.

Developing countries now widely recognise their own responsibility for finding resources for social development and the need to divert resources from economic development to social development. At the same time they went to the Summit with the expectation that it would be an occasion to get commitments from developed countries for making additional resources available for social development. The negotiations at the Summit focussed mainly on three issues:-

a. Eliciting from developed countries a firmer and unambiguous commitment for meeting the U.N. target of the transfer of 0.7 per cent of GNP as official development assistance.

b. Shifting of priority in resources allocation by both developed and developing countries with a view to reaching what was described as a 20:20 pact i.e., developed countries should devote 20 per cent of their ODA for financing social development projects and programmes in a particular developing country with a matching action by that country to devote 20 per cent of budget resources for social development purposes.

c. Reaching agreement on new and innovative ideas for raising funds at the international level which could be earmarked for social development.

The developing countries did not get satisfactory results on any of the above three points. The Summit therefore turned out to be a failure from the point of view of meeting the resources expectations of the developing countries. Resources emerged as the major concern at the Geneva Review Conference also. But there also there was no change in the long held status quo. Both the Copenhagen and the Geneva Conferences reiterated the

0.7 per cent target on a best endeavour basis without setting any deadline. Commitment on this score, therefore, was much weaker than that made as far back as in 1970 in the International Development Strategy for the decade of the 1970s. Both the Conferences adopted identical formulation i.e. a commitment to "strive" for the fulfillment of the 0.7 per cent target "as soon as possible".

The 20:20 formula was suggested by some of the developed countries and international organisations. Developing countries were not very enthusiastic about this formula because it did not carry any promise for additionalities of resources. All that it called for was a shift in the priority for allocating resources. The Copenhagen Summit reached an agreement on "a mutual commitment between interested developed and developing countries partners to allocate, on an average, 20 per cent of ODA and 20 per cent of national budget respectively to basic social programmes." As it has turned out, there are very few agreements between individual developed and developing countries to operationalise the 20:20 Pact. The formulation adopted on new and innovative ideas for raising funds was extremely weak and non-operational in character both in Copenhagen and in Geneva.

In Copenhagen, it was recommended that relevant U.N. bodies, particularly the Economic and Social Council, "should be requested to consider new and innovative ideas for generating funds and for this purpose to offer any useful suggestions". In Geneva, the idea got even more diluted. The governments were advised to conduct a rigorous analysis of "advantages, disadvantages and other implications" of proposals for developing new and innovative sources of funding, for dedication to social development and poverty alleviation programmes. This recommendation carries the implication that such proposals can even be disadvantageous and have adverse implications for the development of developing countries or for the global economy. Thus the idea of new and innovative measures for raising international resources has been shelved for a long time to come. Evidently, given the tenuous and negative character of the consensus on this point, no follow up action has so far been taken.

Both at the Copenhagen and Geneva Conferences, appropriate formulations were adopted on providing debt relief to developing countries. These formulations simply summarise the consensus reached in the World Bank, IMF and other forums. Strangely enough, the Geneva Conference has made a recommendation on the stabilisation of commodity prices. This has come long after the view imposed by the protagonists of free market forces, particularly the Bretton Woods Institutions, that the earlier effort for stabilising commodity prices through inter-governmental agreements or arrangements were ill-conceived and should, therefore, be given up and that commodity prices should be left to be determined by the market forces.

Both the Copenhagen and Geneva Conferences were long on recommending measures for the mobilisation of domestic resources and short on commitment for providing international resources. The Geneva Conference adopted a very elaborate formulation on the mobilisation of domestic resources by developing countries, particularly through good governance, more effective utilisation of resources and restructuring the mechanism for the delivery of basic services. Following are some of the specific recommendations:

a. Enhancing the cost effectiveness of social spending.

b. Attracting private investments so as to free public resources for social development.

c. Encouraging active participation of the civil society in the delivery of social services.

d. Extending access to micro-credits and other modes of financing of that nature, to people living in poverty.

e. Supporting community participation in the planning, provision and maintenance of local infrastructure, and

f. Preventing bribery, money laundering etc.

Family Planning Programme

Over the years, the family planning programme has gradually become more broad-based. What began as a population control program, grew into a welfare programme for the family. Family welfare has come to include welfare of the mother (pregnant and nursing) and children, nutrition, a health conscious environmental component (i.e., pollution etc.) and a focus on the girl-child. Programmes are undertaken for special development of each of these categories. At another level, the credibility of the family planning programme was strengthened by the passing of unanimous resolutions in its support, in several of the State legislatures. It is noteworthy also that greater emphasis was placed in the Seventh and the Eighth Plans on 'Operational Behaviour Research', with a view to popularising existing family planning methods, increasing their acceptability, and removing and reducing the complications or inconveniences associated with various methods of family planning. More recently, family planning targets have been abolished and the emphasis has shifted away to reproductive health.

Nutrition and Child Survival

Nutritional deficiency is a cause of most deaths among young children. 'Approximately half of the deaths in India among children under 6 years of age are due to severe and fatal malnutrition'.Malnutrition was seen in the plans mainly as a problem of poverty, due to which a large number of the poor could not afford a 'balanced diet'. Since the early plans, schemes have been introduced for combating the problem of malnutrition. It was recognised that production of more food was needed to solve the problem of malnutrition and to improve the nutritional status of the population, hence there was a need to stress on agriculture and its allied activities It was recognised also that children and pregnant and nursing mothers were especially vulnerable. Over the years, the range of direct interventions expanded to cover supplementary feeding of children and mothers, production of nutritious foods, fortification of foods, nutrition and health education of mothers, and prophylactic programmes against identified nutritional deficiencies. In the fifth Plan, supplementary feeding programmes were brought under the Minimum Needs Programme (MNP) and also became a component of 21 ICDS. In the Sixth Plan, a substantial increase in allocation for poverty allocation programmes was visualised as a means to increase the purchasing power of the rural poor so as to enhance food intake.

During the first three plans, nutrition formed one of the components of the health sector and was not singled out as such for specific plan programmes. It was only in the Fourth Plan that an Integrated Nutrition Programme was introduced. By 1973, the Applied Nutrition Programme introduced in 1960 was extended to all the States and Union Territories. It aimed at spreading the concept of balanced diets, production and consumption of protective food and proper techniques of cooking. In the Fifth Plan, the Mid-Day Meal programme (MDM) for providing supplementary food to school children was introduced in 1962-63 as a part

3

Public Policy on Poverty Alleviation

Globalization, economic liberalization and decentralization of development administration have generated widespread discussion on the need to reorient public administration capabilities to meet the emerging challenges. The key issues identified in administrative reform commissions constituted by the government and consultations on their recommendations include the following:

— Growth in the size of public administration personnel relative to functions in the context of economic liberalization and decentralization;

— Reorientation of public policy towards creation of an enabling environment for economic growth, poverty reduction and sustainable human development;

— The need to enhance capacity of local government authorities (Panchayats *in rural areas and* Nagarpalikas in urban) to assume responsibilities for delivery of basic services to local communities and mobilize local resources;

— Enhance the capacity of citizens' groups to make responsible and informed demands on the public systems in the interest of improving transparency, accountability and responsiveness; and

— Creation of new core competencies in senior civil service echelons in the areas of economic management of poverty reduction and social sector programmes.

The Government is fully aware that measures need to be taken to ensure that the process of globalization and economic liberalization do not affect the poor and marginalised sections of the society. It is committed to ensure that they receive a boost which would not only enrich their lives but also put them in a better position to contribute to growth and prosperity. To help in this process, the 73rd and 74th Constitutional Amendment Act have been passed in May 1993.

There is a broad consensus that no matter how soundly conceived the New Economic Policy and the Constitutional Amendments are, they cannot be implemented effectively without appropriate organisations, and administrative systems geared to deliver results. Efficient managing of these initiatives will largely depend as much on the changes in knowledge, skills, attitudes and value system of the civil service as on the appropriateness of the initiatives themselves and their design and process.

Four departments, viz. Administrative Reforms and Training, Rural Development, Urban Development and Economic Affairs have already taken the lead and worked, or are working, upon a number of specific projects and proposals. Yet, a small, but significant beginning has been made by the UNDP projects on capacity building in the areas of civil service, administrative reforms and training for the Centre and the States and police and tax reforms. The National Training Policy and its operational guidelines issued in 1996 are another important development aimed at capacity building for responsiveness, awareness and commitment to reform. Some states are attempting to restructure their services and training arrangements in accordance with the National Training Policy.

With the exception of Tamil Nadu, Maharashtra and Madhra Pradesh, no other state has formulated its own Reform and Training Policy. Consequently, the imperatives of these changes have yet to percolate down among the multitude of departments and agencies at the state level and much less to the regional or district levels. In almost all the states not even one half of the departments/agencies have any continuing arrangements for administrative improvements or provisions for training their employees. The voluntary agencies and the other organizations of civic society are vigorously coming forward to address some of the critical and important elements in administrative reform and capacity building. However, it is recognized by the government that there is a need to create an enabling environemt so that their participation in the development process is further enhanced.

National Programme Framework

India's development objectives are spelt out in successive five year plans and the current Ninth Five Year Plan takes into account the national programme framework for reorientation of the public administration towards decentralization, greater citizens' participation in development programmes and ethical standards in public administration. The Plan recognizes that people's participation in the development process has hitherto been inadequate resulting in sub-optimal returns to substantial investment made by the state in poverty reduction and basic social services programmes. The Plan further underscores the need to create conditions by which the disadvantaged are not only empowered to take advantage of the opportunities created by the growth process but also to contribute actively in the process of creation of wealth and well-being. The Plan focusesses on the need to enhance citizens' capabilities through education, information and access to appropriate technology. Empowerment of women and the socially disadvantaged groups, and strengthening efforts to build self-reliance and promoting and developing people's participatory institutions such as Panchayati Raj (PRIs), co-operatives and self-help groups are the key development objectives.

Public Policy and Poverty Alleviation: A Case Study of Kerala

Naturally, Kerala was endowed with certain positive factors such as higher level of education, which in turn promoted social consciousness, class movements and enhanced politicisation. While other parts of the country were not favoured with many of these positive factors, the latter regions have their own strength in other areas like higher levels of industrialisation, emergence of a innovative business community and enhanced international relations through industry and trade. Kerala, however, has been deprived on many of these aspects. Therefore, as indicated earlier, the crucial question is as to what Kerala has gained from the rest of the country, and what the rest of the country have learned from Kerala's experience. Unfortunately, most academic discussions in this area have a "Kerala-mania" The Kerala's experience has been studied largely by Keralites than by outside observers within the country.

Majority of the Indians do have to necessarily wait for an indefinite future for the hump of economic growth to be crossed, for schooling, house-sites, primary heath-care, food at fair prices and so on. Kerala's development experience questions such a sequence of agriculture, industry and subsequently, improvement in the standard of living of the masses. The challenge posed by Kerala relates to this historical sequencing of economic growth and mass welfare sanctified by the developed countries. One of the relatively backward states of India, with per capita domestic production consistently below the national average, Kerala has been able to provide for the basic needs of the majority of its citizens. This is revealed by comparative indicators of health, education and demographic transition..

The comparative index of quality of life, taking into account various factors, place Kerala far above the general situation prevailing not only in other parts of the country, but also in most parts of the Third World. Broadly speaking, there are two schools which try to explain the Keŗala model and have arrived at their prognosis. The first school argues that Kerala has succeeded in achieving a quality of life nearly comparable to the developed countries at a much lower level of resource consumption. Arguing on these lines, they hail Kerala as the best sustainability model. Another variant of this approach hails Kerala as shortcut to development, where quality of life can be improved without economic growth or social change. They call it an ideal cheap model of development. There have also been serious criticisms. As a reaction to the above position, there has been a tendency to denigrate the achievements of Kerala in the social sectors. Alternatively, taking into consideration per capita income, unemployment and other indicators of economic backwarness, it has been shown that Kerala has been slipping sharply down in the rank order of development, as a "growth-less model".

The paradox of Kerala's experience lies precisely in achieving a relatively high quality of life at a low level of economic development. Low economic development is normally associated with low quality of life. This raises the question, if the people of Kerala are worse off because they have better education and health. There is also another extreme position. Kerala's educational and health development has been cited as another variant of the underdevelopment paradigm of colonial and neocolonial conditions. Despite the discussions at the overall level, significant deviation also been suggested. The overall indicators cited above contradicts with the experience of some communities that have been left out of the development process. Such communities include the tribes, the fisher folk etc.

The Kerala economy has been characterised by some structural changes, but these changes demonstrate one of lop-sided development. During the 1980s, the economy of the State demonstrated poor performance of agricultural and industrial sectors, severe power shortage, high incidence of educated unemployment and poverty. The development of the economy during the 1990s may be understood in two phases, i.e., the growth phase of the first half of the decade and the recession since the mid-90s.

During the former period, the State's economy achieved higher growth, which can be attributed to the better performance of the secondary and territory sectors. But, the State could not sustain this tempo of development which was not rooted on sustainable factors. The decline in Gulf remittances, a severe jolt to the industrial sector due to acute power shortage, and a sharp fall in the prices of some commercial crops which form the mainstay of agricultural economy of the State, have led to a significant decline. This was compounded by factors such as enhanced unemployment, inadequate infrastructural facilities, especially against a mounting rate of urbanisation. The structural changes that took place in the regional economy were not capable of addressing themselves to these severe problems.

The era of economic reforms and the revival of migration to the Middle East and consistent increase in inflow of foreign remittances to Kerala, have been remarkable features of the economy of the State during the first half of the last decade. The devaluation of the rupee in 1990 and the changes that have taken place regarding convertibility of rupee have helped migrants to earn more. These factors helped to keep migration as a sustained process even when the wage rate in many of the Gulf countries came down significantly. The number of Kerala migrants to the Middle East increased from 8.25 lakhs in 1971 to 14 lakhs in 1996. The corresponding remittances increased from the 230 crores in 1991 to 550 crores in 1995.

The process of migration virtually promoted a structural changes in the economy through a very basic attitudinal change in the society as a whole. A spurt in price of land, and real estate, a boom in construction activity, enhanced speculative and rent seeking activities were the roles of these new environment. The speculative mind got reflected in the labour market as well. While economic activities got concentrated around the tertiary sector, it created a value system which is anti-entrepreneurial. Within this wider environment, the entrepreneurs themselves got subjected to a process of retarded entrepreneurship. The picture on the economy of the state, as available today, is one of chronic stagnation. The data on Net Domestic Product (NDP) indicates that Kerala economy achieved a marginal increase in growth rate during the first half of 1990s compared to 1980s. The tertiary sector registered a higher growth rate, within which, sub-sectors like transport, storage and communication, registered the highest growth rate during the first half 1990s.

Kerala's industrial sector has undergone stagnation since the mid-1960s. The share of manufacturing sector in the SDP is relatively small and the growth rate recorded has been marginal compared to the all-India figures. Industrial performance in India since the Second Five Year Plan has witnessed three phases: a) high growth rate since mid-1950s; b) a deceleration since mid 1960s; and c) a phase of recovery since mid-1970s. Studies like Goldar and Seth (1989) have analysed the spatial variations in the rate of industrial growth across the country. Such studies indicate that, Kerala, Andhra Pradesh and Karnataka, were three states which experienced continuous deceleration till the mid-1980s. The figures available thereafter indicates that both these states have improved their growth rates, i.e., Andhra Pradesh from 6.03 to 6.76% and Karnataka from 6.85% to 7.68%. Among the Indian states, Kerala showed continues deceleration in the rate of industrial growth since the second half of 1960s.

The lopsided development observed in Kerala has often been explained in terms of high cost of production, labour related problems and the psychological fear of entrepreneurs. Unfortunately, much of the academic discussion during the 1980s - 1990s, were either for or against the 'labourunrest hypothesis'. These debates however, failed to go deeper into the processes that are operating at the grass-root level as well as the mental models developed by Keralites which get reflected in their investment decisions.

Rural Development and Employment

The debate on integrated rural development during the mid-1980s has significantly enriched our understanding of the dimensions of the problems of poverty as well as the nexus between employment and poverty. The need for generation of employment opportunities on a massive scale was emphasised by several debates. Hence, emerged the search for the most suitable strategy of employment generation. The discussions revolved around the two major categories: wage-employment and self-employment. At the operational level, employment generation programmes received an added theoretical focus during 1980s. Subsequently, the concurrent evaluations undertaken by the Ministry of Rural Development and independent studies by several scholars gave a greater boost to debate. The concern of much of these evaluations and debates has been to pinpoint the sustainability of employment generation. While some success stories have been reported from different parts of the country, the various rural development programmes implemented by Ministries and central agencies could not report a significantly high rate of success in achieving the economic objective of sustainability and the wider social objectives.

The achievement of such objectives, as outlined above, is essentially geared to structural changes in the rural economy, ipso facto, does not lead to higher levels of income and employment. It is necessary that these changes should be of the type which promotes positive and appropriate linkages in the economy. The new millennium brings in more challenges than hopes to the rural poor in India. While, latest studies indicate mounting unemployment and poverty as two crucial problems which need to be addressed to on a war-footing, it has become practically impossible to chalk out massive programmes that are capable of responding to these problems.

The latest strategy has been to target the poorest of the poor through anti-poverty programmes of a reoriented nature. In Kerala, these programmes have further been fine-tuned through the people's planning approach. Despite all these initiatives, there has been substantial leakges in programme implementation. Besides, even with the best efforts the impact they can make in the rural economy remain negligible, in relation to the needs.

Development of Health-care

The development in the area of health-care in Kerala has been the kingpin of Kerala model. It has been noted that, "no other large population on earth adequately meets the requirements of small families, combined with modest consumption". While the achievements in the health sector of Kerala has to be appreciated, it is important to examine the reasons for the same as well as the methods by which these achievements can be sustained. Enhanced literacy level, enhancement of status of women in society, land reforms, an effective public distribution system, enhanced political consciousness etc have often been suggested as the key factors. However, an area which has been overlooked by most scholars is health-care infrastructure.

The health-care legacy of Kerala dates back to the 19th Century. The princely states of Travancore and Cochin had initiated steps to set up vital health infrastructure, mainly for the objective of prevention of contagious diseases. Since Independence , this legacy continued. The number of beds in government hospitals increased from 13,000 in 1961 to 20,000 in 1971, and again to 29,000 in 1981; by 1996, it became 38,000. A look at the budgetary documents shows that, during 1985-86 to 1995-96, even under budgetary constraints, government expenditure in health-care has not come down. It is also important to note that, both in terms of the number of beds, and the number of employees, the private sector has outweighed the public sector. Simultaneously, the public sector is facing an unhealthy competition, mainly due to unfair practices by the private sector.

In any society, what is expected of the health-care sector is to contribute to improve the quality of life of the people. Infact, a sound health-care system is the very foundation of a healthy economy. Three of the crucial issues facing the health care system in Kerala are the following:

— Mobilisation of adequate resources for maintenance of the existing infrastructure;

— The deteriorating quality of health services;

— The indiscriminate growth of private sector and its negative implications on meeting the healthcare needs of the people.

An examination of the developments in this sector in the recent past indicates that, unlike in the past there has been excessive focus on the curative rather than preventive aspect of the healthcare in the State. Even while the State bears an important part of budgetary resources for this sector, it has not been able to perform the community health role effectively. As a consequence, the outbreak of contagious diseases has been reported from various parts of the State during recent times. Such problems have often been viewed by planners and administrators simply as a health problem rather than as social costs which have a close bearing on the performance of the economy as a whole.

People's Planning

There has been common agreement that something need to be done urgently to salvage Kerala out of its present crisis. One attempt in this direction was the so-called People's Planning which was inaugurated in 1996. People's planning experiment in Kerala is an extension of debates on multi-level planning as it emerged in 1960s and which appeared in several official documents of the Government of India during the late 1960s and 1970s. The thrust on democratic decentralisation contained in these policy documents were adapted to the situation of Kerala. Hence, a model of People's Planning has been articulated in terms of more efficient administration of physical and social capital for the purpose of development. Democratic decentralistion, has also the potential of nurturing a particular useful state-civil society synergies.

The 73rd and 74th amendments to the Constitution of India formed an opportunity for setting in motion the decentralisation process in Kerala in a new direction. The traditional step-by-step approach of devolution of financial resources and administrative powers from the State to the District, was reoriented by giving substantial powers to the village Panchayaths and the municipalities. The LDF Government, way back in 1996, earmarked 35 to 40% of the outlay to the Ninth Five Year Plan towards programmes and projects drawn up by the local-self governments.

During 1997-98, the resources thus devolved worked out to be Rs. 1025 crores and Rs. 1178 crores 1998-99. This excludes the funds from centrally- sponsored schemes and institutional loans that could be availed by local bodies with government guarantee. While before 1996-97 the share of local-self governments in the Annual Plan was around Rs. 20 crores, this signifies a quantum jump in resource available with local- self government. A major feature of the devolution of financial powers in Kerala under the People's Plan has been that, devolution has taken place in terms of a significant size of the Plan funds into the hands of the local-self government, (in 1997-98, 75% of grant-in-aid, and the rest in terms of sponsored schemes). However in other states of the country, grant-in-aid forms a small component of the so-called untied funds whereas financial devolution takes largely the form of schemes.

Another major feature of the People's Planning model was a thrust given to social mobilisation as an instrument for Plan formulation and implementation. The involvement of ordinary people in the Plan process through the mechanism of Gram Sabha is innovative and probably the first experiment of its kind ever recorded under a democratic set up. This method of drawing up a Plan and its implementation has some positive contribution: Firstly, it helped significantly to raise the illusions of common people regarding decision making at the grassroots level. It is important to note that Kerala's grand tradition of "discussing politics over a cup of tea", which signifies a substantial degree of social consciousness and accountability, got eroded significantly since mid-1970s.

The subsequent experiment of Plan design and implementation proved that expectation of a major departure from the beaten track has been much constrained to begin with, the financial devolution did not lead to a diversification of programmes and projects. Since the Second Annual Plan onwards, a conscious effort was taken by the Government as well as the State Planning Board to initiate greater innovative programmes and projects. However, considering the vast requirements of a thorough restructuring of Plan process, the efforts do not bear significant fruits. This owes to several constraints:

Kerala's thrust during the past several decades has been geared largely to the social sectors. The productive sectors like agriculture and industry got only step-motherly treatment under a welfare-oriented regime which Kerala witnessed since about 1970s. Planning these productive sectors were a bureaucratic exercise with very little people's involvement or expertise. This retarded hegemony continues under the people's planning regime also.

Secondly, the planning process itself operates at two levels with their often less complementary regimes. For instance, macro level planning for industry does not match with counterpart initiatives taken by the Panchayathi Raj Institutions. Thirdly, the People's planning movement could not mobilise the expertise of a large number of people who could have contributed significantly to its success. Unfortunately, several experts who showed substantial enthusiasm during the initial stages of the movement got distanced themselves in the subsequent stages.

Fourthly, Kerala failed to present a clear development agenda before the people of the State. The political parties, unlike in the past gain mandate largely on the basis of short-term programmes and issues, rather than on wider issues of development and long-run programmes. This gradually led to a blurring of the developmental scene where some sort of inertia is rampant.

Fifthly, the intellectual leadership, of the State also got alienated from the mainstream of development. While the lower ranks of academic community, due to their political leanings showed some interest in activities which are largely politically driven, those who could have made use of their expertise, largely chose be silent.

Sixthly, the emergence of non-resident Keralites (NRKs) as a significant group, had it negative implications on the development scene as a whole. While NRKs contributed significantly in terms of foreign exchanges, the NRK phenomenon itself lead to a polarisation in Kerala society. While NRKs received considerable social and political patronage, this was largely at the expense of the morale of sizeable sections of the community who wanted to earn a living on the local economy. This is very clear in the industrial sector where no major effort has been initiated over the last 20 years to raise the morale of the entrepreneurial community. This vicious effect has not received adequate attention in the media as well.

Naturally, while in other parts of the country, atleast selected sections of the society have been aware of the challenges of liberalisation and are taking steps to withstand the evil effects of these challenges, Kerala by and large, has been groping in the darkness. It is against this background that an innovative approach like People's Planning has been placed. Naturally, the enthusiasm it has created does not get translated into concrete action and ideas generated by the people. In a people-centered initiative, it is the enthusiasm, imagination and drive of the people that lead the programmes into success.

While many of these issues are common to several villages in Kerala, the case of Vypeen Island stands out, in terms of the specific history the Island has. While poverty and unemployment are of a common problems of the rural economy of Kerala, the regional diversities are a reflection largely of how the people, and poor people in specific, react to these problems. While comparable literature is scanty, we have attempted to provide a comparative static position in terms of a similar study we have undertaken in Idukki district of Kerala during 1999. The changes that have taken place in the regional economy of Ernakulam district as well as of Vypeen Block has to be understood against the background of these State-level issues. Where Kerala is a rural-urban continuum, highly sensitive to information through a higher average level of education and transport and communication network, it is natural that the developmental issues of Vypeen resembles closely with the wider issues of development at the State-level.

Vypeen, is an island on the western side of the Ernakulam District. With the Kodungalore strait on the

North, the Cochin port and Backwaters on the South, river Periyar and the Cochin city on the East and the Arabian Sea on the West, Vypeen has a size of 87.85 Sq. kms. The Island is demarcated by a sea coast of 26 Kilometers on the West and backwaters extending around 30 Kilometers on the East. A cluster of islands, this Block is constituted by seven Gram Panchayaths, Mulavukadu. Elamkunapuzha, Narakkal, Nayarambalam, Edavanakad, Kuzhupilly and Pallipuram. Of these, Mulavukadu is constituted by three islands, ie., Panambukadu, Valarpadam and Mulavukadu.

Narakkal is constituted by two islands as well ie., Valliavattom and East Manjanakadu. Though it remains separated from the main land, Vypeen is narrowly linked with other parts of the District through an artery road, the Vypeen-Munambam road, which divides this Asia's most densely populated Island into two stretches, i.e., the Western stretch, which is coastal-belt, and the Eastern-belt, which is closer to the Backwaters. Three of the constituent Island, ie., Mulavukadu, Panambukadu and Valarpadam, remain completely isolated with water transport as only access. Similarly, the only direct access to the nearby Cochin city is the Backwaters.

Largely below the sea level, Vypeen is subject the threat of the vagaries of the Ocean, though the Kodungalore strait provides a bulwark. The ecology of Vypeen is unique. The region is endowed with large canals extending over 50 Kilometers and a network of small canals emerging there from. With paddy fields, coconut gardens, marshy lands and waste lands, water in most parts of the Island is extremely saline. Naturally, availability of drinking water remains a major problem. With the mixed topography, improper drainage is a major problem which affects the environment adversely.

Population: The population of Vypeen according to the 1991 census was 1,88,521 which is 9.53 % of the district population of 19,77,142. The density of population is 2158 per square kilometers, which is highest in the State. The total number of households is 35,606 which is 9.10% of the total households in the district. The sex-ratio is 1042 females per 1000 males.

Literacy Level : A distinguishing feature of Vypeen is its higher level of literacy and especially of female literacy. While the district level of literacy rate is 84% and in Vypeen it is 85.5%. Corresponding figures for female literacy is 78.5 and 81.6% respectively. A more distinguishing feature is the higher level of literacy among SC/ST population. It exceeds both the district level rates as well as rates within the Block. Literacy rate among Schedules Castes is 82.9% whereas for Scheduled Tribes is 83.7%. It is to be noted that, the district level rates for Scheduled Castes is only 61.4%, whereas for Scheduled Tribes, it is 47.9%.

Occupational Pattern: The occupational profile of the Block throw light upon the lope-sided development of the Block. Main workers constitute only 8.56% of the total population, whereas the size of non-workers category constitute as large as 10.09%. The share of marginal workers remain low indicating the small size of ancillary employment opportunities.

The decline in agricultural employment is an emerging phenomenon in the Island. Though, this to some extent, has been compensated by non-farm activities, there is a general preference among the younger generation not to go for the traditional non-farm activities like tree-climbing and coir work like, retting, dehusking, and spinning. There has also been an alienation of the younger generation from fishing, which is prominent tradition activity. Fish peeling absorbs a sizeable group of women workers. Carpentry and masonry would have been other prominent areas.

However, due to inadequate mobility of labour, the opportunities remain limited. Other section like masons assistance and casual labourers, move out of the Island to some extent. Besides, there is also a process of entry into the ranks of masons and carpenters from other communities. The Island in general, demonstrates a tendency of a ratchet within which labour circulates without much opportunities for openings outside.

Employment and Unemployment: The Census figures indicate that unemployment is a major problem in the Island. While partial and full unemployment are rampant, the major reason remains the structural factors. Marginalisation of coconut gardens, and enhanced diseases have led to a declined interest in coconut cultivation. Similarly, the entry of massive tribe of Tamil fishermen and their settlement in the region have reduced employment opportunities of local fishermen. The problem has been compounded by limited mobility of labour.

Infrastructure: The Vypeen is endowed with availability of basic social and economic infrastructure. However, many such infrastructure is not adequate in relation to higher density of population. Constraints are largely in the areas of water supply and sanitation.

Education and Culture: Vypeen has a rich cultural heritage. However, its attainments in the area of education are far from satisfactory. Both secondary data, as well as our own field research indicate that the levels of education are much lower in relation to the situation in other parts of the State. Based on secondary and primary sources of data and information, it may be noted that the physical facilities available in educational institutions remain far from satisfactory. This adds to the inadequate number of institutions in relation to the density of population.

Public Health: There are a variety of factors which influence the health standards of the people. These can be categorised as direct and indirect factors.

Transport and Communication: The availability of transport and communication influence the physical quality of life significantly. The availability of these facilities in Vypeen does not match with the state level average. The major constraint of the Island despite its proximity with the main-land is its poor transport facilities. Any major initiative worth mentioning is the bridge connecting Cherai on the North with North Paravoor. Even this connection does not improve the transport situation significantly as the bridge is far away from Cochin. A regular Jungar service linking Fort-Cochin and Vypeen was started in 1977 as an outcome of an agitation under the leadership of Mr. T.A. Paraman, who was then member of the Legislative Assembly. Subsequently, a similar service between Ernakulam and Vypeen started in 1993.

Regional Economy

The regional economy is characterised by pre-dominance of agriculture and fisheries. In tune with the emerging needs of a significantly sized population, there has been a significant growth of the service sector. Large industries are almost nil. Small enterprises are largely of a primitive mould, involved in service activities.

Agriculture: Vypeen is characterised by a peculiar eco-system suitable for paddy cultivation, cultivation of garden crops like coconut and fish farming. The canals connected with the Cochin backwaters on the eastern side facilitates paddy cultivation in most Panchayaths of Vypeen. However, there is a direct inlet, which connects Puthuvypu village with the sea. This prevents paddy cultivation in that village. The estimated productivity of paddy is 600 kgs. per acre. Prawn culture is an off-season activity which provides substantial income and employment. Infrastucture for research and development activities in this area have been set up by the Kerala Agricultural University as well as by the Govt. of India through its Krishi Vigyan Kendra. Coconut is another major crop, distributed throughout the area. It has been estimated that an area of 7136 acres are occupied by coconut gardens. Root-wilt disease is widespread and this has affected productivity of coconut gardens significantly.

Livestock and Poultry: Livestock and poultry which were important subsidiary activities in the village have come down in the recent past. However, programmes like IRDP have attracted more households into these activities. Two Co-operative Dairies, one at Pallippuram and the other one at Narakkal, as well as a number of private initiatives, take care of the processing and distribution of dairy products. Rearing of ducks and poultry also provide subsidiary employment opportunities for many households.

Fisheries

Endowed with rich water resources and with infrastructural support by several governmental agencies, fishing, fish processing and trade have offered an important source of income and employment in the region. Fishing forms the major occupation for nearly 21,000 persons. In addition, there are around 8,000 workers involved in fishery related ancillary activities. Membership in Fishermen's Welfare Societies (which forms the backbone of fishermen's villages in Kerala) constitutes, as per latest data, around 12,500 persons. Fishing equipments also support the village assets significantly. This includes, 1323 fishing boats registered in the area, in addition to about 400 boats which come from outside Vypeen. The fishing craft also includes trawlers and purse-seine boats, amounting 110 in numbers. The infrastructure for this sector include, the state-owned Fishing Harbour at Munambam, in addition to the two private harbours, one at Munambam and the other one at Murikkumpadam. The processing network includes 70 ice plants and 400 peeling sheds located in various parts of the Block.

The public support system for fisheries is significant and widespread in Vypeen. The R&D and extension services are offered by the Fisheries Station of the Kerala Agricultural University located at Puthuvypu as well as by the Fisheries Research Station and the Krishi Vigyan Kendra located at Narakkal. In addition to this, there is a regular support network, largely by the Govt. of Kerala. The Matsya Bhawan of the Fisheries Department has 2 Inspectors posted in this area, in addition to 3 Project Officers of the Matsyafed and 2 Fisheries Officers of the Fishermen's Welfare Board. Most of the government programmes in the area have been implemented through a network of 22 primary Fishermen's Societies operating under Matsyafed, which is the apex Federation.

The public promotional cum incentive system includes, distribution of equipments to primary societies, production and distribution of prawn seeds through hatcheries, and technical training in prawn fishery and hatchery. The relevant institutions are, the Marine products Export Promotion Authority, and state level organisations, the ADAK and the BEFDA

Industries: As already noted, the region has been characterised by lope-sided industrial development. The industrial base is largely constituted by fisheries related industrial activities such as, fish processing units, tiny units which are involved in processing of fish products, peeling sheds, ice plants, boat yards, production, repairing and servicing of fishing equipments etc. Despite this significant resource base and natural advantages, no major structural or organisational changes have taken place in these industries. The government promotional activities in the past include setting up of an industrial estate, registration of 16 industrial co-operative societies and implementation of usual programmes of promotional agencies like the District Industries Centre and the Khadi and Village Industries Board etc. Depsite these initiatives, and the possible market opportunities offered by Cochin city, which is just a few kilometers away, the industrial base has not picked up, nor have any significant diversification taken place in the existing structure.

Services Sector

While there is a lope-sided industrial development as outlined above, the service sector has grown significantly, partly in response to the high density of population. The activity structure of this sub-sector include, a large number of hotels, distribution services, shops catering to household items, financial services etc.

Income Levels and Poverty

Despite significant interventions through official and non-official development programmes, Vypeen stands first in poverty and income inequalities. In terms of the rate of urbanisation as well as regarding the extent of unemployment Vypeen stands out among other Blocks/ regions of the country.

Government Programmes in Vypeen

Unemployment and poverty are major problems which constrain development of Vypeen. These problems have been addressed to by several governmental agencies as well as by NGOs. However, the role played by the governmental agencies is more crucial than that of the NGOs. The governmental programmes can be broadly categorised into two: a) social sector programmes; b) programmes which are addressed essentially to the economic sectors.

Social Sector Programmes

The social sector programmes may be discussed under the following heads:

— Anti poverty/rural development programmes

— Health

— Water-supply and sanitation

— Social Welfare Programmes

— Education and Culture

The social sector programmes have a distributional content in programme design and implementation. This content is more pronounced in the case of the anti-poverty or rural development programmes which are specifically targeted to the people below the poverty-line. The other programmes in this category, such as health, water-supply, education and social welfare, are largely not targeted and are meant to be of an overall impact in the community as a whole.

Antipoverty Programmes

Among the various anti-poverty and rural development programmes, 7 programmes have been implemented in Vypeen. They are, IRDP, DWCRA, TRYSEM, SITRA, IAY, MWS, JRY and CRSP. While SITRA has been implemented only since 1994-95, data regarding all the other programmes are available from 1994-95 onwards. The physical and financial figures on anti-poverty programes themselves do not explain how these programmes have contributed to a structural change in the rural economy of Vypeen. What is more important are: (1) how the new assets created perform in offering a flow of services to the people whom they are meant for; and (2) to what extent the new employment created has led to a structural change in the overall position of household income, savings and investment. An understanding of these aspects requires a more detailed analysis of income flows and assets created.

Implementation of SGSY

The congruence two factors, the newly initiated SGSY programme, as well as the new planning methodology adopted by the State, should offer considerable hopes for the design and implementation of rural development programmes in a novel way. Viewed from this angle, we made an indepth study of selected Activity Clusters identified by the Block under the SGSY.

Water supply and sanitation

Lack of availability of potable water and salinity of the existing water resources, make drinking water a major constraint in Vypeen. The fact that a significantly large population is subject to these problems, caught the attention of the government soon after Independence. Against acute scarcity of drinking water, especially towards the southern part of the Island, steps were taken way back in 1950s to bring drinking water in barges and to supply it in the Island. This continues still. The supply of water through pipelines was started in 1958. Such water was made available in places like Vallarpadam, Mulavukad, Elamkunnapuzha and Narakkal. The LIC-aided Water Supply Scheme was launched by the

Government of Kerala in 1980, drinking water has been made available from Aluva through pipelines.

Social Welfare Programmes

As Vypeen stands first in the District in terms of the percentage of population below the poverty line, social welfare activities assume particular significance. Public programmes in this area form broadly of two categories: (1) programmes targeted to women and children; and (2) special programmes for SC/ST communities. Among the other welfare programmes include, the specific economic programmes targeted to women. Training and support services for women have appeared prominently in the Plan documents of all Gram Panchayaths. Unfortunately, the vital linkages are often missing. For instance, in one of the Panchayaths 50 women were trained in a particular trade called manufacturing of electronic chokes. It has been indicated that none of these trainees have been sticking on to their area of expertise, nor have they been provided escort services.

In the new approach to planning in Kerala, projects/programmes relating to the welfare of SC/STs have been given a special status and thrust. Traditionally, occupation-wise, the SC/ST communities are largely agricultural labourers. Of these, paddy cultivation provided employment to a significant extent. While the area under paddy as well as employment therein has significantly come down during recent times, other activities like fish and crab culture which substituted it, are not capable of compensating this decline. While political and administrative compulsions have necessitated earmarking a fixed portion of Plan funds for the welfare of these communities, there has not been serious effort to chalk out sustainable strategies and programmes. Naturally, there has been significant misutilisation of funds as evident from our field investigation. Besides, most of Gram Panchayaths have spent the bulk of such funds for training activities.

Economic Programmes

The economic programmes are, general programmes which are meant for the overall economic development of the region, though such programmes may have an indirect distributional impact in the community. We may broadly include the following under this category: (a) agriculture; (b) industries; and (c) fisheries.

Agriculture: Vypeen is a basically agrarian economy. The support programmes of the Government relating to agriculture need to be situated against the peculiarities of agricultural economy of the Island. The major peculiarities relate to the ecology itself, i.e., prominence of crops such as paddy and coconut, which requires proper irrigation. Vypeen has this natural advantage, as the whole area is connected with waterways large and small which inturn, are connected with the sea. The direct inlet of saline water at the village Puthuvype, prevents paddy cultivation here. This ecological peculiarity facilitates a diversified development of the agricultural sector.

During the off-season, fish culture is made possible. Despite the opportunities, agriculture remains stagnant in the Island since 1970s. The enactment of land reforms in 1970, and its faithful implementation resulted in access to land ownership for a large number of tenants. The small plots, which, a large number of tenants got entitled, have not been properly cultivated. Besides, the large farmers lost much of their interest in cultivation, due to several reasons such as high cost of production and lack of remunerative prices for agricultural products like paddy and coconut, enhanced vulnerability of crops like coconut to diseases. This situation led to some forms of absentee landlordism by which the farmers increasingly lost interest in periodic maneuvering and planned protection measures.

While cultivation of paddy become unremunerative, the mainstay of the agricultural economy of Island now is coconut. Hence the fulcrum of any agricultural development strategy in the Island need to be to enhance the productivity of coconut cultivation. This requires a sustained effort to maintain and improve agricultural practices according to the changing needs. While in the past cleaning of waterways and gathering of slurry implied an indirect maneuvering for coconut trees. While an almost complete stoppage of this practice has resulted in a virtually demaneuvering process as well as to several environmental problems arising out of blocked waterways. It has been noted by several experts that, a ground of the root-wilt disease itself can be explained in terms of such blockage of waterways.

Considering environmental and human geographic factors of Vypeen, it is vital to evolve relatively large agricultural development project with the active involvement of governmental agencies. While the Gram Panchayath have several constraints, considering their limited resources and expertise, this task need to be performed by District Panchayath or directly by the agricultural department through non-plan funds. We have noted that no such important initiative has taken place in the recent past. Besides, much of the funding for agricultural developments in the are have been spread over several tiny projects, implies poor results. Besides, several of the conventional type of projects (eg. Promotion of vegetable cultivation) are not appropriate to the situation of Vypeen.

Public Assets

The meaningfulness of a public asset depends largely

upon the flow of income that it may create over the years. Such income is both qualitative and quantitative. We have noted that there is an inadequate effort to link the assets created, with the expected ultimate income contributions. For instance, construction of a road requires that it should provide a continuous flow of services to it users over a period of time. Hence, keeping a road open without finding adequate allocations for its maintenance as well as provision for a few culverts which are vitally needed, alternatively means that the efficiency of the assets is stolen away. This also implies questions of investment criteria.

The pattern of assets creation over the two Plan periods and their economic performance indicates a crucial mismatch between the aspirations of the people vis-à-vis what has been realised in the form of assets. For instance, allocations have been made by all the Panchayaths for cleaning the drainage. The drainages remain full, though the allocations have been utilised. However, the explanations given by the Panchayath is that the cleaning work has been done only during the rainy season, because during rains, cleaning is "easier". Such a uniform explanation by all the Panchayaths raise questions as to how they respond to the wisdom of the Gram Sabha. It is important to note that the Development Reports of all the Panchayaths have identified bad environment as a crucial problem, and have identified improper drainage as the villain.

Conventionally, in most discussions on public assets, there is largely as an engineering concept behind . For example, school buildings have been constructed in various parts of Kerala as well as in Vypeen, without regard to the basic comforts required for their inhabitants, ie., teachers and students. The concept of a school building does not often include an airy space for children to take rest or to play, shelves for keeping books, food-packets etc. There has been too much of conceptual rigidity which prevents any sort of informal mingling between teachers and the pupil.

Such perception was observed in the case of construction of shopping complex by two of the Panchayaths also. Shops have been built on some arbitrary criteria relating to the size and facilities and are rented out at nominal rates, which in no way reflect the market rate. It is also important to note that, the subsidy thus given is enjoyed largely by well-to-do people, who manages to rent-in the shops. The same perception applies in the case of other civil constructions like construction of an office for the Krishi Bhavan, and for a Veterinary hospital.

While the services offered by the Krishi Bhavan and the Veterinary hospital remains much to be desired and that the functions of these offices have been conceptually meant to be more fieldoriented, it is difficult to rationalise such investment. However, there have also been encouraging initiatives where support has been given for renovation of a public library by Nayarambalam Panchayath.

Employment: Structure and Changes

The existing structure of employment in the regional economy of Vypeen is dependent on the non-farm activities that have come up in the recent past. An analysis of the employment structure indicates that wage labour and non-farm activities contribute significantly to the survival of the majority of poor households. The antipoverty programmes have only the limited role of performing a largely supplementary supportive role rather than as a major inducement mechanism. It is important to note that a large number of beneficiaries are aged or infirm and their contribution to productive activities is negligible. The low percentage contribution of the respondents income in total household income, has implications on the survival strategies of the household. The other members of the household have to perform a subsidising role. In performing this role, the other members are forced to join the labour market at a relatively early age. This, together with the poor economic status of the household results in a low level of education for these members.

The relative stagnancy of average annual working days and average daily earnings of respondents are important observations which require special attention. The compound growth rate (CGR) for working days is 2%, whereas for earnings per day, the rate is 8%. This finding need to be related to the average age of respondents, which is 36. The broad implication is that, even after years of participation in the work-force, the process of graduation of labour into higher income-earning opportunities is negligible. This has been compensated by the subsidy added to household income by other members of the household. The respondent's meager income is supported by the income of other members. The implication of all these is that the income level of households remains absolutely low and household survival strategies are complex. These results also indicate that the average longevity of labour also is relatively low, probably because of adverse environmental factors.

A comparision of the findings emerging from the research at Idukki suggests some crucial differences. While in Idukki, agriculture contributes significantly to household income, in Vypeen these households are almost exclusively dependent on wage income. However, the average household income in Vypeen remains larger than in Idukki. To what extent this higher household income is beneficial on a relative sense, need to be examined in relation to the expenditure pattern. While agriculture performs a subsidy function in the family budget, this role is totally absent where the households are exclusively dependent on wage income.

Income behaviour

While employment is a spill-over of the process of investment and income generation, inorder to analyse its sustainability, it is necessary to analyse income changes in detail. A comparative static analysis of income structure may give insights into the relationship between income and employment. An analysis of the income distribution in Idukki, on the contrary, indicates anomalies in the selection of beneficiaries. Unlike in Idukki where approximately 33% of the respondents belong to the above BPL category, the respondent in Vypeen belong largely to the BPL category.

Assets are the outcome of past savings or are externally provided. A higher asset position enhances the household's command over productive resources, which in turn, lead to future enhancement in income. Total assets per earning member, can be a meaningful indicator of this process. A comparison with the situation in Idukki suggests that command over assets do not equip the poor of Vypeen to improve their economic position over time.

The average asset per household is relatively low. Likewise, the debt-asset ratio is relatively higher. This reflects on the composition of total assets as well. While in Idukki, productive land is the major form of asset, in Vypeen it is mainly land and houses. Hence, in the latter case of the latter, the flow of income is negligible, whereas in Idukki, land is an important source of income.

Disparities in asset-base, to some extent, explain the disparities in income. This is because the second major source of income in poor households is assets. The following Lorenz curve gives a picture of asset disparities among households.

New assets created through anti-poverty programmes add to the existing asset position of households, and one would expect that they may generate new income which will add to the current income of households.

Asset position in itself does not tell the full story. A more meaningful understanding of the role of assets require relating them with the debt position of the households. Therefore, debt/asset ratio provides a more meaningful explanation of how the assets of households fare in the present circumstances.

Indebtedness

The overall balance of survival and survival strategies is a crucial concern of our study. While many studies on poverty and rural development focus on the indebtedness as an absolute factor, in the present study, we would like to examine it terms of its two dimensions: (a) endogenous dependency; and exogenous dependency. Endogenous dependency (measured by dependency ratio) is a crucial factor influencing the viability and sustainability of households. Exogenous dependency, on the other hand, is the excess of debts which the households have on their assets. While both forms of dependency influence the viability, it is important to examine the structure of such dependency.

4
Public Institutions and Governance

The recent financial crises in Asia have exposed problems of governance and public sector performance in that region. The latest work on aideffectiveness points out the risks of lending to countries with bad policies and poorly performing public sectors. Just as it became evident in the 1980s that potentially good projects often fail in poor policy environments, so it became evident in the 1990s that policy reforms are less likely to succeed when public institutions and governance are weak. Building effective and accountable public institutions is arguably the core challenge for sustainable poverty reduction. The World Bank has increasingly focused its attention in recent years on reform of public sector institutions. The Bank has acknowledged the harmful economic consequences of corruption-a fundamental symptom of public sector malfunction-and is working with partners and clients to address it in both country settings and international forums.

Institutional development and capacity building have been identified as major goals under the Strategic Compact. The Bank's activities in core areas of public sector functioning-such as public expenditure analysis and management, tax administration, civil service reform, regulation, decentralization, and judicial reform-grew rapidly from 1997 to 1999 (Figures 1 and 2). Much of its work in public service delivery (whether in the social sectors or in infrastructure) has focused on institutional concerns, including private provision or decentralization in addition to capacity building. Indeed, virtually all Bank projects approved in recent years try in some way to reform the institutions of the public sector. About one-quarter of the Bank's lending in fiscal 1997-99, equivalent to about $5 billion to $7 billion per year, was allocated to institution-building as broadly defined, with about one-tenth being spent on direct technical assistance.

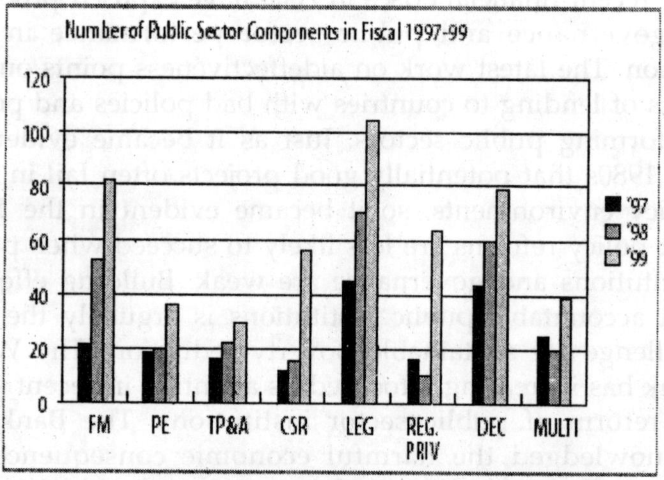

FM:	Public Expenditure and Financial Management
PE:	Public Enterprise Reform
TP&A:	Tax Policy and Administration
CSR:	Civil Service Reform
LEG:	Legal and Judicial Reform
REG.PRIV:	Regulation of the Private Sector
DEC:	Decentralization
MULTI:	Multisector (more than one of the above)

Figure 1. Governance-Related lending has grown rapidly

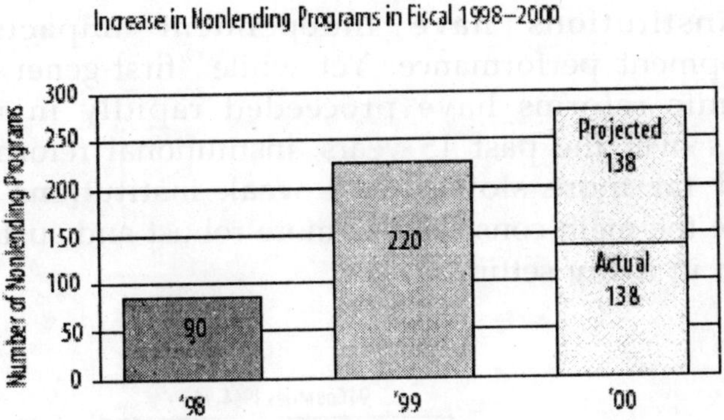

Figure 2. Governance-Related nonlending activity has also expanded

For the first few decades of its history, the Bank as well as other donors addressed development primarily as a technocratic challenge. The implicit model was that good advisers and technical experts would design good policies and projects, which good governments and an adequately resourced public sector would then implement for the benefit of society. As World Development Report 1997 (WDR97) highlighted, however, at least as important as the policies and resources for development are the institutions within which public action is embedded-the "rules of the game" and the mechanisms through which they are monitored and enforced. Institutions can include organizational rules and routines, formal laws, and informal norms. Together they shape the incentives of public policymakers, overseers, and providers of public services.

Following WDR97, this strategy takes as its focus the reform of public institutions, as broadly defined to Institutions and policies interact in complex ways. A focus on institutions complements, but is broader than, the Bank's long-standing efforts to foster policy reform. As Figure 3 (taken from WDR97) shows, both policies and institutions have independent impacts on development performance. Yet while "first-generation" economic reforms have proceeded rapidly in many settings over the past 15 years, institutional reform has moved far more slowly, and weak institutions have become the main constraint to more robust and sustained growth in many settings.

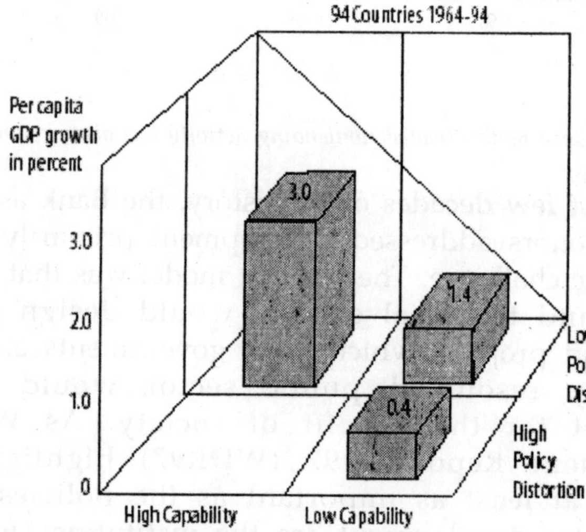

Figure 3. Institutional capability improves economic growth

Policies and institutions are closely interlinked in several ways. First, policy design should take institutional capacity carefully into account. When institutions are weak or dysfunctional, simple policies that limit administrative demands and public discretion work best.Where institutions are stronger, more challenging public initiatives can be effective. Matching policies and institutions is key. Second, policies do not emerge from a vacuum but generally are the result of bargaining among contending groups-with the interplay among them shaped by the institutional and political "rules of the game." Indeed, the Bank's Public Expenditure Reviews (PERs) used to be primarily analyses of expenditure policies, but in recent years they have increasingly focused on institutional issues of budgeting and financial control. A PER is now considered incomplete if it does not address the institu-tions of public expenditure management.

Third, the causation also works in reverse: policy choice can significantly influence the way institutions develop. A decision to reduce tariffs or move from highly varied to uniform tax rates can dramatically shift incentives and responsibilities within customs and tax administrations, making it harder for officials to extract bribes in return for lower taxes. This is one example of why economic reform is a key pillar of an anticorruption program.

Institutional Governance Concerns

The Bank has traditionally classified "public sector management" (PSM) as a sector, focused somewhat narrowly on the workings of core areas of government. The approach proposed in this strategy, however, goes beyond a compartmentalized approach to PSM. It emphasizes the links between core public institutions (including not only the executive arm but also the legislature and the judiciary) and sectoral institutions, and ultimately between reform of the institutional system and the reduction of poverty at the grass roots. The economic functions of the public sector can be broadly classified into three distinct categories, each with its corresponding institutional challenges:

- Making and Implementing Economic Policy: Good performance in designing policy requires more than economic analysis. Institutions are needed that can maintain discipline in fiscal and monetary aggregates, effectively set priorities among competing demands for resources, and mobilize revenues. Institutions for macroeconomic planning and monetary policy should generally be structured to provide autonomy and avoid pressures from spending ministries for over-optimistic forecasting. In contrast, institutions for strategic prioritization are intrinsically political and should be structured to provide participation and buy-in from interest groups, with legislative oversight where appropriate.
- Delivering Services: The public sector delivers or fosters private delivery of a broad range of public services-infrastructure services, social services and also the legal and regulatory services needed for an efficient private sector. This broad range of services can be delivered through a variety of institutional arrangements and with widely varying degrees of effectiveness. A central challenge is to put in place institutional arrangements for service delivery that are workable in specific country contexts and that promote the goal of poverty reduction. This goes well beyond a narrow concern with activities within relevant line ministries-that is, the allocation of sectoral funds or the configuring of ministerial organizational charts.

Accountability for Public Resources and Public Regulatory Power

Well-functioning public sectors do not operate in a vacuum. They are grounded in multiple mechanisms that insure accountability. The key to accountability is the capacity to monitor and enforce rules-within the public sector, between public and private parties, and, sometimes, among private parties. The internal regulatory mechanisms of government- accounting and audit, procurement, and personnel have long received sustained attention as the centerpiece of reforms to promote accountability, and should continue to be a key part of the agenda. Additionally, the monitoring and enforcing functions rooted in countries' constitutional separation of powers have recently come to the forefront of development discourse. These include the mutual monitoring roles of legislatures and executives, the vertical division of power associated with decentralization, and the monitoring function of an independent judiciary and an informed citizenry.

This strategy focuses primarily on core public institutions and their sectoral linkages. The Public Sector Board is also interacting closely with other groups in the Bank working on particular specialized topics of public sector reform in client countries, including OCS (in its work on systemic procurement and financial management reform), Controllers (financial management systems), LEG (legal/judicial reform), OED (evaluation capacity development), and WBI (anticorruption and parliamentary strengthening).

A broad view of capacity building must encompass institutional reform. Institutional reform is sometimes used interchangeably with "capacity building," a term that has become increasingly common in recent years. When more broadly defined to include reforms of incentives and institutions as well as strengthening skills and resources, however, the term capacity building is essentially synonymous with the concept of institutional development. scope of "capacity building" can, however, be ambiguous. If narrowly defined as the provision of training and materials to build skills within organizations, capacity building is only part of the challenge of reforming public institutions. A technocratic supply-side approach does not go very far in addressing the complex political

World Development Report 1997 was the culmination of a long process of learning inside and outside the Bank about the centrality of institutions for development rather than a radical break with the past. The need for institutional reform was on the Bank's agenda in the early 1980s, with the establishment of a public sector management division in 1981 and the World Development Report, 1983: Management in Development.

A 1998 QAG review of four technical assistance projects in the Europe and Central Asia region rated only one of them as "satisfactory" overall and three of them as "marginally satisfactory" in quality at entry and quality of supervision. The Bank's interventions in the area of systemic legal and judicial reform are relatively new and have not yet been formally evaluated, but the general view of practitioners is that their success to date is also mixed.

A recent internal review of the Bank's interventions in the area of tax administration also indicates a mixed record of quality. What led to these mixed results, particularly in the first half of the 1990s? Four consistent messages emerge from OED and QAG reviews, seconded by the "common wisdom" gained over the past decade by Bank operational staff. First, projects are not likely to be successful when they fail to take fully into account the complex political and institutional realities on the ground-and thus the real incentives for implementation. The Bank (not unlike other donors) has sometimes taken a rather narrow and "technocratic" supply-side view on PSM and TA in the past, interacting exclusively with government interlocutors and funding consulting services, computers, and other inputs in the absence of a deep and sustainable demand for institutional reform on the part of the borrower.

In some cases, the Bank has failed to consult with key stakeholders whose support is critical or who could help mobilize pressure for change. Often a few reformers in the central ministries want reform, but they cannot mobilize the support from broader groups in society to push it through. Furthermore, in some cases the Bank has tried to provide technocratic solutions within government when changing the role and scope of government activities (for example, contracting out or decentralizing public service delivery) might have led to more fundamental institutional change.

Second, the Bank has sometimes relied on models of "best practice" that may not be feasible in the particular country setting. Unrealistic optimism is a persistent strand of weakness running through Bank work, as reported regularly by OED and QAG. Bank staff, enthused by some new "best practice" breakthrough in one country, have sometimes rushed to recommend it in an entirely different setting, with little attention to the impact of these country differences on the prospects for success. While comparative knowledge and broad principles can help illuminate options for reform in any situation, they are no substitute for in-depth country knowledge. For example, the recent OED report on CSR concludes that, "the Bank has relied on small groups of interlocutors within core ministries to design and implement one-size-fits-all CSR–blueprints in diverse country settings."

Third, in addition to the shortfalls of a narrow technocratic or one-size-fits-all approach, public sector management interventions have been hampered in the past by shortcomings in traditional lending instruments, which have made it difficult to address systemic problems in the public sector over the medium-term time horizon needed for institutional change. Fourth, some OED reports have also pointed to problems within the Bank, including deficient staffing and weak incentives for timely and cost-efficient delivery of Bank products. A 1998 OED study of Public Expenditure Reviews, for example, surveyed 35 PERs conducted prior to 1998 and found that many had weak analysis or limited ownership and impact in client countries.

In the area of judicial reform, for example, a 1992 project in Venezuela was criticized by the NGO community for not involving a wide range of stakeholders in the design of the project; drawing in part from that experience, more recent projects in Venezuela and Guatemala have been careful to include extensive consultations with the private sector, civil society, and other donors in the design phase. With regard to PERs, extensive efforts are being made to link PERs more closely to country strategies, to increase country participation and ownership of the PER process and outcomes, to focus PER analysis more centrally on institutions for budgeting, implementation, and accountability, and to build stronger partnerships with the IMF and other donors.

Sector-based Institution-Building

Since the late 1980s, Bank support for service delivery in infrastructure, rural and social sectors has begun to move away from an exclusive reliance on public monopolies-because of their operational inefficiency, poor incentives for performance, and inability to meet growing sectoral demand-and has increasingly recommended the participation of both the private sector and private citizens in service delivery. The Bank has focused on "voice" and competition in addition to-or sometimes in lieu of-internal government reforms. Private participation in infrastructure is becoming standard practice, and the Bank is shifting its support increasingly toward policy, regulation, and risk mitigation. More health, nutrition, and population (HNP) projects since 1990 have worked to employ NGOs and civil society in a participatory role in service delivery. The Bank is actively encouraging private participation in the education sector in Latin America, and water supply and sanitation projects such as those in Uzbekistan, Paraguay, and Pakistan have been noted as models of participatory development.

Reforming core institutions of government and addressing governance and anticorruption concerns are extremely difficult challenges, in part because of social and political dimensions. Given the nature of the task, many attempts at reform will fail to meet their full objectives. Some may fail entirely despite the Bank's best efforts, and others may be judged as failures even though the interventions resulted in substantial gains relative to the earlier status quo.

In the area of anticorruption, for example, Bank interventions are unlikely ever to eliminate corruption, and even making a significant dent in the problem may be difficult in certain countries no matter how well the Bank performs. Defining a standard for success is particularly tricky in such a situation. Rather than aim for the same percentage and standard of success in all types of projects the Bank undertakes, success should be measured in part against the difficulty of the challenges addressed, and if possible against what would have been in place without the intervention. Furthermore, a mere yes-no (successful/unsuccessful) indicator will not properly capture the outcome. Not all successes have equal benefits, and the benefits of successful interventions may be particularly high in core areas of public sector reform. A lower success rate may be offset by higher benefits in the cases that do succeed.

Need for Institutional Reform Challenges

The first step in doing better is to recognize the mismatch between the requirements of successful institutional reform and traditional ways of going about the aid business. Effective governments work in integrated, not fragmented, ways. Public decisionmaking is an ongoing process of making choices among competing ends. Recognizing the advantages of integrated decisionmaking by governments poses a fundamental challenge to a core product of the aid business projects. Almost by definition, projects target some specific facet of public action for detailed attention, rather than the broader institutional environment. In so doing, projects can preempt domestic budget decisionmaking by earmarking resources (including technical assistance) for preferred donor objectives. Moreover, to achieve their specific objectives, projects often support specialized implementation units, with higher pay scales than the civil service as a whole. These institutional enclaves deplete government of scarce human and financial resources.

At the same time, in countries where the core institutions of government are very weak, an enclave, project-driven approach may be the only way to get anything done at all and perhaps begin a cumulative process of change. Clearly there is a need to reconcile investment and institution-building objectives, both short-term and long-term. So far, the Bank and other donors have not done so systematically and effectively.

The Bank is only one of many organizations involved in resource transfer and capacity building in developing countries. Other major players include UNDP and other agencies of the UN system, bilateral donors, the regional development banks, the European Union, OECD, the WTO, professional organizations, and the

NGO community. The private sector also has a major role to play in private resource transfer and capacity building. Each of these players brings somewhat different skills and advantages to the development arena, and we can achieve more collectively if we work toward common goals and strategies, respect and build on our respective comparative advantages, and avoid the disruptive effects of disjointed enclave activities.

The Public Sector Board has recently undertaken extensive discussions with the external partners in various locations (including, among others, Abidjan, Copenhagen, Harare, London, Maastricht, Manila, New York, Paris, Stockholm,Warsaw, and Washington) to share strategies, explore the various roles, and build opportunities to work together.World Bank's relationship with UNDP, expanded the work of the MDBs' Governance and Anticorruption Working Group, forged new working relationships with OECD (including the Anti-bribery Working Group and the Public Management Service (PUMA), joined a new governance working group organized by the Conference Board with representatives of major multinational private firms, continued the interactions with Transparency International and other NGOs (including through the EAP and ECA Regions' advisory groups on anticorruption), expanded the dialogue with the professional associations and had extensive discussions and workshops with major bilateral partners.

In some areas (depending in part on the country concerned) numerous donors can make important contributions, and the goal is to work cooperatively through coordinated analytic work, policy advice, resource transfer, and monitoring and evaluation. Given the enormous amount of work to be done and the tight resource constraints faced by virtually all development agencies. The policy of the party is that the people know, the people discuss, the people do, but here people only implement the last part, which is the people do.

While a wide variety of institutional arrangements within the public sector are workable, well-functioning governments are generally thought to have certain important characteristics in common. They are responsive to the citizenry and reasonably efficient in the delivery of public services. Their decisionmaking processes and the decisions they result in are in general transparent and predictable. Oversight mechanisms (checks and balances) exist to guard against arbitrariness and to ensure accountability in the use of public resources, but these oversight mechanisms do not eliminate the flexibility and delegation that are needed to respond quickly to changing circumstances. In sum, they are accountable and results-oriented.

Most governments in the developing world are a long way from this model, although a growing number are devoting great efforts toward reform. Nontransparency, a lack of accountability, excessive intervention, a lack of delegation, and poor results on the ground are commonplace and contribute to arbitrariness, corruption, and poverty. The fundamental and very difficult question is how to move from this current situation toward a better-functioning one, and what the World Bank can do within its mandate to help clients progress toward this goal. Public sector reform requires not only internal bureaucratic change-but also "voice" and competition. WDR97 provides a starting point for translating theory into practice.

It distinguishes among three mechanisms that can help provide incentives for public actors to pursue social ends, hold them accountable for results, and restrain arbitrary action. Looking across the spectrum of countries, and as Figure 4 illustrates, a broad set of arrangements are evident. These include:

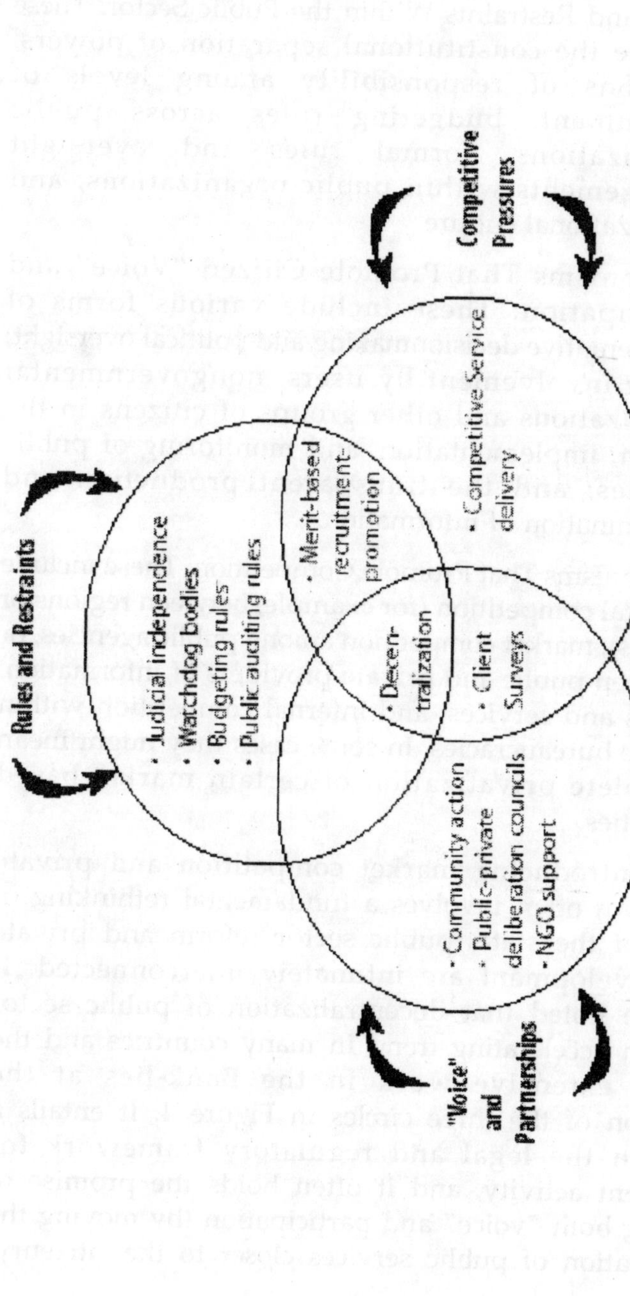

Figure 4. Mechanisms to enhance state capability: three drivers of public sector reform

- Rules and Restraints Within the Public Sector: These include the constitutional separation of powers, divisions of responsibility among levels of government, budgeting rules across public organizations, formal rules and oversight arrangements within public organizations, and organizational culture.
- Mechanisms That Promote Citizen "Voice" and Participation: These include various forms of representative decisionmaking and political oversight; direct involvement by users, nongovernmental organizations and other groups of citizens in the design, implementation, and monitoring of public policies; and the transparent production and dissemination of information.
- Mechanisms That Promote Competition: These include political competition (for example, between regions or parties); market competition among public agencies, or between public and private providers of information, goods and services; and internal competition within public bureaucracies. In some cases they might mean complete privatization of certain market-based activities.

Because introducing market competition and private participation often involves a fundamental rethinking of the role of the state, public sector reform and private sector development are intimately interconnected. It should be noted that decentralization of public sector activity-an accelerating trend in many countries and the focus of extensive work in the Bank-lies at the intersection of the three circles in Figure 4. It entails a change in the legal and regulatory framework for government activity, and it often holds the promise of increasing both "voice" and participation (by moving the administration of public services closer to the citizenry) and competitive pressures (including competition among levels of government and between subnational entities). But while decentralization holds many promises, it also entails risks that must be addressed, including the risk of "capture" by local elites or lack of capacity within local government.

It is not being suggested here that countries must have all of the checks and balances shown in Figure 4 in place to have effective governments. Indeed, countries differ greatly in the relative emphasis they give to different mechanisms-have much to learn about how different systems of accountability work in diverse country settings.

But what is being suggested is that countries need some critical mass of checks and balances to ensure accountability and state effectiveness. It is also not being suggested that active involvement to build all of these types of institutions falls within the Bank's mandate. The question of the Bank's mandate was considered in designing its anticorruption policy in 1997, and the tests and limits set in that policy apply here as well.

If a country requests assistance from the Bank, it is proper for the Bank to respond if the activity will contribute to economic development and if the Bank has the requisite skills and resources to help. And if weak governance and ineffective state institutions are hampering economic development prospects in a country, the Bank should take this into account as it considers the content of its assistance strategy, the size of its lending program, the design of projects, and the program of economic and sector work for that country.

Institutional reform and capacity building in the public sector will succeed only when it is "owned" within the country and driven by a country's leaders, with participation and input from the legislature, the private sector, and civil society. The Bank's role is to support the clients-both committed leaders and their citizenry-and provide assistance and advice to help them succeed.When local conditions are amenable to change, Bank support can be invaluable: Increasing transparency can help to reveal problems and set priorities, and Bank-financed analytic work can help in this regard. Corruption surveys in Albania, Latvia, and Georgia, public officials' surveys in Armenia, Bangladesh, and Bolivia, and the expenditure tracking survey in Uganda are recent examples.

Innovative uses of the internet and other forms of information technology to disseminate information on public spending and procurement, judicial decisions, regulatory activities, and data on service delivery can also help to improve accountability and performance, and undertaking a new initiative in fiscal 2001 to collect information and disseminate experience with E-government. Mechanisms to promote citizen feedback are fundamental to accountability and efficient service delivery, and Bank-supported consultations and citizen surveys can contribute. The strong efforts to promote citizen consultation in strategy preparation for public service delivery in Guinea, project preparation for judicial reform in Guatemala, and budget formulation in Campo Elias,Venezuela, and the growing stress on community action and participation in decisionmaking across all sectors are recent examples.

Well-designed technical assistance and other capacity building efforts can also be very helpful, as long as governments are in the driver's seat. One of many examples is the Bank's recent loan to Guatemala to support development of a customized financial management system. Another is the innovative Partnership for Capacity Building in Africa, initiated by the African Governors of the World Bank and facilitated by Bank staff and Africa's other development partners, which has endeavored to proceed in a substantially more participatory way.

Building on the fiduciary concerns in the own lending to provide broader advice and assistance to build in-country capacity for financial management, procurement, and monitoring and evaluation (including OED's initiatives in the area of evaluation capacity development) can spur systemic reforms and a much-needed focus on results on the ground in the client governments.

Government is not monolithic but is itself a collection of interests. Institutional change can significantly alter the incentives facing politicians, bureaucrats and other powerful groups. Reforms to spur development may not be desired by one or more of these groups, and they may be in a position to block change. At the extreme are countries locked into a dysfunctional political equilibrium, where powerful interests block any actions with the potential to promote development. The experiences of countries as diverse as Argentina, Poland, and Uganda suggest that it can take a major system-wide crisis-and a resulting transfer of power to reform-oriented leaders-to "unlock" dysfunctional equilibria of this kind. Prior to crisis, the prospects for reform to succeed are very low in such situations.

At a less extreme position are those countries where some scope for reform exists, but where there is still significant opposition. In these circumstances parties committed to reform need to find and take advantage of existing windows of opportunity, in ways that progressively build constituencies committed to development. Often the resulting agendas of the reformers may look "second-best" or "roundabout" in their aims from a narrowly economic perspective, but they can result in useful improvements because they take political reality into account.

It is important for the Bank to understand the political economy of a country, to recognize where efforts at reforms might have a chance and where they do not, and to allocate resources accordingly. In countries with strong domestic leadership and substantial capacity, the Bank's main contribution to public sector reform may well be through technical assistance for further capacity building in public sector management. Selectivity in approach is also critical for fiduciary reasons.While general principles are being developed and can help, this inevitably requires balanced and informed judgment on a case-by-case basis.

Certainly, action within each activity calls for specialized skills that are appropriately the responsibility of the relevant technical networks. But applying those skills in individual country settings must start with a thorough and broad understanding of the realities as they exist on the ground. Against the backdrop of these realities, the reform challenge is to identify specific actions that support change and continued momentum for development, even if the actions themselves may seem quite imperfect from the perspective of some ideal notion of "best practice." While broad end goals may be similar, "best practice" in achieving them is not uniform across countries; rather "good fit" that builds on basic principles is in essence "best practice."

An emphasis on "good fit" in the reform process has two implications for Bank work. First, it means that in the preparation of Bank projects and adjustment loans, the clients undertake whatever analytic work is necessary on the ground to identify reform options that are feasible, can be readily implemented, and have a positive long-term effect on institution-building. Institutional analysis to understand realities on the ground-including, for example, the capacity of local institutions and the extent of political support for reform-should be a routine part of the design of Bank projects.

To help address this need, a draft Operational Policy (OP) has been prepared on institutional assessment in Bank projects. A second implication of the emphasis on "good fit" is that need to be more attuned to how the range of public institutions fit together and reinforce (or undermine) each other in any particular setting. Sector institutions (such as public health providers, transportation ministries and schools) and institutions at the core of government (such as parliaments, cabinets and finance ministries) do not operate separately but rather interrelate in complex ways. This strategy proposes that where possible and try to understand linkages in institutional systems and integrate this knowledge into country assistance strategy formulation.

Country Assistance Strategies (CASs) play a central role in allocating resources for country programs and are thus a key focal point for ensuring that the Bank's programs within individual countries-both the choice of operations and their design-reflect a deep understanding of existing institutions and a well-considered approach to reforming them. A growing number of country strategies (such as those for Albania, Armenia, Azerbaijan, Bangladesh, Bolivia, Bulgaria, Cambodia, Kenya, Mexico, Mozambique, Papua New Guinea, Philippines, and Thailand) are already designed around a core goal of improving public sector performance and governance. Given the Bank's current direction and the findings of the aideffectiveness literature, most CASs can be expected to address this goal in the future. Pursuant to the fiscal 1999 Anticorruption Action Plan, all CASs must at a minimum diagnose the state of governance and the risks that corruption poses to Bank projects in the country concerned. As corruption is a symptom of public sector dysfunction, an effective strategy to address corruption will inevitably involve reform in public institutions.

While there are clearly lessons that are important in all settings-such as the importance of focusing on accountability, transparency, and outcomes and of building the capacity for incountry monitoring and evaluation-even these must be approached with a full understanding of nuances on the ground in each setting. Where should one start in trying to build institutional capacity?

The long-term goal is to strengthen institutions-not just to operate within the constraints of what is currently workable. But where to start and what sequence to move in is not always obvious. Is an enclaving approach likely to help or hurt over the long run?Where the institutional starting point is very weak, or where the political window of opportunity for reform is narrow, a common approach is to begin by creating institutional "enclaves". Project implementation units are one example, but there are many others.When judicial systems are weak, for example, the temptation is to bypass the judiciary and set up special courts or out-of-court mechanisms for problem resolution (such as debt workouts or bankruptcy, for example).

Or when government procurement or financial controls are unreliable, donors establish special rules to govern their projects. Such enclaves can create highly visible islands of success on which to build and can help loosen constraints to sustained development (for example, in taxation, mining, or agribusiness).

Yet the potentially harmful longterm effects described earlier of an "enclaving" approach, especially if multiplied over many donors, must also be taken into account. Furthermore, bypassing mainstream structures takes away the "demand" that can put pressure on them to improve. The costs and benefits of enclaving, in both the short and the longer run, should be carefully weighed in every relevant case, and enclaves should in general be avoided.

While important knowledge gaps remain, the immediate priority is not more fundamental research but rather a systematic effort to codify, adapt, and make accessible to practitioners the insights that already exist-albeit often in fragmented and haphazard forms-on the political and institutional dimensions of development. PREM and WBI are currently working to develop several types of country-focused diagnostic tools for public sector reform, including:

- tools that evaluate the quality of a country's institutions (including those at the "core" of government) and help measure the severity and pattern of institutional dysfunction, and
- tools that assess a country's readiness for specific reform initiatives and likely political and institutional obstacles to implementation.

There are two core types of economic and sector work-Public Expenditure Reviews and Institutional and Governance Reviews-to provide a full range of public sector analysis to underpin the Bank's lending and assistance programs.

Public Expenditure Reviews

PERs have been in use in the Bank since the 1980s, and the Bank now undertakes about 30 to 40 annually, primarily in the Africa Region. In addition, the IMF and other donors have expressed concerns about the availability of timely budget information needed as input to their programs. The Public Sector Board and the Public Expenditure Thematic Group have developed new draft guidelines for PERs, which are currently being discussed with the sector and IMF colleagues, that will bring better clarity to their scope and better quality to their content, taking the needs of partners into careful account.

With regard to content, PERs will continue to provide information on budget allocations as needed but will also focus increasingly on institutions for budget decisionmaking and implementation. As noted earlier, the purpose and scope of PERs has broadened in recent years from an economic analysis of public spending allocations to a broader analysis of both spending patterns and the institutions for public expenditure management. For example, a recent China PER focused on institutional reforms in budget management and won a wide hearing, while the Macedonia Public Expenditure and Institutional and Governance Review will analyze the sustainability of the fiscal program and its institutional drivers.

The fiscal 1999 West Bank and Gaza Public Expenditure Review, Jordan Public Sector Review, and PERs in the Pacific Islands and Cambodia also have an institutional focus. While maintaining these constant core themes, each PER may also look at specific expenditure topics of particular importance to the country, and they will necessarily vary somewhat in scope, size, and timing, depending on country demand. In some cases (such as Ethiopia), PERs may be undertaken annually but may have a rotating focus that covers individual topics only once every few years.

With regard to quality, the Public Sector Board is working with the Regions (particularly AFR) to develop stronger criteria for task team leadership and membership, more thorough monitoring programs, and stricter peer review procedures to complement the guidelines on scope and content. Half-day public expenditure clinics are now offered by the Public

Expenditure Thematic Group to teams about to embark on PER field missions.

With regard to country ownership, some PERs are now undertaken by clients themselves with Bank assistance, with both client and Bank staff participating in any pre-mission training provided. In the recent case of Argentina, the country carried out the PER on its own, and the Bank provided a clinic for country staff. In some cases there may be tradeoffs between objectives of quality, timeliness, and ownership.

For this reason PERs (particularly those focusing more heavily on assessments of spending programs) must not be the only elements in the public expenditure program through which the Bank engages with clients; other forms of technical assistance, training, and analysis may also be appropriate as complements to PERs. A focus on results-moving beyond budget allocations to what those allocations actually buy-must also increase as part of the improvement program for PERs. A recent PER for Uganda included an innovative "tracking" survey to determine how much of the funding budgeted for schools and clinics actually reached them.

It identified significant gaps between amounts budgeted and amounts spent, and this has resulted in a strengthened effort at citizen monitoring of budget disbursements in that country. Similar surveys are planned in Albania and Macedonia, and over time they are expected to become standard instruments for monitoring expenditure outputs and outcomes on the ground.

Another initiative that several countries have undertaken is an effort to analyze the incidence and impact of public spending from a gender perspective through "gender budgets". PERs and facilitate institutional analysis in other areas of public sector reform, in fiscal 2000 to pilot variants of a new family of analytic instruments, called Institutional and Governance Reviews (IGRs), in four countries: Armenia, Bangladesh, Bolivia, and Indonesia. At least five more are being undertaken in fiscal 2001.

These IGRs attempt a broad assessment of the quality of accountability, policymaking or service delivery institutions in a country, and propose a comprehensive strategy for institutional change. Two particular characteristics tend to distinguish the family of IGRs from PERs and other analytic work done in the Bank to date:

First, they focus heavily on actual performance, starting from a problem (such as inadequate health service delivery in the Armenia case) and working backward to establish a chain of causation that links sector problems to upstream weaknesses in public expenditure management, policymaking, judicial oversight, intergovernmental relations, or other systemic functions of the public sector.

Second, they attempt to enrich the understanding of actual incentives on the ground and may include analysis of the political economy of the situation, and they draw on local knowledge and expertise to provide such knowledge to the extent possible.

Such analyses can help support CAS preparation and the design of lending programs. The individual toolkits that underlie them should also be useful in further downstream analytic work and the design of individual projects in specific areas of institutional reform. These institutional analyses complement the analytic instruments (Social and Structural Reviews) being developed for wider country analysis; one of the key areas of concern in the Social and Structural Reviews (SSRs) is public sector effectiveness, and the tools being developed for IGRs and PERs can be straightforwardly used in the SSRs.

The tools also complement the Country Procurement Assessment Reports (CPARs) and the Country Financial Accountability Assessments (CFAAs) being undertaken by OCS and Controllers as part of the Bank's fiduciary mandate to improve procurement and disbursement mechanisms both system-wide and for Bank projects. These various analytic tools all deal with accountability institutions in the client countries, and are taking steps at the regional level to integrate them more closely. Finally, all of these tools need to feed into Poverty Reduction Strategy Papers (PRSPs), and a toolkit for governance and poverty analysis to help clients bring these various strands together with an explicit poverty focus.

The Bank has also sought to promote public sector reform through transferring knowledge and building capacity in client countries. This is critical if clients are to take on the ownership role envisioned in the CDF. Traditionally, the main instruments for this knowledge transfer have been economic and sector work (ESW), research, training, and policy dialogue with client governments. ESW and research have worked well to raise the level of country-Bank discussion by providing transparent, empirical documentation on public sector issues and offering new ways of thinking about difficult problems. ESW, research, and training have also been effective in transmitting global and crossregional lessons and in distilling accumulated wisdom in a systematic way.

For several reasons, however, the Bank's knowledge transfer has not always been fully effective in fostering public sector reform. In research and ESW, institutional analysis has sometimes been an add-on to more traditional policy analysis. Knowledge disseminated through WBI training has sometimes been poorly coordinated with country program priorities. Knowledge has not always been available when most needed because of delays in research and ESW.

Furthermore, these instruments have not always been linked to sustained and continuous dialogue with the government. Rather, the ESW may have been done to fill a need for a one-shot operation or single policy issue. By contrast, the process of reforming public sector institutions takes time, often requiring a social and political consensus that must be nurtured and developed incrementally with short but punctual interventions on the part of the Bank. The new forms of IGRs and PERs outlined earlier provide one means to work more actively with the clients to focus knowledge generation and transfer on operationally relevant institutional concerns in the public sector.

Institute are another important means of knowledge transfer and stakeholder involvement, and the formation of the networks and closer integration of staff and client learning will help link such programs more closely with operational concerns, as is already being done in the area of anticorruption. DRG has a rich research agenda, and the network boards (which include active membership from DRG) will need to continue to foster close coordination between this agenda and operational needs. DEC's and WBI's expanding efforts to support the development of local research institutes in client countries are also valuable initiatives to transfer knowledge and build capacity. In addition, some countries may from time to time want technical advice on specific topics but be unable to pay for it, and the Bank should have a way to provide the advice without tying it to a project.

A model is the SIGMA program in Central and Eastern Europe, which has proven popular among policymakers and reformers. Sponsored by the European Union and administered by OECD, SIGMA provides financing for a network of professionals (ranging from senior government officials to academics and practitioners) in the area of public sector reform that can be activated at the request of beneficiary countries. A technical secretariat helps prioritize the requests and can offer initial technical assistance.

Although the same services could perhaps be provided by the Bank through an IDF grant, the advantage of SIGMA has been its flexibility and the continuity of advice and institutional memory that it can provide. The Commonwealth Secretariat provides similar technical assistance to countries belonging to the British Commonwealth, and donors such as DFID also provide large amounts of assistance. The Bank should work with these organizations to tap into or build more of these types of flexible nonlending services.

Long-Term Institution-Building

To have a bigger impact on poverty, the Bank must make a quantum leap in its ability to address critical systemic concerns. Does the Bank have an appropriate mix of lending approaches to this end? The Bank's traditional approaches remain useful in certain circumstances. The Bank's traditional lending instruments include quick-disbursing policy loans, technical assistance loans, and investment project loans. Each has played an important role in promoting institutional change, although each also has inherent limitations.

Structural Adjustment Loans (SALs) or Structural Adjustment Credits (SACs), are used to encourage policy shifts that are needed to set new "rules of the game" for public sector institutional behavior and governance. Frequently, they reinforce government actions that are on the critical path to reform but, for political economy reasons, are too difficult to undertake without external urging and assistance. Through the leverage they provide, adjustment loans have been effective at focusing country political leadership on important policy issues, at bringing a strategic framework to otherwise disparate reform measures, and at triggering crucial initial steps in a reform process.

For example, a structural adjustment credit and supporting TA in Albania is tackling two key sources of corruption: patronage in judicial appointments and the civil service. A structural adjustment credit in Georgia is supporting the creation of a legal and institutional framework for procurement. And a planned SAC in Vietnam will have a substantial focus on state enterprises and financial sector reform.

Quick-disbursing loans are ideally suited to discrete policy actions, such as the reduction of trade barriers. In contrast, institutional programs that require ongoing attention and support can fit awkwardly within a short-term adjustment framework. The timeframe of an individual adjustment operation often forces us to focus on those tasks that can be accomplished in the very short span of the loan. Sometimes "the tail wags the dog": SALs typically form part of comprehensive macroeconomic programs, so a disbursement may in practice be deferred only for major violations. Formal SAL conditionality tends to be narrow and specific, thus often too limited in scope to foster sustained institutional reforms.

Technical Assistance (TA) loans provide an alternative and complement to adjustment lending. In principle, technical assistance can provide needed help in performing tasks that are beyond the capacity of local governments and can help train country personnel to carry on with activities after the loan is completed.And its timeframe affords a more extended window in which to realize institutional objectives.

The Economic Law Project in China has influenced the crafting of legislation to enable the market-driven sector to flourish in a modern system of business regulation. The TA for fiscal policy in China is contributing to the development of a more modern budget system and new regulation for fiscal management and macroeconomic planning. Technical assistance loans have also promoted an institutional agenda in Korea, Thailand and Indonesia.

As it is currently practiced, however, the impact of freestanding TA is often limited, lacking the influential weight of SAL resources and the policy leverage to bring off difficult reform measures. TA loans for institutional reforms in different areas or sectors of government often end as uncoordinated activities without a strategic or programmatic impact. Even when used in tandem with SALs, ongoing technical assistance often sputters when the SAL has been disbursed and highlevel attention has waned. In resource-poor environments, TA sometimes amounts to "substitution" assistance, where tasks are performed by experts with little transfer of capacity or even involvement of host country clients. Increasingly, technical assistance lending is considered too expensive by those countries where other donors provide assistance through grant aid.

Traditional investment lending and, increasingly, sector investment programs (SIPs) can also be instruments for institutional strengthening, and indeed a substantial percentage of investment loans have contributed to sustainable institutional development. SIPs offer a promising approach to integrating institutional programs in particular sectors and provide a more demand-driven vehicle for institutional reform. They also create incentives for greater results-orientation, because they force governments and donors alike to focus on sectoral outputs and outcomes rather than individual donor inputs.However, they do not address the need for cross-sectoral integration or coordination with reforms of central government institutions.

The Bank has relied for several years on Institutional Development Facility (IDF) grants for initiating upstream, non-project work on public sector reforms. These grants use indigenous capacity as much as possible and have proven useful in stimulating early work on institutional topics. The separation of IDFs from subsequent lending can impede the continuity of institutional work, however, and raises concerns about scaling up from these small initiatives to larger programs with greater impact.

Several new approaches look like promising adaptations of existing instruments in situations where government commitment is strong. Adaptable Program Loans (APLs) or Credits (APCs) can provide a flexible approach to institutional reforms in individual sectors or at the core of government, lengthening the timeframe for reform and promoting a more programmatic rather than project-oriented approach to reform. APL/Cs have recently been chosen as an instrument for promoting public sector institutional reform in Bolivia, Ghana, Tanzania, and Zambia. In Bolivia, for example, the government, project team, donors, and Bank management agreed that an Adaptable Program Credit (APC) was preferable to a traditional Technical Assistance Credit to support Bolivia's public sector reforms, because of the need to address systemic reforms (including a fundamental reform of human resource management and compensation) and to ensure flexible long-term commitment by both the borrower and the Bank.

The APC is phased in three operations over 10 years. Phase I, the Institutional Reform Project, supports reforms in human resource management, national integrity, budgeting by results, and performance evaluation, to be implemented in several pilot agencies through a program of organizational restructuring and change management. Specific trigger indicators will be used to assess achievements at the end of each phase and to decide on the financing for subsequent phases that extend the reforms to additional entities. Project design is being informed by a Public Expenditure Review and an Institutional and Governance Review, and the operation has attracted considerable donor co-financing.

The operation is a keystone of the Bolivia CDF pilot. Learning and Innovation Loans (LILs) offer a new instrument that allows for more experimentation and piloting of promising but unproven reform approach-es. Given the uncertainties of applying lessons from developed to developing countries, LILs provide an excellent opportunity to "get it right" at a pilot level before investing on a wider basis. The first LIL, the 1997 Venezuela Supreme Court Modernization Project, supports judicial reform. In Georgia, the Georgia Ministry of Transport Project is a LIL aimed at reorienting the Ministry from an old Soviet-style entity to an agency charged with policymaking and regulation of private transporters. In China, a LIL is being used to promote pension and enterprise reforms.

APLs and LILs are both investment loans. A series of Programmatic SALs or SACs (PSALs or PSACs) offers an alternative vehicle for supporting coherent public sector reform. PSAL/Cs are a series of typically two or three one- or two-tranche adjustment operations that together support a medium-term government program of policy reforms and institution-building. Their design relies on a solid foundation of completed or parallel analytic and advisory work, especially in the areas of public expenditure management and public sector governance and reform. Key features of PSAL/Cs are as follows:

The medium-term reform program supported by a PSAL/C series is laid out at the outset in the government's Letter of Development Policy for the first PSAL/C. It is reflected in a multi-year matrix of policy and institutional reforms with monitorable indicators and progress benchmarks for each loan. The corresponding multi-year framework of Bank support is also articulated at the outset. Typically it includes a notional (non-binding) multi-year envelope, with individual PSAL/Cs phased annually in line with the borrowing government's budget cycle.

The conditionalities of the first PSAL/C in the series are agreed up-front. Each subsequent PSAL/C builds on the previous ones; its conditionalities are formulated and agreed when it is negotiated, drawing on the progress benchmarks laid out at the outset as a part of the mediumterm framework. Each individual loan in the PSAL/C series depends on satisfactory progress with reforms against agreed benchmarks, based on a review by staff, and on a continued satisfactory macroeconomic framework. Programmatic SALs were recently approved for Thailand and Latvia. A subnational loan with programmatic features was approved for the state of Uttar Pradesh in India. Loans with similar programmatic features are also under consideration for Benin, Jordan, and Uganda. This approach allows objectives to be laid out over a longer time horizon, but allows "multiple paths to get there," accommodating the fact that reforms of various agencies and institutions are likely to proceed at different paces.

For example, the Public Sector Reform Loan I (PSRLI) for Thailand, approved by the Board in October 1999, is designed as the first of three annual loans that together constitute the PSAL program. This first loan disburses in a single tranche to support the initial steps of reform in five areas of the government's reform program: public expenditure management, human resources management, revenue management, decentralization, and accountability and transparency. Subsequent loans, PSRLII and PSRLIII, will depend (in addition to a continued financing need) on the continuing strong commitment of government to reform and on the satisfactory progress of reform measured against a detailed set of specific monitoring indicators. Reform progress will be measured against semi-annual benchmarks the government has set for itself.

Programmatic lending approaches also carry risks. The country's institutional context is critical to the success of programmatic lending operations.Weak financial management and institutional capacity can undermine performance, yet these are precisely areas that programmatic lending seeks to help build. In addition, the broader scope of such lending-typically involving several sectors or regions and counterpart agencies-increases the risk of diminished focus and implementation problems. Design and country commitment are critical, and clear accountability arrangements and monitoring mechanisms must be built into such programs. In view of these generic risks, the CAS will need to focus on the suitability of the use of programmatic instruments in a particular country or sectoral context.

In sum, the various types of Bank lending instruments available to client countries all offer advantages in certain circumstances, and a major challenge of a CAS is to find a "good fit," that is, to tailor the mix of instruments to country conditions. The programmatic approach embodied in institutionally oriented APLs and PSAL/Cs provides a longer-term perspective that is likely to prove useful as the Bank moves to strengthen its institutional development and capacity building focus. As the Bank gains experience with programmatic lending, it can further identify good practices and delineate important aspects of design and implementation.

The fundamental challenge-is to use both the lending and nonlending instruments in ways that not only reform internal rules and restraints, but that also bring competition to bear when feasible, and that enhance the voice and participation of the citizenry, drawing on the range of fundamental drivers for public sector reform. An innovative assistance program for Guinea and a push in the Africa Region more generally for programs of community empowerment provide examples of recent innovations.

Staffing, Organization, Incentives, and Partnerships

The second skill is the ability to understand the forces that shape institutions at a deep conceptual level. People with this second skill have a broad understanding of the way formal and informal incentive systems and political conditions drive behavior within organizations, especially public agencies in developing countries. This skill does not derive primarily from academic training, although some academic fields (including economics, political science, public policy, public administration, or anthropology) can provide a solid foundation. It is usually developed through in-country experience and can be strengthened through in-house training. The Bank's move to decentralize its operations can help in this regard because it is better able to incorporate local staff with in-depth knowledge of institutions and culture in client countries.

Because institutional reform is inherently complex and interdisciplinary, a good institutional specialist will be open to knowledge of different disciplines Initiatives to mainstream the reform of public institutions and to expand the use of more appropriate lending instruments will succeed only have in place staff who are capable of taking advantage of these new opportunities-and have the incentive to do so.And Bank staff will need to make a special effort not to over-reach, but rather to step back in favor of the development partners for those aspects of institutional reform which they are better positioned are to take on.

Traditionally the Bank has lacked a sufficient number of specialized staff with extensive knowledge and practical in-country reform experience in most if not all of the following specialized areas: public financial management (tax policy, tax administration, expenditure policy, budget process, information systems, accounting, auditing); administrative and civil service reform (policymaking, service delivery, agency structure, and civil service regulation, pay and employment); legal and judicial reform; subnational government reform; and regulatory and public enterprise reform. Some of these skills can be hired on the market on a short-term consulting basis, and there has also been a need for some increase in in-house expertise in these specialties in the past three years. Of course, as is illustrated by some of the best practitioners already in the Bank, functional specialists will be most effective when they also have a broad understanding of the interplay between their specialty and the broader array of formal and informal incentives that shape behavior within the public sector.

Addressing remaining deficits in the second and third skill categories requires actions on several fronts. First, we need to continue (to the extent budgets allow) to externally recruit people with relevant academic training and public sector experience. Second, we need to strengthen the capabilities of existing staff (including general economists and sector specialists) to address questions of public sector institutional reform. This requires training and experience aimed at increasing staff capabilities to analyze the incentives of public officials and the institutional arrangements that shape these incentives. In organizing this training, a special effort to include as trainers officials from developing countries who have led successful reforms of public institutions. Third, we need to revisit the incentives and organizational arrangements that encourage task management at the expense of specialization.

The Bank's matrix structure implies that may need special arrangements to recruit new staff. Regional budgets rest with the Country Directors, and there is inevitably a lag between their expression of "demand" for work from the sector units and the ability of those sector units, to expand their staff if demand exceeds current supply. Country Directors are sometimes understandably hesitant to commit funding to tasks without commitment from pre-identified, well-proven staff. This situation can create impediments to expanding the staff skills in new and somewhat untested areas of high priority. The Public Sector anchor can help to some extent by bringing new staff into the Bank for an early "tryout" phase; if the staff prove to fit well in operations, they can move to a Region after a period of time. To date, the anchor has had the funding to bring in 2 to 3 new staff per year, and the regional units have also been able to augment their staff, albeit incrementally and with some lag. The Public Sector Board has recently agreed to pilot a new recruitment initiative, through which the Sector Board will collectively work to identify and hire 3 to 5 new fixed-term recruits in fiscal 2001.

The recruits' salaries will be partially funded by a central human resources budget during their first year on the job and will be located in specific VPUs while maintaining a group identity for purposes of orientation, training, and support. The initiative is designed to foster a more worldwide search for talent, a greater focus on diversity objectives, and a better ability to provide support and training to new hires, without these new hires being obliged to support their positions fully with operational activities from the first day on the job.

Country directors are more apt than under previous organizational arrangements to demand "value for money" and thus not contract for analytic and lending products with little immediate impact. Furthermore, the existence of the network and associated thematic groups has clearly enhanced the incentives and ability of staff working on public sector reform across the Bank to cooperate and share knowledge. Important efforts were made in fiscal 2000 to strengthen the matrix structure across the Bank, particularly to increase the authority and flexibility of sector managers with regard to the specific use of budget resources allocated in work program agreements.

The experience of the past three years points to the benefits of having sector board members who are clearly accountable in their Regions or central units for delivering effective programs of support across the range of relevant topics to country directors or other clients, and who have the authority and resources to hire and manage the staff needed to do the job. The network family should then be jointly accountable to the whole of the Bank to set strategy and priorities, recruit and train staff, and oversee quality. The cohesiveness and sense of shared vision of the Public Sector Board and the overall quality of management and staff in relevant public sector units have grown considerably over the past three years.

Even with strengthened staffing, the tension and ambiguity between the role of the World Bank as a lending institution and its role as a development institution may nonetheless constrain the ability to address the challenge of reforming public institutions.

Institutionbuilding is difficult and time-consuming. It requires detailed country-specific information, and its success can be difficult to measure.

Furthermore, difficult institutional components of projects are often the first to be dropped in a pinch. And in times of tight budgets, the ability of Bank staff and country counterparts to undertake the analytic work needed to gain country knowledge and undertake effective institutional work may be constrained. An important way to keep governance and institution-building on the forefront of the Bank's agenda is to continually emphasize these goals in reviews and evaluations of CASs and country lending programs.

The emphasis on the quality of institutional work has definitely increased in recent years as an outgrowth of the Wapenhans report and the subsequent creation of QAG and reorientation of OED. The emphasis on governance has also grown dramatically, and all CASs are now required to diagnose the state of governance and the risks that corruption poses to Bank projects in the country concerned.While substantial progress has been made, still more emphasis on evaluation and development impact is needed if the Bank is to have a deep and serious commitment to public sector reform in its client countries. The Public Sector Board will continue to work actively with OED and QAG to enhance the Bank's ability to measure success in institutional development, and it will continue to work closely with country teams to help strengthen the coverage of governance issues in CASs.

Over the medium term, the networks will work to upgrade the quality of institutional and governance work through staffing, professional development, and knowledge management. With better measurement and deeper focus on quality should come greater selectivity-that is, the willingness to reduce activity when conditions are not conducive to reform. Such selectivity is already part of the Bank's anticorruption strategy, but it needs to be continually reinforced in individual country situations.

Partnerships

Several types of partnerships are worth highlighting:

- with clients. The most important partner is of course the client, and the Bank's primary responsibility is to serve its clients. Although the proximate client is the government in the borrowing country, the ultimate client is the public interest, that is, the citizenry of a country. "Serving the client" is often but not always synonymous with serving the interests of the government, and the Bank needs to be sensitive to the broad public interest and the ultimate objective of poverty reduction in all cases. When feasible, the Bank (and other donors) should support the client government as the government designs and implements strategies for development, and this situation is envisioned in the CDF process. In the worst case scenario, when the Bank and the government do not share a common view of the country's needs, the Bank may need to devote its resources elsewhere. One key to effective partnership is selectivity.
- across the Bank: Because virtually all of the Bank's operational activities involve institutional development and capacity building, internal Bank units must be willing and able to work together to share ideas, experiences, and staff resources as needed. In addition to the sector families, key groups in the Bank include the Public Sector Group in PREM (reforms at the core of government), WBI (external and internal knowledge transfer and capacity building), OCS and Controllers (procurement and financial management), LEG (legal and judicial reform), DRG (knowledge creation), and

OED (evaluation capacity development). The various perspectives and disciplines all bring important contributions to the table, and we must continue to seek interaction and mutual support and avoid creating "cylinders."

- with other donors: Different donors bring different skills and comparative advantages to recipient countries. Because of their size and leverage, the Bank and regional multilateral banks may be best suited to undertake high-level policy dialogue and broad interventions to reform institutions. In the case of civil service reform, for example, the Bank's comparative advantage is likely to lie in stimulating major reforms (such as downsizing, contracting out or privatizing service delivery where appropriate, changing the rules for civil service hiring and promotion, or institutionalizing citizen feedback mechanisms) rather than in specific capacity building activities (such as civil service training).

In contrast, the comparative advantage of some bilateral donors and the private sector is often seen to lie more in longer-term organizational strengthening, because of the technical skill-bases they can tap into in their countries and their ability to commit to sustained involvement and careful monitoring. Furthermore, many donors bring more expertise in certain areas than the Bank. In some cases the Bank simply has not built expertise, while in others (particularly certain areas of political governance) the Bank does not have a mandate like some of its partners. Public sector reform requires work at all levels, and donors must keep trying to find better ways to recognize and coordinate the unique and complementary contributions of each other.

The Bank's partnership with the IMF is particularly critical in the area of public sector reform. The Bank and

Fund are both active in fiscal policy and administration, albeit with somewhat different emphases. The Bank has more in-depth involvement in many other aspects of institutional reform, such as civil service reform, judicial reform, decentralization, and reform of sectoral institutions, although many Fund programs have important impacts in these areas. The Bank is very supportive of the Fund's work on the Code of Fiscal Transparency and is working with clients to facilitate its dissemination and application.

The Bank's partnership with UNDP is also a critical one, particularly as both organizations have recently expressed heightened commitment to helping client countries improve governance and build institutional capacity. UNDP's grant-making ability, its close client relationships built through long-term in-country residence, and its expanded mandate (reaching, for example, to issues of political governance) all make UNDP's role both important and in many cases complementary to that of the Bank. Countries where there is already substantial collaboration between UNDP and the Bank include, among others, Bolivia, Ghana, Indonesia, and Vietnam-and intend to highlight these and other good examples in order to stimulate further work in that direction. The Public Sector Board is in close touch with the UNDP counterparts, and are undertaking a series of meetings over the current year toward this end.

Bilateral donors are also important partners of the Bank in the area of public sector reform.Many bilateral donors focus extensively on issues of governance. Like UNDP, bilateral donors often work in areas of political governance (such as election monitoring and political party development) that the Bank is not involved in. They are able to draw on experience and expertise in their own countries that can deepen their contributions to development.

5 Politics of Governance

Since at least the time of Independence, the reduction of poverty and the empowerment of poor and politically marginal groups in India have been strongly associated with at least some form of decentralization. Perhaps the most enduring image of decentralization in India was Gandhi's vision of village swaraj, in which universal education, economic self-sufficiency and village democracy would take the place of caste, untouchability and other forms of rural exploitation. Although this vision has been hotly debated since (at least) the time of Independence, Gandhi's vision has had an enduring effect on the ways in which decentralization has been articulated and defended in Indian politics.

Beyond the symbolic imagery of the independent 'village republic,' an important element of this relates to the idea that the panchayats can and should serve as a forum that would represent traditionally marginal groups (such as women, backward castes, etc.) and a vehicle for social advancement. Procedurally, the 73rd Amendment to India's Constitution contains a number of provisions that would facilitate the achievement of these norms. Principal among these are the stipulations that:

— Representatives at village, sub-district and district levels be elected to five year terms;

— One-third of all seats be reserved for women;

— There must be reservations for SCs and STs proportional to their population;

— Such reservations must apply to elected village chiefs, the sarpanches;

— The voting public—the gram sabha—has constitutional status as a formal deliberative body at the village level;

Individual States may enact further provisions creating reservation status for other backward groups. At the village level, the gram sabha, which constitutes all eligible voters within a gram panchayat area, is meant to serve as a principal mechanism for transparency and accountability. Among its principal functions are:

— To review the annual statement of accounts;

— To review reports of the preceding financial year;

— To review and submit views on development programmes for the following year;

— To participate in the identification of beneficiaries for some government schemes.

This last provision is particularly important because it confers substantive authority over an area that is particularly prone to misallocation and corruption. The 'Eleventh Schedule' of the 73rd Amendment identifies 29 areas over which panchayats can legitimately have jurisdiction. Many of these - such as agriculture, minor irrigation, animal husbandry, fisheries, social forestry, small-scale industries, and implementation of land reforms - focus on particular sectors within the rural economy. Others—such as rural housing, rural electrification, transportation and communication linkages—are primarily concerned with the provision and maintenance of rural infrastructure.

Some cover the provision of key rural services, such as health, sanitation and primary, secondary and vocational education. Others still govern the provision of targeted welfare benefits - such as the PDS, and benefits for scheduled castes and tribes, women and children and the handicapped. In short, the 73rd Amendment covers many areas that would enable the panchayats to improve the lives and wellbeing of poor and vulnerable groups.

Moreover, it contains specific provisions that guarantee the inclusion of traditionally excluded groups, such as women, SCs and STs, and transparency for local institutions such as the gram panchayats and the gram sabha. However, studies of decentralization have consistently highlighted the fact that the 73rd Amendment and earlier attempts at decentralization have failed to prevent a local (and primarily landed) elite from controlling local panchayats. Micro-level studies have shown that gram sabha often fail to fulfil their role as deliberative bodies or as a mechanism for accountability. This is partly attributed to low levels of participation among the electorate as well as the non-cooperation of local officials. Examples of the latter include officials delaying or postponing gram sabha meetings, officials not attending gram sabha, and, more generally, official decisions having no bearing on decisions reached during the gram sabha.

Even when there are reservations to ensure that marginal groups have a place in the panchayat system, there is evidence to suggest that these formal institutions have been usurped by more informal patterns of domination and power. Reservations for women, for instance, are notoriously prone to corruption by male relatives, excluded from formal participation by their lack of scheduled status. Similar patterns have been observed among SCs and STs, whose economic well being is dependent on the patronage of local elites.

There is thus a substantial gap between the normative principles on which the panchayats were founded and the procedural ways in which they operate in practice. Explanations for poor performance include the centralizing tendencies of State governments, the incentive structure of the non-elected bureaucracy, and rural inequalities rooted in land holdings, caste, religion and gender. Such findings highlight the difficulty of transposing formal models of democracy onto societies in which power and politics are determined by highly informal systems of inequality and domination. Moreover, they suggest that the ideals that panchayati raj aims to uphold - transparency, accountability and democracy - are somewhat inconsistent with the ways in which the Indian state has traditionally operated in rural areas.

Specifically, the notion that state interventions would be guided by pluralist pressures institutionalized in elections, public meetings and the like, underplays the relationship that often exists between public office and private commerce. This is not to suggest that elements within the Indian state would never uphold the public interest - just that it is difficult.

Reflecting on the decentralization process that took place in Karnataka in the early 1980s, that 'bureaucrats at all levels were made considerably more accountable to elected politicians than they had ever been before,' This, they argue, was due to the fact that mandal (sub-district) councillors were far more vigilant in demanding and monitoring a wider distribution of public resources from non-elected officials within the bureaucracy. Particularly important to this process was the level of public (as opposed to private or 'back room') contestation that transpires over the allocation and distribution of public resources.

Accounting for the subsequent re-centralization of power in Karnataka, the political orientation of the party in power (i.e. the political and ideological terms on which it draws electoral support) had strong bearing on its commitment to decentralization. Such assertions are very consistent with the experience of the two "models" most commonly associated with good governance in India: Kerala and West Bengal. In 1996, the Left Democratic Front government in Kerala launched the People's Campaign for Decentralised Planning, an exercise that resulted in the devolution of 35 to 40 per cent of plan (i.e. non salary) expenditure to local bodies . This involved unprecedented planning and co-ordination among the gram sabhas, as well as block and district-level panchayats.

Although there were problems of co-ordination and some resistance from the non-elected bureaucracy, the process was notable both for the sheer scale of devolution as well as the political mobilisation that transpired around the issue of decentralised planning. However, it is vital to stress the fact that this process took place in a context of competitive party politics, in which the legitimacy of the ruling government (a CPI (M) coalition) was highly dependent on a re-distributive agenda.

The experience in West Bengal suggests that political parties can and will challenge the interests of dominant groups when they develop and pursue a programme that is ideologically committed to the goal of social redistribution. Central to the ruling Left Front government's decentralization agenda in the late 1970s was a two-pronged strategy aimed at strengthening the panchayats and redistributing land to the rural poor.

Left Front's ability to penetrate the countryside and to challenge the interests of landed elites was highly dependent on a party with a coherent leadership, an ideological and organizational commitment to exclude propertied interests from the process of governance, a pragmatic attitude toward facilitating a non-threatening environment for propertied interests, and an organizational structure that was both centralized and decentralized, allowing the regime to maintain contact with local society, without becoming beholden to local propertied elites.

The Left Front government appears to have been able to strike an ideal balance between local governance and a central executive, whose power and legitimacy helped to maintain a minimal sphere of autonomy from local elite capture. Specifically, policies aimed at strengthening the enforcement of land ceilings, abolishing bonded labour and providing poor people alternative sources of credit had the largely unintentional effect of dismantling the decades-old system of debt, bondage and vote buying that had defined electoral politics in the village of "Mallannapalle." Significantly, the credible threat that land ceilings would now be enforced encouraged the two main landlords out of moneylending, thereby removing a principal means of bonding local labour.

During the same period, the introduction of the Indebtedness Relief Act and the availability of new sources of income and credit (arising largely from central government programmes) further severed the links between landlord and tenant/labourer. The end result was that by the 1977 Parliamentary elections, the principal village leaders were "no longer in control of the Mallannappalle vote bank but neither was anyone else. Recent assessments of decentralization in Andhra Pradesh (AP) have emphasized a State that has become decidedly hostile to the interests of panchayati raj. In Madhya Pradesh's ambitious 'experiment' in direct democracy, the AP government has been associated with a system of governance that has undermined the panchayats in favour of line departments and 'parallel bodies' such as water user groups, joint forest management committees, self-help groups and the like.

A principal vehicle in this process has been the AP government's wellpublicised janmabhoomi programme. Introduced in 1997, janmabhoomi aims to reduce poverty through the establishment of community development programmes, such as watershed rehabilitation, joint forest management, thrift and credit, and so on. Central to the programme is the idea that poverty reduction is contingent upon the active participation of poor people, both in terms of self-employment through subsidised credit but also in terms of contributions in kind, such as voluntary labour. The assumption here is that poor people require both the resources and the incentive to lead healthy and productive lives. Whether or not it has been able to achieve these aims, janmabhoomi is believed to have undermined the autonomy and functioning of the panchayats in two important ways. First it has been alleged that the AP Government has diverted public resources intended for centrally-sponsored schemes into the janmabhoomi programme, thereby 'starving' the panchayats of funds which are rightfully theirs.

Second, janmabhoomi is perceived to have used the village gram sabhas as a means of organising and identifying beneficiaries, creating a situation of confusion for recipients and for the panchayats. As G. Krishna Reddy points out, "there is a heavy dose of bureaucratic involvement in running janmabhoomi." Nodal officers at district and mandal levels are centrally involved in selecting works, channelling resources and organizing user committees.

Chandrababu Naidu, the former Chief Minister of Andhra Pradesh, has argued that because they are organised on the basis of class, caste, gender, etc., SHGs are actually more participatory than panchayats. His principal assertion is that SHGs conform with the divisions that already exist in rural society. Panchayats, on the other hand, aim to encourage democratic ideals, such as equality, transparency and freedom, but fail to enforce them, thereby creating a situation in which the local bodies are systematically captured by powerful elites. G. Krishna Reddy argues that janmabhoomi . . . has not brought any substantial change in the way the bureaucratic functionaries are positioned vis-à-vis people except that the officials are asked to visit the villages periodically . . . In fact, precisely because of this reason, it has become yet another officially sponsored ritual . . .

As numerous observers have pointed out, policies of this kind were extremely popular with international donors, such as the UK Department for International Development and the World Bank, but very unpopular with the large class of farmers (particularly those using bore well irrigation) who have traditionally benefited from state subsidies. In rural areas, the dual commitment to good governance and painful reform has created strong incentives to shore up political support among traditional constituencies. Partly for this reason, populist policies on rice, janmabhoomi and micro-credit for women, have endured. Moreover, in the wake of the 2001 panchayat elections, in which the TDP suffered substantial losses to the rival Congress Party, the TDP undertook a "massive review" of its policies and programmes, resulting in two important outcomes.

One was a change to janmabhoomi in which rounds were held bi-annually instead of quarterly. A second was the introduction of a new nonelected official at the village level: the village secretary. Hired, promoted and rotated from Hyderabad, the village secretary was explicitly designed to provide a systematic source of administration which draws its authority and legitimacy from the State bureaucracy. In this way it is highly consistent with the Chief Minister's public commitment to organised and accountable government (personal communication with senior officials in the GoAP).

In sum, party politics in Andhra Pradesh have produced a government and a Chief Minister whose political fortunes have become strongly tied to an image based on transparency, accountability and good governance. The progressive 'weakening' of the panchayats has been construed as a reflection of the Chief Minister's autocratic 'style' and the ruling Telugu Desam Party's strategy of creating and maintaining political control by channelling funds into local user groups. In contrast to AP, Madhya Pradesh is often portrayed as a pioneer in the field of decentralization.

Since 1994, the State government has introduced a series of legislative reforms, which have expanded the formal authority of the gram sabha. In 1999, an important reform was the 'Right to 16 Recall,' which gave the gram sabha the power to dismiss the GP chairman (the sarpanch) in the event of wrongdoing. In 2001, the State government expanded the gram sabha's authority to include greater powers of planning, consultation and accountability. Significantly, the gram panchayat has the ability to choose and select the site of the school and the schoolteacher. Once a village provides the space for the school and identifies a teacher, the MP government guarantees to create and fund a school in the GP area within 90 days of the application. In contrast, panchayats in AP do not have this authority.

Another important difference between the two States is the MP government's 1999 decision to create District Planning Committees (DPCs). The principal function of the 17 DPCs is to co-ordinate, evaluate and oversee the plans and budgets of subordinate municipalities and panchayats. The Government of MP also reserves the right to devolve additional powers to the DPCs 'from time to time,'. A key component of district government in MP is the requirement that DPCs have a State Minister serving as Chair. The explicit aim of this stipulation is to expedite district-level allocations of government funding. Other members of the DPC include the president of the ZP, the District Collector, a pre-determined number of scheduled representatives, 'special invitees' from the Lok Sabha (union lower house), Rajya Sabha (upper house) and State Legislative Assembly, and elected representatives, four-fifths of whom shall constitute the entire DPC.

Such 'high-level' participation within the DPCs and the large discretionary powers that still rest with the State government have prompted some analysts to conclude that DPCs actually constitute a threat to lower level GPs and JPs, as well as the ZPs. In the words of the World Bank study of decentralisation in MP, ministers, MPs and MLAs have 'completely usurped the powers of the ZP,' and 'completely undermined beneficiary selection of the GP, JP and ZP,'. As in AP, decentralization in Madhya Pradesh has been used by the ruling Congress Party as a means of maintaining political support in rural areas, as well as within the ranks of its own party. In theory, the constitutional amendments legislated by the MP government therefore create a village structure with strong mechanisms for downward accountability. The principal mechanisms include:

— Powers of appointment and approval in the hands of the gram sabha;

— The right of the GS to 'recall' or dismiss the sarpanch;

— Minimum requirements governing the GS quorum;

— Direct elections of GP councillors and sarpanch;

The legislation also provides important opportunities for upward accountability, in particular the guarantees provided through the EGS and the ability to appeal to subdistrict officials. The Government of AP has not devolved power to the extent that proponents of decentralization would have liked, its populist approach to certain forms of poverty reduction has empowered the poor in ways that the more ambitious decentralization agenda in MP has not.

Governance and Politics in the Gram Panchayats

Focus group discussions (FGDs) and key informant interviews were designed to understand the extent to which the GPs and GS were able to affect the implementation of 2 general types of government scheme: employment generation (largely EAS and JRY) and self-employment programmes (largely SGSY, formerly IRDP). FGDs were conducted with major caste, class, religious and age groups, as well as in separate groups of men and women. The principal questions were designed to understand:

— How the selection process works (informally) with respect to principal social groups in the villages (e.g. caste, class, gender, religion, age);

— How people perceive the role and quality of the panchayats in general and with respect to their particular group;

— Levels of awareness about the nature of the schemes being discussed, how the programmes and panchayats are supposed to function and what rights they are entitled to under these programmes and in relation to the panchayats;

— Whether and to what extent they have used formal mechanisms (such as the gram sabha in both states, the right to recall in MP) to ensure accountability of government officials;

— Which formal and informal mechanisms have been most effective (if any)

Key informant interviews were conducted with elected representatives (sarpanch, upasarpanch, all ward members), non-elected officials (e.g. the VAO, BDO, the patwari, etc.) and villagers, selected on the basis of caste, class and gender. These were principally designed to understand:

— The political, administrative and fiscal powers that the GPs and gram sabha have to ensure the appropriate and accountable delivery of employment and self-employment schemes;
— How the selection process takes place, especially among GP members (representing different wards and therefore different caste constituencies) and the non-elected bureaucracy (e.g. the BDOs, VAO, VDO)

The extent to which the PRIs have the power to ensure that programmes are implemented according to the letter of the norms, rules and laws under which they were meant to be governed.

Village Assemblies

The gram sabha were strongly tempered by the large gap that is known to exist between the rhetoric surrounding the ideals of direct democracy and the actual performance of the gram sabha. Interviews with villagers did little to dispel this scepticism. In both States, the gram sabha was widely perceived as a powerless forum, in which panchayat leaders would simply confirm decisions already taken by the sarpanch and other GP leaders. Interviews with ward members, sarpanches and villagers in all of the six villages in MP suggest that the 1994 reforms had little impact either on the day to day functioning of the panchayat or on the relationship among villagers, elected representatives and government officials. Under the gram swaraj reforms, the 8 user committees are meant to be selected by the gram sabha and then empowered to decide matters in accordance with the needs of their constituents.

Moreover, a quorum of at least 20 per cent of the GS is required on matters relating to development planning, village expenditures and beneficiary selection. In practice, the committees and the gram sabha in the MP villages appeared largely dysfunctional. According to the 1994 reforms, members of the 8 committees were meant to be selected by the gram sabha. Evidence from Mandla, Ujjain and Tikamgarh suggests that the gram sabha was involved in the election of committee members. In practice, however, the selection process was dominated by the sarpanch, often in collaboration with the line ministry officials whose projects were being implemented in the village. "Selection" here was essentially a matter of compiling a list of names, and submitting 23 them to the relevant line departments.

In one village in Ujjain, for instance, a forest committee was formed on the basis of a 20 minute meeting between the mantri and the gram sabha, whereby the former instructed the latter to form a committee, documented eight names and then left the village. In many cases, committee members were completely unaware that they were even on a committee. In our household surveys, the number of respondents who said they were members of a village committee was less than 2 percent. Finally, the committees in question appear to have been highly ineffectual. Forest committees in Ujjain, for instance, showed no resistance to illegal logging around the village; water conservation committees had no powers to curtail the extraction of groundwater and the sinking of borewells.

The only committees that appear to have had any role in local development initiatives were the educational and agricultural committees principally because they were connected to the allocation of government programmes and resources. In this respect, the functioning of the committees was far more a matter of bureaucratic procedure than it was one of democratic representation. Interviews with sarpanches in the MP villages revealed high levels of confusion and derision arising from the gram swaraj reforms. Sarpanches in the Tikamgarh villages told us that they "were forced" to decide matters outside the gram sabha because it "takes too long" to reach consensus and to achieve the 20 per cent quorum, as the legislation requires. In best case scenarios, the gram sabha served as a "final stamp of approval" for decisions about the location of projects, the selection of beneficiaries, and the distribution of state resources. However, the "vote" or voice of the GS had little power to alter or challenge the decisions presented within this village forum.

Interviews with the villagers in question reveal an opaque process in which the sarpanch would accept the relevant documentation, providing little information about whether and how the claim would be processed. Many respondents told us that their claims were still outstanding, and that they had received no follow-up information about their status. Moreover, sarpanches were highly adept at manipulating the gram sabha to meet the requirements of gram swaraj. Signatures of villagers and ward members were commonly added to the register; gram sabhas were arranged with very little time or notice for ward members to organise opinion or support on a particular issue. The ward members and villagers were completely unaware that gram sabhas had in fact been held.

A number of interesting differences between the functioning of the gram sabha in AP and the processes encountered in MP. First, it was clear that levels of participation in the GS were significantly higher in AP than they were in MP. This appears to be primarily the result of the fact that the GS was used as a means of selecting beneficiaries and announcing allocations for the State's janmahboomi programme and during 2002 for the State's FFW programmes. In AP, the /rates of attendance and participation in the gram sabha (a very crude indicator of political inclusion) were substantially higher (73%) than those for MP (48%), a State in which the gram sabha has been vested substantive powers and responsibilities stemming from the "gram swaraj" reforms of 1999. A second and related difference between the two States was a much stronger presence on the part of mandal-level officials in the gram sabha.

Interviews with mandal officials, representatives and villagers revealed that the mandal development officer (MDO) and more rarely the mandal revenue officer (MRO) were consistently involved in GS meetings. Once again, this is primarily due to the fact that mandal officials were responsible for implementing and coordinating janmahboomi and FFW programmes in the villages, and that the GS served as a principal vehicle in this process. Finally, gram sabhas in AP followed a more rigid and systematic schedule than did their counterparts in MP. Sarpanches, ward members and villagers in Chittoor reported that the gram sabha would convene on the 5th of every month, and that GP councillors would attend meetings at the mandal office every three months. In Medak and Krishna, GS meetings appear to have been somewhat less frequent, although representatives, officials and villagers all reported that gram sabhas would operate according to a fairly rigid schedule.

In sum, the most important variations in AP and MP are ones relating to levels of participation in the GS and levels of interaction between our respondents and elected and non-elected officials. In terms of the GS, a crucial point that needs to be made at this early stage is not that participation in MP was all that low (48 per cent), but that levels of participation in AP appear to have been exceptionally high (73 per cent). At first glance, findings of this kind appear highly consistent with the image of an AP government committed to principles of transparency, accountability and a professionalized bureaucracy. Upon closer inspection, it is clear that although interaction between "ordinary villagers" and non-elected officials was higher in AP, it is not at all clear that the relationship was any more transparent or accountable. This is due in part to the fact that mandal officials were not necessarily listening or responding to the needs of their plaintiffs.

Moreover, the active role of non-elected officials appears to have come at the expense of the power and autonomy of elected representatives in the AP panchayats. In MP, the testimony of villagers and ward members in the AP villages gives the impression that the gram sabha was little more than a public forum in which announcements about janmahboomi and other government programmes were made by the sarpanch. Evidence that the gram sabha was used to select beneficiaries or to identify BPL households was non-existent. As in MP, villagers in the AP villages used the gram sabha to make claims and requests about government schemes and entitlements (such as white cards), largely to no avail. Reports of opaque processes, ambiguous responses and the like were very common among our AP respondents.

The enthusiasm for decentralisation in MP puts an emphasis on village level institutions, particularly the sarpanch, as the gatekeeper of all resources. However, the result is the (over) empowerment of the sarpanch, which gram swaraj has tried to dismantle, and a reduction of power players (and thus political competition) at the village level, with most information and patronage channelled through fewer people. This also reduces the options by which people can seek redress, especially given that the block level is meant to be the watchdog of the GP. Although they are by no means a vibrant democracy, the high levels of participation in AP do suggest that citizens are engaged in some sort of political discourse with the bureaucratic state. Relation of this kind have a legacy in AP, reflected in the State government's policies (and electoral strategies) on reservations and targeted poverty reduction.

Reservations

As noted earlier the 73rd Amendment stipulates that panchayats at all levels "reserve" seats for women, Scheduled Castes (SCs), Scheduled Tribes (STs) and other backward castes (OBCs). Findings from our studies in both States suggest that reservations of this kind had a limited impact, and that powerful families and elites were able to control the agenda and decisions of the GPs, in spite of reservations. However, longer standing policies of targeted reservations in AP appear to have produced important forms of political empowerment in the sample villages.

Beyond the limitations imposed by the panchayat voting system, the formal powers and responsibilities of scheduled sarpanches and ward representatives were often easily undermined by the informal authority of local elites and powerful families. KO in the coastal district of Krishna is probably the most illustrating case in point. In this village, a woman had achieved the seemingly unusual distinction of winning the election of sarpanch on an open ticket (i.e. it was not reserved for women). This was unusual in at least two ways. First, she was from a caste (yadav) whose power has not traditionally been strong in this part of AP. Second, she was a woman. However, any optimism about the empowerment of women was quickly tempered by interviews with the individual in question, which revealed that she was the mother of a very powerful shipping magnate from the coastal city of Vizag, who was keen to extend his influence (and that of the TDP) in his home village.

In MB, a village in which power relations were particularly unequal, the female sarpanch was visibly subservient to her husband, who once again conducted our interviews on his wife's behalf. The same cannot be said of caste. An important point to emphasise here is that all but one of the GPs is controlled by caste groups whose economic and political trajectory has been moving upwards. Moreover, they have done so in part by taking advantage of the reservations that exist outside of the panchayat system.

Sarpanches in the Andhra villages of OP, VP, KO and KA were all elected on tickets reserved for OBCs. Here it is notable that all of the sarpanches were from caste groups whose economic and political fortunes have improved in the last ten to fifteen years. In OP and KO, the sarpanches were from the upwardly mobile yadava caste. The Yadava, also known as Golla, are one of the largest BCs in AP. They were traditionally livestock keepers and have accumulated much wealth through dairy and meat production, both sectors are expanding due to urban demand and changing food habits. In the coastal districts they were among the groups that benefited from the transfer of land from the higher castes because of their good links with patrons through trade;

they were suppliers of milk and ghee. The Yadava have been able to take advantage of reservations for BCs more than many others because they have been relatively better off in physical asset ownership. They were wooed aggressively by the TDP because of their numerical strength and their Sheep and Goat Rearers Primary Societies were given preferential treatment in access to grazing.

Social Growth

Gram panchayats in India have long been portrayed as "clearing houses" for the Ministry of Rural Development and for other line agencies, with no substantive powers of their own. This is frequently attributed to the fact that the vast majority of States devolved few substantive resources or powers of revenue collection to the panchayats. It also reflects the administrative structure that underlies the panchayat system. As Dasgupta et al. point out, the vast majority of revenues among the 12 GPs were either tied to centrally sponsored schemes, such as JRY (Jawahar Rozgar Yojana, a wage employment poverty programme), Food for Work (FFW), etc. or were transferred from superior bodies in the form of 11th Finance Commission Funding or in AP, the State government's janmahboomi programme. This is not to say that local revenues were non-existent; just that they were negligible.

For most GPs, the most important sources of revenue were centrally sponsored schemes, such as JRY, EAS and FFW. In terms of planning, identifying needs and representing interests, evidence of GPs or their constituents developing plans that they would one day implement in their villages was very rare. In some of the MP villages, sarpanches and ward members said they were involved in a series of "village action plans," but these were essentially requests for funding developed by the GP and then sent to the block and the district for approval, according to pre-existing programmes, such as JRY or IAY (a centrally sponsored housing scheme for the poor). Such planning exercises were only reported in the district of Tikamgarh, and appear to have had no clear connection to the eight village committees which were meant to be empowered by gram swaraj legislation or to the gram sabha.

E-Governance in India

The nature of governance often changes depending on the intensity and speed of transition in some of these surrounding factors. In the current age, one of the most significant contextual phenomena affecting public governance is the revolution in Information and Communication Technology (ICT). Internationally, this revolution in ICT has facilitated the globalization of the economy, business, finance and culture. Today ICT constitutes the fastest growing component of the global economy and the revenue generated by the interactive information industry may have reached $3.5 trillion. Internally, within each society, the conventional forms of communication (print media, motion pictures, radio, telephones, records) are increasingly being replaced with digital and wireless technologies such as cellular telephones, satellites, electronic mail and, above all, the internet.

However, the most influential dimension of this revolution is the worldwide proliferation of access to the internet. It is observed that the number of internet hosts increased from 100,000 in 1988 to over 36 million in 1998; and the number of internet users rose from 26 million in 1995 to 143 million in mid-1998, and it might reach 700 million by the end of 2001. This contextual phenomenon, which has changed the nature of the workforce, human relations and public expectations, represents a considerable challenge to the state to adjust its public governance.

In response to this transition in the context of governance, in almost every country, the state has taken the necessary initiatives to restructure political and administrative institutions by adopting ICT in order to enhance electronic interaction and service delivery. Today public servants are encouraged and trained to be familiar with the tools and languages of ict. In fact, there have emerged many buzzwords - including digital governance, smart governance, net-governance, cyber-management and digital democracy - which overlap with the notion of electronic governance or egovernance. Although the advocates of e-governance tend to define it as something that is always beneficial, a value-neutral perspective may interpret it as a new mode of governance that extensively uses advanced forms ofICTin pursuing public policies, maintaining organizational relations, interacting with customers and delivering services.

However, one of the most significant dimensions of e-governance is the creation and maintenance of websites by legislatures, ministries, agencies, political parties, local institutions, and so on. The main rationales behind this opting for e-governance are that egovernance will reduce costs and delays in delivering services, expand citizens' access to public sector information, reinforce innovation in public agencies, increase transparency and public accountability, weaken authoritarian tendencies and strengthen civil society and democracy.

In line with this global trend, India has undertaken massive initiatives to introduce e-governance at the national, state and local levels. In terms of the total number of government websites, although the advanced industrial countries top the list, India is ranked seventh in the global list. Similar to the previously mentioned common rationales, the top policy-makers in India tend to justify the adoption and expansion of e-governance on the grounds that it costs less, reduces waste, promotes transparency, eliminates corruption, generates possibilities to resolve rural poverty and inequality, and guarantees a better future for citizens.

In short, the government tends to portray e-governance as the panacea for all ranges of problems confronting India. But there are critics who, in general, suggest that the whole enterprise ofICTmay have created a new class of 'untouchables' living in 'information poverty', compromised equal access to government services and eroded accountability and individual privacy. This dimension is crucial, because what matters most is whether the adoption of e-governance has been able to create relationships between these stakeholders - between citizens and politicians, between politicians and public servants and between citizens and public servants - based on accountability, equality and fairness.

Unlike developed nations, India is one of the poorest countries in the world with severe problems of poverty, inequality, illiteracy and external dependence, which represent major impediments to the effectiveness of e-governance in ensuring equal public access to state institutions, empowering ordinary citizens to exercise their basic rights and obliging political and administrative officials to be responsive and accountable. However, before examining the impacts of e-governance on the nature and structure of citizen-politics-bureaucracy relations in India, the next section is devoted to an analysis of the major policies, initiatives and institutions related to e-governance in this country.

Policies, and Initiatives

India is one of the leading countries venturing into e-governance. Recently, the Indian Government has set the target of delivering at least 25 percent of its dealings and services electronically. In this regard, the Indian Government's major policy measures have been defined in terms of computer density, connectivity, content, cost and cyber laws. More specifically, the Indian Government has decided to boost 'computer density' by making computers easily affordable; to increase 'connectivity' by improving the telecommunication system based on optic fibre networks; to upgrade 'content' by making government sources on computers readable by ordinary citizens; to cover the 'cost' of ICT by ensuring adequate allocation in the national budget; and to introduce 'cyber laws' by adopting the Information Technology Act. Under this overall policy framework, the government has introduced various measures for e-governance, which can be categorized into national- and state-level initiatives and institutions.

One of the most important initiatives undertaken by the central government is the Information Technology Act, which is to regulate cyberspace and define offences and penalties related to information technology (it) such as tampering with computer source documents, breach of confidentiality and privacy, publication of false digital signatures and so on. The Indian Government has also drafted the so-called Freedom of Information Bill that requires all public authorities to maintain information and records, and appoint Public Information Officers to assist citizens in gaining access to such information. The Government has also planned to produce a series of documentaries to generate awareness of the advantages of it and electronic service delivery. Furthermore, it has introduced citizens' charters under which the ministries and departments at both national and state levels are required to adopt charters specifying their respective service provisions, time frames, service standards and channels for redressing grievances.

In order to implement this vision, policy initiatives and legal measures related to e-governance, there has emerged a series of institutions and official positions in India. For instance, the Government has introduced a National Task Force on IT and Software Development, a Committee on Improving Efficiency in Government Through IT, a Ministry of Information Technology (MIT) and a Centre for Electronic Governance in order to promote it and e-governance in the country. In particular, the MIT plays a crucial role in facilitating e-governance by reinforcing knowledge-based enterprises, encouraging coordination among users, adopting procedures based on international standards, promoting the internet and introducing it education. However, the main functions of the Centre for Electronic Governance are to identify the appropriate forms of ICT necessary for better service delivery, to conduct training for generating it awareness among government officials and to help state governments in implementing policies and reforms based on best e-governance practices.

Government has also decided to establish a National Institute of Smart Government in order to enhance capacity-building in egovernance at all administrative levels. In addition, various ministries and departments have created Information and Facilitation Counters as one-stop shops to make varieties of information available to citizens through electronic links. An essential institutional aspect of e-governance in India is also the government decision to appoint it managers (all are ranked as Joint Secretary officers) in the ministries or departments - they are responsible for adopting and implementing it in their respective organizations. In line with the institutional requirements of e-governance, the ministries and departments have undertaken initiatives to introduce and expand the structures and processes of e-governance.

For example, the Ministry of Finance, Ministry of Labour, Department of Agriculture and Cooperation, Ministry of Environment and Forests and the Ministry of Chemicals and Fertilizers now provide computers, email facilities, advanced software, local network connections and internet access to all their officers holding positions from the Secretary to Section Officers. These organizations also maintain their own websites, and often have Facilitation Centres to disseminate information to the public. Similar information infrastructure and communication facilities can be found in most other ministries and departments under the central government.

Although the central government has adopted certain measures to assist various states in pursuing e-governance, the state governments themselves have undertaken massive initiatives to transform their governance systems based on it. At a recent conference on e-governance in Bangalore, IT Secretaries from 32 states and union territories expressed their strong commitment to e-governance. In September 2000, Bill Gates, the chairman of Microsoft, advised 10 Chief Ministers on the role of it in improving governance. Of the total 25 states and seven union territories in India, some of the leading examples of e-governance include Andhra Pradesh, Gujarat, Karnataka, Kerala, Madhya Pradesh, Maharashtra, New Delhi and Tamil Nadu.

More specifically, the Andhra Pradesh Government took the initiative of e-governance known as the Andhra Pradesh State Wide Area Network, which is a network for data, voice and video communication. Through this network, it launched the Twin Cities Network Services to provide various services to citizens in two main cities (Hyderabad and Secunderabad) through onestop Integrated Citizen Services Centres (ICSCs). Through ICSCs, the citizens can access information about state and central governments; pay utility bills and property taxes; purchase certificates and licenses; and receive information regarding building permits, property registration and transport procedures.

Madhya Pradesh followed Andhra Pradesh's example by introducing its own e-governance with some modifications. In particular, the government in this state has introduced extensive computerization in dealing with payrolls, the budget, accounts, personnel, official communications, land records, public programmes and relief operations. It trains public servants in e-governance at the Academy of Administration. Initiatives have also been taken to use Hindi as a popular medium to communicate among governments, provide information to the public, use email services and maintain government web pages.

Karnataka is another state that has undertaken an ambitious e-governance programme. This state government has begun to computerize most departments, especially the education department. Its major city, Bangalore, is known as an it hub attracting over 1500 it companies from advanced industrial nations; and its Indian Institute of Information Technology has a very advanced infrastructure and it facilities. Furthermore, under its Department of Information Technology, the government plans to create a centre for e-governance. It has recently signed a Memorandum of Understanding with the Microsoft company with a view to computerizing all departments.

Similarly, the Government of Tamil Nadu is strongly committed to transforming the state into an advanced system of e-governance by computerizing its major departments and building technical capacity, with the ultimate objective of restoring public confidence and creating an effective relationship between government and citizens. To reinforce its mission of restoring citizens' confidence, the Government has adopted projects to ensure computerization of land records, registration, the education system, transportation, and so on. It has also established a Tamil Internet Research Centre to promote the use of Tamil on the internet in order to increase access for citizens.

In Kerala, however, the state government uses selected nodal officers in each department to accelerate the application of it. In this regard, one unique feature of Kerala is its comprehensive programme aimed at decentralizing e-governance to the district level - many district cooperative banks and credit societies have been networked. Activities and documents which have been put on the internet may cover tax collection, accounting, welfare schemes, court rulings and government orders and directives. Moreover, the government is using a transliteration technology that allows its web pages to be available in the local language (Malayalam). It launched a project called 'A PC for Every Home' through the Kerala Electronics Development Corporation, which aimed to reach the target of 10 personal computers (pcs) per 1000 people by the end of 2001.

There are other states that are also pursuing e-governance. For example, the Rajasthan Government has taken measures to strengthen e-governance, proposing the creation of a statewide network to provide information and video communication to both public and private organizations. The Department of Information Technology in Rajasthan has developed such programs as RajSWIFT to facilitate the use of online data and email communication among officials; and RajNIDHI to provide services to citizens in a transparent and responsive manner. The Government of Gujarat has introduced a state-wide network (Wide Area Network) connecting all office complexes and corporations in the state. However, beyond the overall state-wide agenda for egovernance related to land revenue, transport and rural development, the Uttar Pradesh government has taken a special interest in transforming its Allahabad district into a Smart District.

Similarly, the Government of Maharashtra is trying to develop Mumbai and Pune into major it hubs while pursuing the state-wide expansion of e-governance. It has taken on the responsibility for developing it skills and awareness among employees through training, and to link all district-level offices through the Wide Area Network. Although the status of e-governance in other states has not been discussed, they also have their independent agendas for e-governance, which include, in particular, Haryana, West Bengal, Orissa, Tripura, Meghalaya and Himachal Pradesh. Beyond these state-level initiatives, e-governance has been pursued at the local community level. A good example of local-level initiatives in e-governance is a rural intranet project known as Gyandoot, which was adopted by the district panchayat of Dhar district in Madhya Pradesh to extend it services, including both e-governance and ecommerce, to rural areas in a people-centred manner.

In Kerala, the so-called Information Kerala Project was adopted to computerize and network about 1214 local bodies. In this state, a district panchayat known as Ernakulam has adopted a model of e-governance that provides guidance to three village panchayats in the district to build an information network covering information related to land holdings, age structure, health, tax payments, and so on. In Maharashtra, the Warana Wired Village Project, executed by the National Informatics Centre, covers 70 villages: it allows internet access to cooperative societies and aims to deliver information relating to agriculture, health and education to the people by creating networked 'facilitation booths' in these villages. The Indian central government also plans to set up about 500 Community Information Centres in a hilly northeast part of India to let the local people have access to the internet.

The scope of e-governance, it can be safely concluded that despite the relatively rural-agricultural nature of its economy and the high levels of poverty and illiteracy, India has undergone a fundamental change in terms of the application of ICT to its public governance. There are diverse implications of this recent transition in governance in various domains, sections and relations in society.

Impacts of E-governance on Citizens, Politicians and Public servants

The key issue in evaluating egovernance is the way in which it affects the nature of the relationship between political institutions, bureaucracies and citizens; and whether it facilitates a relationship based on public accountability and participation. The cyber-optimists believe that e-governance does contribute to better relations among these three actors by making information available on government operations and public services, facilitating public feedback or reaction and allowing more direct participation by the ordinary citizen in decision-making. In the case of India, for the current generation of policy-makers, e-governance facilitates the dissemination of information to citizens, ensures greater access to government administration, enhances public participation in the formulation and implementation of state policies and thus strengthens the government-public interface.

But the cyberpessimists believe that the use of it in governance may worsen inequality in access to government services due to the lack of an adequate infrastructure, unequal ownership of computers, language constraints, and so on. There is also a concern that e-governance may disempower citizens by individualizing them, eroding their common bonds and endangering their privacy.

In India, e-governance creates an avenue for its citizens to communicate with top political leaders and local ministers through such tools as video-conferencing, online grievance channels and complaint cells. A major means through which such interaction between citizens and politicians occurs is the parliamentary website, which is supposed to facilitate the top-down flow of information from the legislature to citizens, allow a bottom-up channel for feedback from citizens to the elected members, increase transparency by providing detailed information about legislative procedures and activities, expand the number of avenues for greater public scrutiny of the nature and processes of public policies and thus enhance the accountability of these elected politicians to their constituencies.

There are 98 countries in which the national parliaments have their own websites; of these the most comprehensive ones are from Scandinavia, western Europe and North America. Among the developing countries, the website of the Indian Parliament (alfa.nic.in) is quite comprehensive. It encompasses a list of basic information regarding the House of People (Lok Sabha) and the Council of States (Rajya Sabha). The menu includes such items as parliamentary activities, parliamentary committees, budget matters, national constitution, legislative acts, prime minister's office, web addresses of all ministries and states, bulletins and publications, economic surveys, citizen services, and profiles and speeches of parliamentary members. It also provides an option for citizens to send feedback and suggestions through email.

The Prime Minister's Office also has a website, which provides information regarding his policy initiatives, maintains an option for surveying opinion regarding current political issues and offers opportunities for the public to send queries and comments. These online sources of information and avenues for public expression are supposed to be more conducive to a stronger relationship between citizens and politicians. Another dimension of e-governance that has implications for the citizen-politician relationship are the websites maintained by various political parties. The traditional mode of interaction between party leaders and the public has changed in this age of it, because in most countries, political parties are putting online information about their ideological positions, policy choices, political messages and campaign issues. However, there are significant regional and crossnational variations.

Although the number of parties online has reached 1250 worldwide, on average, there are 41 party websites per country in North America, 24 per country in Western Europe and less than five per country in the Middle East and Sub-Saharan Africa. There seems to be a positive correlation between the levels of democracy and income, on the one hand, and the number of political parties online, on the other. Although India is a relatively low-income country, it has as many as 20 party websites, perhaps due to its strong democratic tradition. However, taking into account its population size, this number may appear less sufficient.

In terms of content, there are differences among political parties in the information put on the website. Among the major parties, the Bharatiya Janata Party (the current ruling party) covers quite a number of items, including its history, philosophy, leadership, members in parliament, interviews, press releases and write-ups on certain issues. It also provides an option for citizens to send feedback. The Communist Party of India, Marxist has a website that includes the party programmes, constitution, party structure, statements, elections and documents. The Samajwadi Party (www.samajwadi-party.org) presents its history, constitution and achievements, and an option for citizens to send feedback. The Akali Dal Party (www.shiromaniakalidalmann.org) covers such items as party resolutions, interviews, historical documents and news archives.

However, the Communist Party of India (www.cpofindia.org) has a website that not only presents its background, programme, constitution, press releases and journals, but also maintains a guestbook and an email option for citizens to send feedback. These are a few examples of the menus offered by various political parties on their websites in India. These provide some useful information regarding these political parties, so that citizens can make informed choices when they support or oppose any of these parties, especially during elections. Despite all these websites maintained by Parliament, the Prime Minister's Office and political parties in India, their effectiveness has yet to be evaluated. In the case of the Indian Parliament, there is no way of knowing how much information is put online and how much is concealed; and whether these elected politicians have the time and motivation to respond to all the public queries and comments, especially when these are too critical.

With regard to the politicalparty websites in India, apart from those launched by the Bharatiya Janata Party and the Communist Party of India (Marxist), they are not as comprehensive as those found in North America or western Europe. There has been hardly any studies on whether the electronic mode of governance in the political sphere of India, especially the use of the internet and email, has been effective in deepening the relationship between politicians and citizens. The critics may point to the fact that electronic means such as websites, in fact, can be used by political parties and leaders to publicize their achievements, construct positive images and direct public opinion in their favour. After all, this is a great opportunity for them to mitigate or reverse traditional public scepticism towards political parties, institutions and leaders.

The emergence of e-governance has significantly changed the nature of the relationship between citizens and public servants. The e-governance movement not only promises higher quality and better delivery of services and a greater realization of entitlements, it also claims to offer stronger bonds between public servants and citizens based on transparency and accountability. With regard to this new mode of relationship, Schware emphasizes that it in governance provides equal access to government and speedy and transparent responses from public servants.

E-governance may strengthen a top-down bureaucratic process by posting information about the structures and functions of public agencies and reinforcing the existing mode of interaction through documents and reports. In the case of India, it is mostly the favourable view of e-governance that is echoed in various print and electronic media, especially government websites. In line with the common optimist picture of e-governance, it is pointed out that in India, compared to the previous citizen-administration relations characterized by bureaucratic rigidity, long delays, unnecessary complexity and public suffering, this relationship under e-governance is now characterized by higher speed, greater access, less cost and less public harassment. At the Conference of Chief Ministers on 'Transparent and Accountable Administration', the potential of e-governance to realize transparency and accountability was strongly emphasized. One way to decipher how e-governance has transformed the nature of the relationship between citizens and the administration is to explore some of the major policy initiatives recently undertaken by the Government, and examine the official websites maintained by various ministries, departments and state governments.

First, the Indian Government has undertaken major policy initiatives at the national, state and local level. In this regard, the previously mentioned Information Technology Act provides privacy for personal information while the Freedom of Information Bill offers them rights to information when interacting with public agencies and officials. However, the adoption of citizens' charters and the creation of Information and Facilitation Counters by various government departments or agencies are initiatives that may provide citizens with specific guidelines regarding what to expect and whom to approach in their interaction or relationship with public agencies and employees.

Another major administrative initiative mentioned earlier is the appointment of senior civil servants as it managers in various ministries and departments -these it managers can not only facilitate the realization of e-governance in their respective organizations, they can also enhance the relationship between these public organizations and citizens. Similarly, most state governments have put senior public servants in charge of it, who now have an avenue through which to interact directly with citizens via electronic means. In order to strengthen the citizen-administration relationship, many state governments have taken other measures such as the introduction of local languages onto their websites (e.g. Hindi in Madhya Pradesh, Tamil in Tamil Nadu and Malayalam in Kerala); and the decentralization of information networks to various district and village panchayats (e.g. those in Kerala and Madhya Pradesh).

Second, the websites maintained by different ministries, departments and state governments have considerable implications for the interaction of ordinary citizens with public servants, especially with public servants involved in the direct delivery of services related to agriculture, health and food supply. A comprehensive website is maintained by the Department of Agriculture and Cooperation (www.nic.in/agricoop), which includes information relating to its various programmes and schemes, prices of agricultural products, weather watch, basic statistics, announcements and documents. More importantly, it has clickable feedback and email options and a helpdesk, which provide citizens with an opportunity to express their opinions, needs and problems.

Although the Ministry of Health and Family Welfare website (mohfw.nic.in) covers only its schemes and programmes, a database of parliamentary questions and staff profiles without an option for sending feedback, it includes gateways to its major departments that have their own websites. A similar website structure can be found in the case of the Ministry of Consumer Affairs, Food and Public Distribution (fcamin.nic.in). However, in addition to the gateways to its departments, the Ministry of Finance (finmin.nic.in) has an option for feedback on its website. Beyond these ministries and departments, there are other major nationallevel government institutions, including the supreme court, public service commission, election commission, planning commission, and so on, which maintain their respective websites.

For example, the Supreme Court of India (supremecourtofindia.nic.in) has a website that covers such menu items as the constitution, rules, profiles of judges and, more importantly, an option for citizens to send feedback. But the web menu of an essential public service institution, the Union Public Service Commission (www.upsc.gov.in), only includes items such as examination schedules, interview details, final results and notifications; it does not have an option for citizen feedback. However, the Directorate of Public Grievances (dpg.bharatsarkar.nic.in) has a website that maintains a clickable option for citizens to send their grievances against any government department or agency.

At the state level, the web menus of state governments cover some major items in various combinations - including profiles of governors and ministers, ministerial statements, facts and figures, structures and activities, gateways to various departments and district offices, email addresses, press releases, tourism and investment information and, above all, contact addresses and feedback options.

The websites of public sector organizations (ministries, departments, courts, commissions) at the national and state level not only provide information about their activities, programmes, reports, statistics and publications, many of them also offer feedback options on their websites. These are apparently favourable changes toward a more interactive relationship between public servants and citizens. However, beyond how many hits each of these government website recieves, it is difficult to assess the actual quantity of feedback and suggestions and the frequency at which public officials genuinely respond to them.

An important consideration in this regard is how relevant the online discussion items and information sources are to the needs and interests of various segments of the population in India. Not all citizens are interested in receiving information or providing feedback about ministerial speeches, leadership profiles and reports and documents on current issues. Even the practical information and application forms for services such as public utility bills, agricultural inputs, registration of driving licenses, pension schemes and housing and property taxes, may not interest certain occupational or income groups. Thus, under the electronic mode of governance, the interaction between the public and public servants becomes need-based and service-specific.

A common feature of the relation between politicians and the administration highlighted in most advanced democracies is the political neutrality of public servants and their accountability to elected political representatives. Following the liberal democratic model of governance, India inherited the tradition of political neutrality of public servants, although in reality, its bureaucracy was often found to be too powerful to be neutral and accountable to political representatives. However, compared to many developing countries, India did not experience excessive bureaucratic politics in the form of interventionist civilian and military bureaucracies, and it preserved a certain degree of separation between the political and administrative spheres.

In general, unlike the conventional democratic system of governance emphasizing a balance of power based on neutrality and separation among the various branches and levels of government, the current system of e-governance gives more importance to the 'connectivity' between the public and private sectors, between government and non-government organizations, between departments or agencies and between elected political executives and appointed senior civil servants. These increasingly blurred boundaries between the domains and levels of governance are endorsed by the advocates of e-governance on the ground that such a trend would increase efficiency and coordination in information-sharing, and reduce intragovernmental duplications and conflicts. This global trend toward increasing networks and connections among various layers and realms of governance can also be found in the case of India.

As far as the linkages between politicians and public servants are concerned, there is a growing tendency in India toward a blurred or fused relationship between them, especially due to their common mission of e-governance that stresses connection rather than separation. In fact, there has emerged in India a new breed of politicians possessing skills in it and behaving like bureaucratic experts. This is often the case at state-level governance. The recent speeches of Chief Ministers invariably include technical languages related to it understood and shared by technical bureaucratic experts rather than ordinary citizens. In fact, the elected Chief Ministers of such states as Andhra Pradesh, Arunachal Pradesh, Gujarat, Maharashtra, Meghalaya and Punjab, are themselves in charge of adopting it in governance. In the case of other states - including Bihar, Haryana, Himachal Pradesh, Karnataka, Madhya Pradesh, Orissa, Rajasthan, Uttar Pradesh and West Bengal - other elected ministers are assigned with this task.

There is no serious problem with the elected politicians managing the whole range of activities related to the use of it in governance, but it implies an increasing tendency of these politicians to play the role of technical experts and thus means a certain degree of bureaucratization of the political sphere. Conversely, there is a new generation of public servants in India who are well trained in ICT to generate, maintain and disseminate information. Despite the greater level of technical skills possessed by current political leaders, they are often dependent on these bureaucratic information experts. In the past, it was widely known that the power of a bureaucracy based on information and technical expertise always posed a challenge to its accountability to the non-expert political leaders in developing countries like India.

The current addition of a more sophisticated form of information power to the bureaucracy under e-governance brings back the question regarding the accountability of such an informationexpert public bureaucracy to elected politicians who are much less skilled in this new game of it. In addition, e-governance provides a wider opportunity for public servants to interact directly with the public in the process of receiving feedback from citizens and responding to their queries and complaints through electronic means. By entering into this domain of shaping public opinion, ict-skilled public servants may have assumed a certain political role. Thus, egovernance may not only increase the power of bureaucratic experts in relation to elected political leaders, it may also lead to the politicization of the overall bureaucracy.

Even if these politico-administrative consequences of e-governance - i.e. the bureaucratization of it-driven political leaders and the politicization of information-smart bureaucrats - imply a greater connectivity or interaction between them, it is likely that the latter (bureaucrats) will have a more favourable position in sharing power. After all, the new governance tends to privilege those with greater expertise and experience in it. This is an interesting situation in which greater connectivity does not necessarily mean stronger cooperation between the stakeholders: it may, in fact, imply more competition between them. In any case, if there is a stronger alliance between politicians and public servants based on their common interest in it-intensive governance, it may compromise neutrality as a principle of their relationship and alienate the information-poor public in India.

However, if the information-expert bureaucrats become too influential in relation to elected political representatives, it may undermine their accountability to these elected politicians. In other words, under e-governance, the nature of the relationship between politicians and public servants may have changed from one based on neutrality and accountability to one of a fused power structure with the dominance of bureaucrats empowered by information expertise.

6

Urban Development

The Constitution (74th) Amendment Act, 1992 was intended to give a more focussed thrust to decentralisation and the creation of a democratic governance structure with local responsibilities being assumed and managed at the local level. It was to address the inadequacies of the existing system of municipalities, redefine the relationship between the states and municipal bodies and lay the foundations of a new approach to urban management and governance that could fulfill the needs and aspirations of urban residents for development. Article 243W of the Act mandated the setting up of elected municipalities - urban local bodies (ULBs) - as the 'institutions of selfgovernment'. The important features of the Act are well-known but bear repetition since all of them have not been acted upon. These are :

— Regular elections under the supervision of the state Election Commission;

— a clear tenure of five years for the elected body;

— protection for the elected body against arbitrary dissolution;

— constitution of Wards Committees for greater proximity to the citizens;

— mandate to state legislature to endow the ULBs with such powers and authority as may be necessary to enable them to function as 'institutions of selfgovernment';

— the Twelfth Schedule which illustrates the range of responsibilities to be given to the ULBs;

— the constitution of State Finance Commissions (SFCs) to review municipal finances and make recommendations regarding distribution of the proceeds of state-level taxes between the state governments and the ULBs, criteria for grants-in-aid, measures needed to improve the financial position of the municipal bodies, etc.;

— setting up District Planning Committees and Metropolitan Planning Committees for integrated as well as coordinated planning for urban and rural areas by the various agencies involved in providing civic, transport, economic and social services.

It is significant that apart from the traditional municipal functions, Article 243W allocates to ULBs the function of 'preparation of plans for economic development and social justice', and the Twelfth Schedule contains 'urban poverty alleviation' as a municipal responsibility. These take municipal bodies from being mere providers of civic amenities to a much wider arena of action encompassing economic and social planning. The Constitutional amendment has designed the ULBs as comprehensive institutions of urban selfgovernment, and has left the details to be worked out by the state legislatures.

The state governments have carried out the required amendments to the municipal laws in accordance with their own requirements and some states have even enacted fresh legislation. Elections under the new dispensation have been held in most states, more than once in many. The enthusiasm among urban residents for the ULBs has been amply demonstrated by the fact that voter turnout in elections has been in the range of 65 to 70 per cent, much higher than the participation in elections to Parliament and state legislature.

There are around 73,000 elected representatives in the ULBs all over the country. It has, therefore, rightly been observed that 'the democratic structure of the country is no longer limited only to the Parliament and the state legislatures'. Now there is no denying the fact that the elected ULBs are full-fledged institutions of local self-government, a key part of democratic decentralisation in the country.

The challenge to be met in the Tenth Plan period is to assist these elected bodies to grow organically to fulfill the demands of urban residents for a quality of life in line with world standards. There is no doubt that the urban governance will progressively be managed at the local level ensuring better opportunities for people to express their needs and expectations, and with professional competence and capacity supplementing the democratic nature of the ULBs. The credit for this goes to the 74th Constitutional amendment, though it has been the subject of much debate from the outset.

Urbanisation in India

The Provisional Census Data of the 2001 Census reveals several significant facets of urbanisation over the last decade. Of the 1.02 billion population, 285 million or 27.8 per cent live in the urban areas which comprise 5,161 towns, an increase of 2.1 per cent over the proportion of urban population in the 1991 Census. Table 1 gives the proportion of urban population to total population between 1961 and 2001:

Table 1. Proportion of Urban Population & total Population

Year	Percent
1961	17.97
1971	19.91
1981	23.34
1991	25.71
2001	27.78

There is wide variation among states in urbanisation. At one end of the spectrum is the National Capital Territory of Delhi, with 93 per cent of its population living in urban areas. At the other end, Himachal Pradesh is the least urbanised state with only 9.8 per cent of its population in urban areas. Tamil Nadu is the most urbanised among the larger states with 43.9 per cent urban population, followed by Maharashtra with 42.4 per cent and Gujarat with 37.4 per cent. Among the larger states, Bihar has the lowest proportion of urban population (10.5 per cent), below Assam (12.7 per cent) and Orissa (14.9 per cent).

In terms of absolute number of persons living in urban areas, Maharashtra leads with 41 million persons. Uttar Pradesh comes next with 35 million followed by Tamil Nadu with 27 million.

There are 27 cities with more than one million population, while the Urban Agglomerations (UAs)/ Cities with population of more than one million number 35. About 37 per cent of the total urban population live in these Million Plus UAs/Cities. In Maharashtra, West Bengal and Gujarat, more than half of the urban populations live in the Million Plus UAs/Cities.

The decadal growth of population in rural and urban areas during 1991-2001 is 17.9 per cent and 31.2 per cent respectively, indicating a relatively higher growth in urban populations. However, it has been observed that the degree of urbanisation in India is among the lowest in the world. United Nations estimates for 2000 show that 47 per cent of total population of the world live in urban areas. While the proportion of urban population in developed countries range between 75 and 80 per cent, it is 36.7 per cent in Asia. Within Asia, countries like China and Indonesia, starting from lower levels of urbanisation in 1950, have now overtaken India with urbanisation of 32.1 per cent and 40.9 per cent respectively.

This is partly explained by one demographic fact : In India the decadal growth of urban population has been declining, from 46.1 per cent in 1971-81 to 36.4 per cent in 1981-91 to 31.2 per cent in 1991-2001. Correspondingly, the average annual exponential growth in UAs/Towns has also dropped from 3.8 per cent to 3.1 per cent and 2.7 per cent respectively. While this, to some extent, reflects a declining trend in total population growth, the fact still remains that urbanisation in India is proceeding at a fairly modest pace, though some states and cities are reporting exponential growth.

The moderate growth rate gives some breathing space to set the house of urban governance in order. However, there are cities where there is no time to lose.

Issues in Urbanisation for The Tenth Plan

Attitudes to urban growth within the country tend to swing between two extremes. Cities are seen either as an unavoidable evil or in a more positive way as 'engines of growth'. The former view is held by those who focus on the growth of slums and squatter colonies, the congestion on the roads and environmental degradation. The others, in contrast, focus on the bustling formal and informal sectors in urban areas and their contribution to the economy, the diversification of occupations away from traditional land-based ones to newer forms of production and services, and the lower levels of poverty as compared to rural areas.

There is, in fact, evidence to show that urbanisation is likely to have been a key determinant of economic growth in the 1980s and 1990s, boosted by economic liberalisation. From this point of view, the moderate pace of urbanisation in the country has been a cause of disappointment. There is, however, no rural vs. urban conflict either in terms of national growth, or in development priorities. In fact, perhaps because of the success of rural development programmes along with the limited availability of land for squatting in central urban areas, there seems to be no runaway migration from rural to urban areas.

Growth of Population

The impact of the growth of population on urban infrastructure and services has mostly been adverse. Cities with high rates of growth would be expected to have more resources for investment in the cities, but the fact is that much of this potential has remained untapped. On the other hand, smaller cities with less economic growth face inadequacies of financial and other resources to cope with increasing demands on services, and this may call for supplemental support from the budget.

Urban Governance

Urban governance today is characterised by fragmentation of responsibility, incomplete devolution of functions and funds to the elected bodies and ULBs, unwillingness to progress towards municipal autonomy, adherence to outmoded methods of property tax and reluctance to levy user charges. State governments continue to take decisions on such matters as rates of user charges, property tax, octroi, role of parastatals in water supply and sanitation services, etc., with little reference to the ULBs that are affected by these decisions.

Far from strengthening the constitutional role of the elected ULBs, such developments only reinforce the perception that ULBs are subordinate entities under the day-to-day control of the state governments, beholden to them not only for the development of the cities but often for their very survival. There appears to be a lack of confidence that many of the ULBs are capable of meeting their obligations as institutions of local self-governance. In the present set up, initiatives for local developmental activities rarely come from the ULBs.

The role of the ULBs in the immediate future will be:

— To be responsive and accountable to the community;

— to develop cities with standards of service comparable to the best in that particular category;

— to constantly improve their capabilities so as to equip themselves to undertake their tasks in resource-raising, service provision, and poverty alleviation,

Good urban governance calls for adequate policy and legal frameworks, the existence of regulatory and planning authorities, human skills, a sound revenue base, accounting and accountability. Substantial work has already been done to upgrade the urban infrastructure and several parastatals and urban development authorities have acquired considerable skills in planning and executing projects.

Programmes such as the Mega City project for five selected cities, the Integrated Development of Small and Medium Towns (IDSMT), and the Accelerated Urban Water Supply Programme (AUWSP)have shown varying degrees of success in meeting some of the urban needs. In particular, parastatal agencies and bodies such as development authorities, need to play a supportive role to the elected bodies rather than taking over functions which properly belong to the ULBs. The objective of devolution and decentralisation should be carried forward by making parastatals and authorities partners and agencies of the democratically elected ULBs, thus making a gradual transition to local management while continuing to use the expertise of the organisations set up and supervised by the State Governments. Initiating the necessary processes for partnerships between the State and its agencies on the one hand, and the ULBs on the other, is a part of the exercise of 'capacity building' in the ULBs.

Transparency and Right to Information

Since ULBs are closer to the tax-payers who depend on and are affected by the standards of services and infrastructure, there is need for a greater accountability in matters relating to municipal management and transparency in their functioning. The urban development sector is required to develop processes whereby information on all important decisions impinging on the life of urban residents are made available to them.

Citizens must be kept informed about the application of funds and other assets and resources of local bodies, decisions relating to land use, construction and other development activities in the cities, taxation/ user charge policy and performance and facts of financial health of the city. The people can be kept in the picture through the media, the Internet, and by the participation of municipal councilors and other personnel in meetings of residents' associations, as well as through more formal means of public information to be laid down in municipal rules.

Urban Finances

The system of a smooth sharing of resources between the State Governments and the ULBs on the one hand, and between different municipal bodies on the other, which is one of the objectives of the institution of the SFCs must ensure that the transfer of funds to the municipalities is both adequate and stable. The second round of SFCs are in place in most states and, hopefully, as the system evolves, there will be greater simplicity and transparency in the process of devolution of resources to local bodies, without undue transaction costs.

The objective of the system of SFCs would be fulfilled if an adequate level of resource transfers to ULBs takes place. It would, however, be unrealistic to expect ULBs' finances to be healthy when State Governments themselves face acute fiscal and resource constraints. Further, the allocations by SFCs may well tilt towards areas like rural development, irrigation, etc., and may not adequately meet the needs of the cities. The Finance Commissions at the Centre are now increasingly alive to the growing needs of urban areas.

The effectiveness of the system of SFCs will depend on adoption of certain healthy conventions by the State Governments. The conventions relate firstly to the choice of persons with adequate knowledge and expertise for appointment to the Commissions, and secondly to the practice of willingly adopting and fully implementing the recommendations. The different approaches adopted by the SFCs in various States to the tasks of assessing the critical needs of urban areas and making recommendations, and the policy of states in regard to acceptance and implementation of these recommendations, would be an area for study. Such a study would also show how far the objective of autonomy of the ULBs is being fulfilled.

Striking a balance between own resources of the ULBs and transfers from the state, is of critical importance. The system of transfer from the State Government should not lead to dilution of the seriousness and adequacy of the ULBs' own effort to raise resources. Misguided 'populism' is a game that the ULBs can also play, and inefficiency in collection, leakage of funds, and violations of fundamental financial principles, are dangers which have been experienced in our municipal entities. There is, therefore, every need to link the transfers under SFC formulations to the degree of efficiency ULBs exhibit in raising resources which the law allows them to generate, and in conforming to proper accounting and financial principles.

In order to help ULBs raise their own resources, the reform of the property tax system should be completed during the Tenth Plan period. The coverage of the property tax net is far from adequate, and this calls for serious attention. Alternatives to the 'annual rateable value', frozen in fiscal terms and discredited in implementation, are available in the form of area-based assessment, and capital value-based assessment. These initiatives should be further refined to develop transparent and buoyant systems of assessment with total coverage of all properties in a city, for which self-assessment by the property owner can be a useful instrument.

The levying of user charges, increasing non-tax revenues, control of costs and in particular of establishment costs, and better utilisation of municipal assets are essential measures to make ULBs financially stronger. Municipal accounting systems should be overhauled and made acceptable to lending agencies and financial markets by making it accrual-based. This is especially important for those ULBs wanting to access debt funds.

Infrastructure Assistance

Assistance from the Centre is an important addition to ULBs resources, though thus far it has been visibly less effective in bringing about reforms in the urban sector. A larger degree of central assistance, including external assistance routed through the Centre, as well as institutional finance from agencies like the Housing and Urban Development Corporation (HUDCO) would be necessary during the Tenth Plan in order to take up a vigorous programme of upgrading infrastructure and services. It is also necessary that these forms of assistance strengthen the elected ULBs as the legitimate institutions of governance at the local level. The assistance must be made conditional on sector reforms, in particular, better standards of service and the collection of user charges.

The coverage of central assistance in the past has been uneven and inadequate, both because of procedural issues as well as limited budgetary allocations. The number of cities/towns which received central assistance under IDSMT, AUWSP, and Mega City scheme up to the end of the Ninth Plan are:

— *AUWSP* : Between 1993-94, when it was initiated, and 2001-02, 654 schemes have been sanctioned with central assistance worth Rs. 337.37 crore;

— *IDSMT* : Since it was launched in 1979-80, 1,172 towns have been assisted and central assistance worth Rs. 531.62 crore released;

— *Mega City Scheme* : Initiated in 1993-94, the scheme covers only Mumbai, Kolkata, Chennai, Hyderabad and Bangalore. Central assistance to the tune of Rs.714.75 crore has been released.

Other programmes through which the Centre channels funds for urban improvement are:

— *NCR PLAN* : Rs 360.92 crore have been released as Central contribution towards provision of infrastructure in the National Capital Region.

— HUDCO, which received substantial injection of fresh equity during the Ninth Plan and has been used to leverage funds from market sources, is the other source of loan assistance to urban infrastructure projects.

— The Tax-Free Bonds scheme was introduced in February 2001, rather late in the Ninth Plan period. Since then, two ULBs (the Ahmedabad Municipal Corporation and the Hyderabad Municipal Corporation) have got approval to raise Rs 100 crore and Rs. 82.5 crore respectively.

— External assistance for the urban sector has continued to flow in from multilateral lending agencies like the Asian Development Bank (ADB), World Bank and bilateral agencies.

Infrastructure assistance through the IDSMT and Mega City schemes should aim at overcoming the worst features of neglect of urban requirements, take care of unmet needs in water supply, sanitation, solid waste management, urban transport, and the development of new extensions like residential colonies and satellite towns to relieve congestion. There is a wide variation in the availability of infrastructure and services, between cities and within the cities. The bigger cities tend to have better institutional arrangements and quality of service. In the hierarchy of cities, capital cities tend to get more attention, followed by other cities with greater economic activity, while the very small towns with extremely limited resources rarely see any improvement. The larger cities often have the capacity to raise resources from the market and from domestic as well as international funding agencies. Planning and financial support will need to be targeted at reducing the notable disparities of urban centres with significant limitations resources and glaring lack of civic amenities.

During the Tenth Plan, it is necessary to achieve a substantially higher, if not, total coverage of cities in need of infrastructural upgradation. A substantial step up in Central allocation to the urban sector is, therefore, required. This assistance should be contingent on the achievement of certain reforms, and an overall improvement in the ULBs' own efficiency in resource mobilisation, both through taxes and user charges, as well as service delivery. Municipal bodies need to be motivated to reduce expenditure, and improve the productivity of employees. A review of the working of on-going schemes, in particular IDSMT, Mega City, AUWSP, and Tax-Free Bonds schemes, will be undertaken in order to improve their working. The existing schemes for assistance for infrastructure such as the IDSMT and the Mega City Project, leave a significant number of cities between them without any Central support. During the Tenth Plan, these schemes will be extended to cover the cities which have been outside their purview.

Urban infrastructure cannot be funded by budgetary support alone. While market borrowings are not yet a viable source of financing for urban infrastructure in most instances,. a beginning has to be made for building up creditworthiness in ULBs. If this cannot be done for ULBs as a whole, then it should be attempted at least for individual sectors such as water supply, and wherever else user charges and the general resource position makes for it feasible to use debt funds to supplement grants or own resources. Assistance should be provided from budgetary sources as well as from external funding agencies, to defray the costs of implementing reform measures. This will enable the utilities to improve their performance and their finances. A City Challenge Fund was announced in the Union Budget 2002-03 and is in the process of being designed.

Broad-Based Reforms in the Urban Sector

The objective of reforms in land and housing policy, and of pricing of utilities, should be to augment the resources of the ULBs, provide for adequate maintenance of civic services, and undertake expansion of infrastructure to meet growing needs.

Cities everywhere are recognised as contributing substantially to economic, social, educational and infrastructural needs of the country. While they offer a higher standard of amenities to city-dwellers, they also have an important role in providing a range of services to the rural hinterland creating demand for rural output and providing inputs. Towns and cities act as nodal centres for providing services in marketing, health-care, education, and providing a window to the wider world, serving people other than their permanent residents.

In the past, the approach to urban growth, and in particular urban land issues, has been restrictive, based on the rigid comprehensive development plans, zoning and regulation of land use, with a predominant role in land assembly and development for urban development authorities. The role of the private sector was extremely limited. The inability of the urban development authorities to meet the total housing needs of the urban residents has driven large numbers of people in need of housing in every city, to seek housing in unauthorised colonies. These colonies are now posing a serious problem in urban management. Slums are only the most extreme form of this problem.

It is necessary to set in motion a virtuous circle of urban growth leading to better resources which are then used for improving infrastructure, which, in turn, will lead to further growth of the cities, resulting in enhanced economic activity and growth. Meeting the needs of the urban poor also necessitates ULBs having more resources at their command. The impediments to urban growth, as well as the necessary policy reforms, have been broadly identified.

Land Policy and Housing

The repeal of the Urban Land (Ceiling and Regulation) Act, 1976 has been a significant step towards reform in the urban land market. Following the repeal of the central legislation, a number of state governments have also repealed the state-level law. However, the Act still exists in some states, while several other state laws like the Land Revenue Act, Land Reforms Act, Stamp Duty Act, and Urban Development Authorities Acts/Town Planning Acts continue to hamper the availability of land for housing and other construction, pushing up land prices.

There is a need to take measures to ease the availability of land so that growth can take place through increased construction and housing activity, and land prices can be brought down to moderate levels making affordable shelter available to the lower income groups. This will also help prevent the proliferation of unauthorised colonies. This is by no means a measure to dilute urban planning, where enforcement has often been the weakest link. On the contrary, it will make urban planning more in tune with the changing nature of cities.

More flexible zoning regulations to permit change of land use where justified, easier subdivision regulations, and extension of trunk services to new areas/new townships will help to reduce congestion and develop the cities in an orderly fashion. Innovative measures for land assembly, land pooling, and use of land as resource to build up infrastructure will need to be continued and their administration made more efficient and transparent.

Since 2001, 100 per cent foreign direct investment (FDI) has been permitted in the development of integrated townships. However, investments may not materialise unless the conditions relating to land procurement are made simple. In urban areas, especially those with Master Plans, the needs of urbanisation should have precedence over land revenue and land reforms legislations in which restrictions on land ownership, transfers, and land use are incorporated in order to prevent the conversion of agricultural land. Other problems relate to the lack of clear titles, old, protected tenancies and rent control. All these problems, working together, have made it impossible for land to be procured for development in city centres, barring in small quantities. In prime areas, much of the land is used well below its potential.

The system of maintenance of land records and registration of property transactions are outmoded and need to be modernised through computerisation so as to speed up the process. There is need to develop and implement a system of authentication of property titles on the lines of the Torrens system now in vogue in many countries. This will make it easier for interested parties to enter into land transactions confidently. Together with the rationalisation of stamp duty, these measures will help in the development of a genuine property market, which ultimately will prove beneficial for the assessment of taxes where property values are the basis.

Rent control and tenancy laws also prevent the development of rental housing, thus contracting housing stock. Reform of these laws is a politically sensitive issue, as as evidenced by the history of recent efforts to amend the Delhi Rent Act. However, there is some awareness that rent control at absurdly low levels with virtually no relation to market rates and extraordinary protection to tenants over generations not only hinder the development of rental housing but also act as barriers to the growth of cities. Dilapidated structures cannot be renovated because of the difficulty in evicting tenants, with the result that rejuvenation of inner city areas is not taking place. Transitory arrangements can be made to help those who will face hardships, but zoning regulations should take into account the changing nature of inner city areas and permit their redevelopment.

Fiscal Balance

Poor management of assessment and collection has ensured that the yield from properties in the form of property tax is a fraction of the potential. In many cities, either property tax is not levied at all, or the rates are extremely negligible, as a result of which the resource position of the municipal bodies is extremely poor. On the other hand, stamp duty levied on transactions in land at 8 to -10 per cent is too high, in comparison with other countries. This has resulted in the use of 'black money' in property transactions and the practice of 'power of attorney 'prevent the emergence of a genuine property market, with resultant losses to the exchequer. A further fall-out is the unreliability of information on property values.

Another cause of the fiscal imbalance of ULBs is the highly subsidised supply of services, in particular, water and sewerage. Insufficient revenue income prevents civic authorities from investing in services, leaving existing and future needs unfulfilled and this, in turn, hinders growth. During the Tenth Plan, emphasis will have to be placed on initiating and furthering broad-based reforms to overcome the impediments to urban growth. The reform agenda, initially mooted through the new programme of Urban Reforms Incentive Fund, will, in order to make a serious impact, need to leverage all schemes in the urban sector. Therfore the conformity to an agreed reform programme will be made obligatory for Central assistance to the sector during the Tenth Plan.

Capacity Building

Capacity building in urban institutions is one area which is much talked about but has been relatively neglected in terms of action. The restructuring of the roles of the elected ULBs has to initially come about in the form of partnerships with the parastatals which have been handling a variety of services. The public service element needs to be made more professional and accountable to the people. As resources are the biggest problem of ULBs, measures for comprehensive and rational levy of property taxes and user charges are needed urgently. Adoption of modern accounting systems, improved practices of budgeting and planning, effective use of wards committees and other means of peoples' participation, and programme assistance under the schemes such as the SJSRY, should be put to use for improving urban governance.

Studies have emphasised that in a programme such as Low-Cost Sanitation, provision of subsidies and loan assistance have to be backed by substantial work on designs and materials relevant to each regional context, and by education, training, and propagation in the basic concepts of sanitation and hygiene. Water supply schemes have been transferred to ULBs from parastatals but without creating an ownership structure or building up the capacity to undertake operations and maintenance functions. Participatory management is still a relatively novel concept as bureaucratic approaches insulate public functionaries from public scrutiny or accountability. These are all areas that any programme of capacity building has to tackle.

Water supply and sanitation are the biggest challenges before ULBs and there is an urgent need to step up investment in this sector during the Tenth Plan. The tasks include efficiency improvement, better customer satisfaction, levy and collection of reasonable user charges, accessing institutional and market borrowings to provide sufficient investment funds, and institutional improvement at all levels.

A number of states have shown interest in arranging public-private partnerships in this sector and these must be pursued prudently to enhance service quality and efficiency. The Low Cost Sanitation programme needs a new thrust as the sanitation problem has defied a solution so far. While encouraging the entry of the private sector, the key role of public functionaries should not be overlooked as the progress towards private sector participation is bound to be slow and may not happen at all in many urban centres.

The growth of urban capabilities has to be ensured with the support of bodies such as the Central Public Health and Environmental Engineering Organisation (CPHEEO), HUDCO, National Environmental Engineering and Research Institute (NEERI), NIUA, Regional Centres at Hyderabad, Mumbai and Lucknow, the IIPA, and the various training institutions relating to the urban sector.

Where needed, the institutions need to re-orient their approach with a view to strengthening the ULBs in the performance of their tasks. The leading role of parastatals has to be scaled down to give the initiative to the local bodies themselves.

Poverty Alleviation and Slum Improvement

Reduction and alleviation of poverty, if not its complete eradication, including poverty in urban areas, has long been one of the objectives of planning. There have been encouraging trends in urban poverty in both percentage and numerical terms, though the urban poor still face age-old problems at the ground level. Besides, there are wide regional variations as well as differences among different size-class towns with regard to the extent and nature of urban poverty.

According to the 2001 Census, the total urban population is 285.35 million, which accounts for 27.78 per cent of the total population. While the total population in the country increased by 21.34 per cent in 1991-2001, urban population grew by 31.36 per cent during the same period. The somewhat moderate growth of the urban population is explained by the declining rate of urban growth in the last two decades: (Table 2)

Table 2. Growth of Urban Population

	Percentage of urban to total	Decadal urban population growth
1981	23.34	46.14
1991	25.72	36.46
2001	27.78	31.36

(Figures in percentages)

The encouraging feature is that apart from continuation of the fall in the proportion of the urban poor, for the first time in the 1991 Census, there is also a reduction in the absolute numbers of the urban poor. According to the large sample survey data on consumer expenditure (55th Round) of the NSSO using a 30-day recall period, 67.1 million or 23.62 percent of India's urban population were below the poverty line in 1999-2000. As is evident from the Table 3, while the percentage of persons below poverty line in urban areas had been steadily declining since it was first estimated at 49 per cent in 1973-74, the absolute number of persons below the poverty line had been rising, touching 76.3 million in 1993-94. This trend has been reversed in the latest Census.

Table 3. Percentage of Number of Poor

Year	Poverty Ratio (percentage)			No. of poor (million)		
	Rural	Urban	Combined	Rural	Urban	Combined
1973-74	56.4	49.0	54.9	261.3	60.0	321.3
1977-78	53.1	45.2	51.3	264.3	64.6	328.9
1983	45.7	40.8	44.5	252.0	70.9	322.9
1987-88	39.1	38.2	38.9	231.9	75.2	307.1
1993-94	37.3	32.4	36.0	244.0	76.3	320.3
1999-2000	27.1	23.6	26.1	193.2	67.1	260.3

Though, at the national level, the percentage of the poor in rural areas is significantly higher than in urban areas, only a few of the larger States conform to this pattern. States such as Andhra Pradesh, Goa, Gujarat, Haryana, Karnataka, Kerala, Madhya Pradesh, Maharashtra, Rajasthan, Tamil Nadu, Delhi and the Union Territory of Pondicherry have reported levels of urban poverty that are higher than rural poverty. States where rural poverty is higher than in urban areasare Arunachal Pradesh, Assam, Bihar, Himachal Pradesh, Orissa, Uttar Pradesh and West Bengal. Analysis shows that poverty reduction among States has been uneven.

The most important point about the interstate variations in poverty is that it shows no correlation with per capita income or other development indicators like per capita consumption, levels of industrial and infrastructural development, etc., in urban areas during the nineties. While the lack of development is the cause of urban poverty in many States, the nature and sectoral composition of development is responsible for poverty in others.

Unemployment data show that the overall unemployment rates are not high, though they are higher in urban areas than in rural areas. The unemployed person-day rates are higher than the rates obtained for persons, thereby indicating a high degree of intermittent unemployment. This is mainly due to the absence of regular employment for many workers. Studies have shown that casualisation of labour is the main, and increasing, source of urban poverty. The dynamics of development in urban areas of many States during the past two decades has been such that rapid economic growth has not led to a corresponding decline in poverty. While income levels are rising to meet the basic nutritional needs, other equally basic needs of shelter, civic amenities, health care, educational and social needs, etc. are not being met in an adequate fashion. Urban poverty, thus, emerges as a more complex phenomenon than rural poverty. Some aspects of the complexity of urban poverty are:

Level of basic amenities: There are serious deficiencies in urban infrastructure as a result of the rapid growth of urban population and low investment in urban development. In general, the smaller the town, the less likely it is to have a wide coverage of amenities, and the poor in such towns face correspondingly higher deprivation. It has been noted that the percentage of households having flush toilets exhibits a strong positive correlation with economic development, much more than any other indicator of amenities. The coverage of civic amenities, specifically electricity, drinking water and toilets, is uneven and variation across size class of urban centres shows regularity and a distinct pattern. The shortages are very serious for urban centres with population of less than 50,000. This emphasizes the need for greater involvement of the State and Central Governments in upgrading the infrastructure of the small towns. Most of the small and medium towns are not in a position to generate funds to provide civic amenities to all sections of population. These towns, particularly those located in less developed states, should, therefore, be the major focus of government policy in terms of providing basic amenities.

Town or city size: There is evidence to show that the incidence of poverty in a town, as measured by Head Count Ratio (HCR), declines steadily with increasing size. In 1987-88, the HCR in towns with less than 50,000 population was 47.40 per cent while that in towns with population of more than one million was 26.73 per cent. In 1993-94, the corresponding figures are 43.16 per cent and 20.57 per cent. The National Capital Territory of Delhi (where the urban population accounts for 93 per cent of the total population according to the 2001 Census), experienced a population growth of 51.3 per cent during the decade of 1991-2001. The percentage of people below the poverty line in Delhi stood at 49.61 per cent in 1973-74 and declined steadily over the years to 16.4% in 1991 and now stands at 9.42 per cent. A larger incidence of secondary and high-value tertiary activities in large cities gives people residing there a higher level of income.

In contrast, the income levels of people in small and medium towns tend to be low because of the poor economic base and lack of employment opportunities in the organised sector. In the changing economic scenario, care has to be taken to ensure that the process of structural adjustment does not lead to an increase in urban inequality. For poverty alleviation in the broader sense, encompassing both income and environment, within a framework of balanced regional development, it would be important to restructure priorities in favour of small and medium towns and slums in larger cities, where a large majority of the urban poor live.

Household size : The fact that household size affects the poverty status of a household is well known. Larger households tend to have a higher probability of being poor.

Slum Upgrading

Action taken so far for slum improvement or in situ upgrading is inadequate. Re-designing and re-constructing settlements with the participation of residents and assistance from public bodies is a viable option with the least amount of disturbance to the settlers or their livelihood. This method of slum improvement needs to be practised on a much wider scale. The VAMBAY project permits in situ upgradation, and it is necessary that an early decision is taken regarding land on which slums are situated in order to facilitate upgradation.

Various Central Government schemes - National Slum Development Programme (NSDP), Swarna Jayanti Shahri Rozgar Yojana (SJSRY), VAMBAY, Night Shelters, Two Million Housing Scheme, Accelerated Urban Water Supply Programme (AUWSP), Low-Cost Sanitation - provide for a wide range of services to the urban poor including slum-dwellers. They include identification of the urban poor, formation of community groups, involvement of non-government organisations (NGOs), self-help/thrift and credit activities, training for livelihood, credit and subsidy for economic activities, housing and sanitation, environmental improvement, community assets, wage employment, convergence of services, etc. What is needed is to ensure that the task of meeting the needs of the slum-dwellers is better organised and effectively administered, and duly monitored at both State and Central levels. There are also many instances of successful implementation of urban poverty alleviation/slum upgrading and services programmes in the Indian situation.

The National Slum Development

Programme (NSDP) initiated in the year 1997 as a scheme of Special Central Assistance, has been providing additional central assistance to State Governments for slum improvement. However, its performance has not been satisfactory mainly because of the delays at the State level in releasing the funds to implementing agencies. The monitoring of the programme at the Central level requires strengthening. To ensure proper utilisation, during the Tenth Plan the NSDP funds should be released for specific projects. States should submit annual plans for projects which will upgrade selected slums to get over the slum characteristics. The existing practice of releasing the funds to the states should be modified to this extent.

7

Civic Amenities in Urban Areas

The traditional role of municipal bodies had been one of providing basic amenities of civic life. Services such as water supply and sanitation, roads and drains, street-lights, collection and disposal of solid waste, maintenance of public places, burial grounds and crematoria, cattle pounds, registration of births and deaths, maintenance of markets have long been seen as the function of municipal bodies. In addition, they performed certain regulatory functions relating construction of buildings, public health areas such as eating places, slaughter houses and tanneries, etc.

The 74th Constitutional Amendment has substantially broadened the range of functions to be performed by the elected urban local bodies (ULBs). The Twelfth Schedule brings into the municipal domain among others such areas such as urban and town planning, regulation of land-use, planning for economic and social development, 'safeguarding the interests of weaker sections of society including the handicapped and mentally retarded,' slum improvement and upgradation, urban poverty alleviation, and 'promotion of cultural, educational and aesthetic aspects'. The subject of 'cattle pounds' has been extended in the Twelfth Schedule to include 'prevention of cruelty to animals'. The

Constitution thus envisages urban local bodies as being totally responsible for all aspects of development, civic services, and environment in the cities, going far beyond the traditional role.

Provision of basic amenities will continue to be among the core activities of the ULBs. The efficient performance of these responsibilities requires proper institutional structure, unambiguous decentralisation of powers, adequacy of resources, support of the State Governments and their entities, and a concerted effort to build up capabilities in the various sections of the ULB machinery. During the Tenth Plan, some key areas of water supply and sanitation, urban transport, alleviation of urban poverty, the housing needs of slum-dwellers, and reforms in the urban sector with a view to strengthening the institutional and resource base of ULBs will have to be taken up for special attention.

Urban Water Supply and Sanitation

As in the Eighth and Ninth Plans, in the Tenth Plan also the approach to the water supply and sanitation sector will take into account the guiding principles suggested in the New Delhi Declaration, which was adopted by the U.N. General Assembly in December 1990. these are:

a) Protection of the environment and safeguarding of health through the integrated management of water resources and liquid and solid waste;

b) Organisational reforms, promoting an integrated approach and including changes in procedures, attitudes, and behaviour, and the full participation of women at all levels;

c) Community management of services, backed by measures to strengthen the capacity of local institutions in implementing and sustaining water and sanitation programmes;

d) Sound financial practices, achieved through better management of existing assets and extensive use of appropriate technologies.

Water needs to be managed as an economic asset rather than a free commodity in the same way as any other resource. The regeneration of sources shall be the responsibility of every user agency, whether they use water for drinking, irrigation or other purposes. Supply of water to consumers should normally be based on the principle of effective demand that should broadly correspond to the standard of service which the users as a community are willing to maintain, operate and finance. At the same time, special provisions should be made to meet the needs of the poor who have less capacity to pay.

Within this overall perspective, the Tenth Plan envisages completing the task at hand, namely, 100 per cent coverage of rural and urban populations with safe drinking water as per the stipulated norms and standards on a sustainable basis. However, the focus should not only be on the investment requirements to augment supplies or install additional systems in sanitation and water supply. Instead, greater attention must be paid to the critical issues of institutional restructuring, managerial improvement, better and more equitable service to citizens who must have a greater degree of participation. Tenth Plan must also focus on achieving sustainability of the sector through the adoption of adequate measures in operation and management (O & M), the financial health of the utilities through efficiency of operations and levy of user charges, and conservation and augmentation of water sources.

In view of the 73rd and 74th Constitutional Amendments, the task of providing and managing water supply and sanitation cannot be separated from the issue of functional and financial autonomy and strengthening of capacity in both rural and urban local bodies. External assistance, involvement of the private sector, and institutional/market finance are necessary to augment resources and to encourage participatory and innovative management practices.

According to the 54th round of National Sample Survey (NSS) an estimated 70 per cent of urban households reported being served by tap and 21 per cent by tubewell or handpump. Sixty-six per cent of urban households reported having their principal source of drinking water within their premises, while 32 per cent had it within 0.2 km. Forty-one per cent had sole access to their principal source of drinking water, which means that 59 per cent were sharing a public source. Fifteen per cent of households did not get sufficient drinking water from their principal source, between April and June, May being the worst month. In the aggregate, 91 per cent of urban households reported the quality of drinking water served by their principal sources to be satisfactory. 18 per cent reported using some supplementary source of drinking water and 96 per cent reported storing their drinking water.

Since independence there has been sustained effort at providing, on a priority basis, potable water to all habitations, and this has been successful to a large extent as seen from the NSS data. Almost all urban centres have been provided with some public water supply scheme which is the primary source of potable water for most urban inhabitants. State level data show that on an average 88 per cent of the urban population were provided with water supply through a public water supply facility, with many States reporting 90 per cent and more coverage. However, official reports tend to give greater weight to physical and financial progress rather than the quality, reliability and sustainability of services. The picture will be incomplete and misleading if the many and significant lacunae in the existing scenario are not highlighted:

State of Water Supply Services

The urban population faces an increasing demand-supply gap, wholly inadequate and unreliable supplies particularly in settlements of the urban poor, and deteriorating financial and technical performance of systems. To take only the metropolitan cities, according to a World Bank study, of 27 Asian cities with populations of over one million, Chennai and Delhi share the same rank as the worst performing cities in terms of hours of water availability per day, while Mumbai is ranked as the second worst performer and Kolkata as the fourth worst.

The problems of the sector are manifold. Transmission and distribution networks are old and poorly maintained. Consequently, physical losses are high, ranging from 25 to 50 per cent. Low pressures and intermittent supplies allow backsiphoning, which results in contamination of water in the distribution network. The utilities are overstaffed. Intermittent supplies for only two to eight hour places a burden on the women who have to fetch water from public taps. The urban poor, who constitute one-fourth of the urban population, and the slumdwellers, who may range from onethird to half of the population in certain cities, are the worst affected. Ensuring equity in distribution of available supplies is one of the key challenges of the urban water supply sector.

According to various studies, most cities are unable to operate and maintain the existing systems to the full capacity. The capacity utilization has been reported to be less than 50 pe rcent in 40 per cent of the towns, and less than 75 per cent in a further 20 per cent of towns. There is grave danger that cities may, in many instances slip back to lesser levels of water supply, due to poor maintenance and depletion of sources even as the population continues to grow. This may lead to a situation where the per capita availability of water by 2020 may actually decrease, unless corrective action is taken expeditiously.

There are wide variations among towns in terms of quantity of water supplied, per capita supply, achievement of normative supply, duration of supply, etc. In the case of slums, which are generally provided public stand-posts, there are wide variations in the availability and average number of households per stand. Wherever ground water is the main source, the over-exploitation of aquifers, depletion of water resources, and pollution by urban human wastes, are causing serious problems. Water supply and sanitation are, above everything else, issues in environmental health. There is a close link between water and sanitation requirements because availability of adequate water is essential for proper sanitation practices.

Finances of Water Supply and Sewerage Services

The general financial position of the urban water supply and sewerage sector is very poor. Only a few providers in large urban areas generate sufficient revenues to make any contribution to investment. In medium and small towns these entities typically do not collect sufficient revenue to cover operating expenses. There is no matching of revenues against expenditures. Collection efficiency is very low. A major cause of poor financial health is low tariff, resulting in direct subsidy. There is an attempt at cross-subsidization from commercial and industrial consumers to domestic consumers. According to one study, 76 percent of the responding towns did not raise sufficient revenues from water supply to cover the revenue expenditure on the service.

Institutions dealing with water supply and sanitation have very little autonomy on personnel and financial matters. Information systems necessary for effective management are generally lacking.

Water tariffs and the methods of levying them vary considerably from very low to reasonable rates. The methods in vogue in Indian cities include any or a combination of the following : water tax, flat rates, slab rates and volumetric rates.

In the past, when municipal functions were few and the pressure on infrastructure was not as intense as today, many local bodies found it possible to meet the costs of water supply from general revenues. Property owners who paid taxes were assured of water supply free of any charges, up to an agreed level. With additional demand being met from water supply schemes executed at higher costs, the free supply became infeasible, but there was resistance to paying more in the absence of a demonstrated improvement in service quality. The prevailing 'subsidy culture' has been largely responsible the reluctance to raise tariffs, notwithstanding the fact that lack of resources is one of the major causes for poor standards of service and maintenance, and inability to expand the system to cater to additional demand.

The resultant unsatisfactory service standards has now created a vicious circle of poor service-leading to low tariff because of less willingness to pay-leading to poor resource position -leading to poor maintenance and poor service. Although surveys show consumer willingness to pay higher tariffs, increases, if they are to be acceptable, must be accompanied by substantial improvements in service quality.

Water supply and sanitation schemes are capital intensive and, consequently, they are financed from the budget, borrowings from financial institutions or the market, and external funding agencies. Most State Governments have a policy relating to the financing pattern of the schemes, with shares for the ULB, State Government, and institutional finance. The Central Government provides assistance through the centrally sponsored scheme of Accelerated Urban Water Supply (AUWS) programme. The five cities covered under the Mega City scheme have been able to avail its funds for water supply and sanitation, and in the Tenth Plan, it is proposed that the scheme of Integrated Development of Small and Medium Towns may permit a similar facility.

The rationale for financing water supply schemes fully or partly through grant funds, is not always clear or consistent. In instances where the capital costs per capita are excessive due to distance of the source, multi-stage pumping or water quality problems exist, and where the number of urban poor requiring targeted subsidy is large, there is need for a capital grant from the Government. Grants ranging from 20 to 50 per cent of the project cost are being provided, but many large cities have received external assistance which has been passed on fully as grants.

Instances where ULBs have raised funds in the domestic financial markets on their own strength, have been very few. HUDCO has been financing water supply projects for the past 30 years, especially those in small and medium towns, against State Government guarantee. As much as 28 per cent of the cumulative loan sanctions for urban infrastructure of HUDCO is towards water supply. During the Ninth Plan period, HUDCO has sanctioned 101 water supply schemes for financial assistance of Rs 4,828 crore. The schemes include water supply augmentation, rehabilitation, extension as well as new schemes with development of source for unserviced areas. State Governments have routinely stood guarantee to borrowings from HUDCO and have in many instances, also undertaken to bear the repayment obligation of such loans.

Water supply and sanitation works are generally executed by the state public health engineering division which is a Department of the State Government, or a state- level Board or Corporation dealing exclusively with water/ sanitation or infrastructure in general. In the metropolitan cities with their own water supply and sewerage boards, these bodies have executed the works with financial assistance from the sources mentioned earlier. Though water supply and sanitation are essentially municipal functions to be discharged by the ULBs, these bodies are unable to take any significant initiative because of their weak financial position. As a result action is rarely taken to augment supplies or effect improvements when they are most needed.

In most states, there is an unhealthy overlapping of responsibilities between the and the state-level Board/ Department/Corporation, which leads to dilution of responsibility for project and service quality and accountability to the consumers. ULBs who are the ultimate owners of the schemes, have little say in project specifications, project cost or quality control, or given assistance for subsequent operation and maintenance (O & M) of the scheme. It is quite common to see the individual city water supply schemes being tossed around between the parastatal and the ULB for O & M, customer service, billing and collection, etc.

The main problem in financing of urban water supply and sanitation is the sustainability of the present model which is heavily dependent on the State Governments' willingness and capacity to provide guarantees for institutional finance, apart from meeting the agreed state share of the project cost. Inability of the states to provide committed shares of project costs, and the tendency to sanction more works than financially feasible, has led to a situation of large numbers of incomplete works, project delays, and cost over-runs.

Some ULBs have initiated innovative cost recovery mechanisms, such as advance registration charges, connection charges, betterment charges, water tax, and application of general revenues and other receipts to meet part of the cost of capital works. However such instances are relatively rare. To encourage reform measures and prompt ULBs to become viable entities to access market funds, instruments such as the City Challenge Fund and the Pooled Finance Development Fund have been proposed in the Tenth Plan. Under the Urban Reforms Incentive Fund, financial strengthening of the municipal bodies through reforms and better enforcement of both property taxes and user charge, is a key objective.

Conservation, Augmentation, and Recycling of Urban Water

So far, there has been little or no thrust on conserving water either in the mega cities or in the smaller ones. For example, Delhi claims to supply water at the rate of 225 lpcd whereas cities like London supply only 150 lpcd In most cities, large quantities of potable water is used for non-potable uses, while treatment of waste water and its re-use continue to be neglected. The following measures should be taken by all ULBs in order to optimise available water and conserve water sources:

— Water tariff should be set at levels that discourage excessive use. Water-efficient systems for flushing should be made mandatory. Conservation of water should be a recurring theme for both users as well as those managing the water supply system.

— Leakages and unaccounted for water is another constraint in cities. Due to old and rusted pipes or poor maintenance of the system, these losses sometimes go up to 50 per cent. These must be controlled and brought to the minimum level. Severe penalties should be levied on those found responsible for leakage and wastage of water.

— Reuse of treated sewage must be given priority in view of the fact that water is going to become more scarce in the near future. With tertiary treatment, water from treated sewage can be used even for airconditioning, industrial cooling and other non-potable uses. This should be made a thrust area.

— Use of potable water for purposes like washing of vehicles, maintenance of gardens, etc. should be prohibited. In urban concentrations, dual supply of potable and non-potable water should be undertaken. For non-potable domestic uses, tubewells should be permitted to be sunk, subject to the construction of a percolation structure in the premises. This will conserve potable water without affecting ground water availability.

— Rainwater harvesting should be implemented widely. This has been taken up as a thrust area in Chennai and Delhi and must be given priority in all towns in the country. The Delhi Jal Board has taken up more than 80 works to harvest rain water and intends to cover about 200 buildings. The Delhi Government has approached the Ministry of Urban Development and Poverty Alleviation to amend building bye-laws to make rain water harvesting mandatory in the Capital. During the Tenth Plan, it shall be made obligatory for all urban areas to adopt rainwater harvesting as a part of the building bye-laws.

— Central Ground Water Board (CGWB) is engaged in developing techniques for artificial re-charge of ground water, which should be implemented where conditions are appropriate. Similarly the exploitation of ground water in urban areas must be constantly monitored in order prevent the drying up of this important source.

Meeting the Needs of the Urban Poor

There is a need to modify the approach to the supply of water to the clusters of the poor. Instead of making them dependent on public standposts, households willing to take individual connections should be giventhese, subject to normal payment conditions. Funds under the National Slum Development Programme (NSDP), Valmiki Ambedkar Awas Yojana (VAMBAY), and EIUS funds could, however, be used to meet part of the cost of individual connections also. This will reduce the drudgery related to collection of water from the public stand-posts, and enable the poor to reach a higher standard of hygiene and health.

Where stand-posts must continue to be the source of water, the number of such stand-posts should be adequate for the population being served. There are successful examples of community supervision of the stand-posts. Community groups should be made responsible for maintenance of hygiene around stand-posts, for maintenance including prevention of wastage, and for collection of user charges from each household attached to the stand-post.

Centrally-Sponsored Accelerated urban water Supply Programme (AUWSP)

The Centrally sponsored Accelerated Urban Water Supply Programme was launched in 1993-94 during the Eighth Plan. It aims at providing water supply in towns with a population of less than 20,000 as per the 1991 census. A total of 2151 towns qualify for consideration under the scheme. The project funding is shared equally by Centre and State, the latter including a 5 percent contribution from the beneficiary town. The Centre meets the entire cost in Union Territories. State-wise share in the Plan allocation is based on a weightage system based on population, incidence of poverty, etc. Priority has to be given for towns with special problems such as very low per capita supply, very distant or deep water source, drought-prone areas, areas with excess salinity, fluoride, iron content in water source and high incidence of water-borne diseases. The per capita unit cost is normally limited to Rs 1000, which can be relaxed if thee is sufficient justification.

Till 15th March 2002, schemes have been approved in 654 towns with an estimated cost of Rs 817.70 crore. Of this 223 schemes at an estimated cost of Rs 212.01 crore were approved during the Eighth Plan. A total of Rs 337.37 crore have been released by Government of India, of which Rs 68.624 crore were released in the Eighth Plan. The State Governments have released an amount of Rs 244.1 crore towards their share. The expenditure reported is Rs 390.33 crore. A total of 240 projects under the AUWSP are reported to have been completed.

Both sanctions and project completion have fallen short of the targets. The average time taken from sanction to completion is about two to three years. Insufficient flow of project funds from the State Governments, land acquisition delays, and inadequacies in project management in some of the executing agencies have been responsible for the delay in project execution, resulting in a large number of schemes being carried over into the 10th Plan.

Out of 240 completed projects, 98 are in the State of Uttar Pradesh. Other States which have made substantial progress in completed projects, are Madhya Pradesh (30), Tamil Nadu (25), Rajasthan (15), Maharashtra (12), Karnataka (8), Chattisgarh (9), Punjab (8), Gujarat (6), Orissa (6), and Manipur (5), and Himachal Pradesh (5). Haryana has completed four projects, West Bengal three, and Goa and Mizoram two each. In the States of Jammu & Kashmir, and Nagaland, one project each has been completed.

The Working Group on Urban Development for the Tenth Plan has recommended continuation of AUWSP in towns with population less than 20,000 as per the 2001 Census. This will make 2,433 towns eligible for assistance under the scheme. Given the many factors causing delays in projects, advance planning for all projects to be taken up during the Tenth Plan should be undertaken in the first year of the Plan period. Each state's indicative allocation of Central assistance under the scheme during the Tenth Plan period should be communicated during 2002-03 so that the states can also make corresponding provision in their Tenth Plan, and proceed with project selection and preparation. Additional funds should be provided to states who excel in performance.

At the time of Plan discussions itself it should be ensured that the state share in the scheme is provided in adequate measure in yearly budgets. The State should preferably deposit its share in advance into the account of the implementing agency before the Central share is released. States should be encouraged to use their allocation under the Urban Reforms Incentive Fund for execution of urban infrastructure schemes. In order to simplify the procedure for sanctioning projects during the Tenth Plan, state level Project Sanctioning Committees will be formed instead of referring projects to the Central Government. It is also proposed that the Central grant be given directly to the State implementing agencies.

The Working Group on Urban Development, Water Supply and Sanitation, and Urban Environment, has recommended that 100 per cent Central grant may be given for implementation of water supply schemes in small towns under AUWSP. However, rather than increase the outlay for individual water supply schemes, in view of the relative neglect of sanitation issues in the past, there is need to enlarge the scope of the scheme to include sanitation, especially basic sanitation such as waste water / sewage treatment, solid waste disposal, and surface drainage. The town which is provided assistance under AUWSP (to be renamed Accelerated Urban Water Supply and Sanitation Project - AUWSSP), should be bound by an agreement to take up such a comprehensive package of sanitation and water supply augmentation, and the subsidy under the scheme should be made available to these components also. Simultaneously, the town should also implement Low Cost Sanitation (LCS) programme in parallel, for which the allocations available under LCS should be utilized.

Urban Sanitation

The 54th round of NSS reported that 26 per cent of households reported using no latrine, 35 per cent reported using septic tank, and 22 per cent reported using sewerage system. This indicates that as many as 43 per cent of households in urban areas either had no latrines or no connection to a septic tank or sewerage. As regards waste disposal, 71 per cent of urban households reported removal of household waste by household members, 14 per cent by local authorities, and 12 per cent by private agreement among residents. Forty-seven percent of urban households reported removing of their waste to community dumping spot, and 30 per cent, to individual dumping spots. Ninety per cent of urban households reported concern regarding mosquitoes, 66 per cent regarding flies and 50 per cent regarding problems related to foul odour.

Estimates of access to excreta disposal systems in urban areas vary from a low 48 percent to a high 70 percent. Out of 300 Class-I cities, about 70 have partial sewerage systems and sewage treatment facilities. Levels of sewage treatment are reported to be very low. A study by the Central Pollution Control Board in 1994-95 shows that the total waste-water generated in 300 Class-I cities is about 15,800 million litres a day (mld), while the treatment capacity is hardly 3,750 mld. In the 23 metro cities, over 9000 million litres of sewage is generated daily, of which about 60 per cent is generated in the four mega cities of Mumbai, Kolkata, Delhi, and Chennai. Of the total waste water generated in the metro cities, hardly 30 per cent is treated before disposal. Most of the cities have only primary treatment facilities. Thus, the untreated and partially treated municipal wastewater finds its way into water sources such as rivers, lakes and ground water, causing water pollution. On the other hand, the programme of Low Cost Sanitation, which offers an affordable alternative technology, has made very little progress, despite being linked to the social problem of manual scavenging, which is prohibited by law.

The poor sanitary conditions, particularly in slums, are often linked to outbreaks of cholera and gastro-enteritis. Water-borne diseases are a major cause of mortality throughout India and impose a huge burden in terms of loss of lives and productivity. According a case study, water and sanitation diseases are responsible for 60 per cent of the environmental health burden and over 11 per cent of total burden of disease in Andhra Pradesh. The single major cause of this burden of disease is diarrhea, which disproportionately afects children under the age of five.

Low Cost Sanitation

The centrally-sponsored scheme of Urban Low Cost Sanitation for Liberation of the Scavengers started from 1980-81, initially through the Ministry of Home Affairs and later through the Ministry of Welfare. From 1989-90, it came under the jurisdiction of the Ministry of Urban Development. The main objective of the scheme is to convert the existing dry latrines into low cost pour flush latrines and provide alternative employment to the liberated scavengers. The rehabilitation component is dealt with by the Ministry of Social Justice and Empowerment.

Low cost sanitation is rightly seen as an important solution to the dehumanizing practice of carrying night-soil, and the legislation prohibiting manual scavenging and its enforcement in turn strengthens the movement for installation of sanitary latrines in urban areas. Low cost sanitation is also the appropriate solution where resources do not permit the provision of underground sewerage, or septic tanks. The scheme covers all the households which have dry latrines and households having no sanitation facilities including households in slums and squatter colonies.

Under the scheme, loan and Central subsidy are extended simultaneously by HUDCO. Subsidy is graded according to economic status, being set at 45 per cent for EWS, 25 per cent for LIG, and nil subsidy for middle and high income groups. Loan ranging from 50 per cent to 75 per cent of the cost, is given at 10 per cent interest repayable over 15 years. Loan is also given for construction of community latrines on 'pay and use' principle, shared latrines in slums, housing chawls. Subsidy is limited to the cost of the sub-structure, but the HUDCO loan can be availed for the construction of super-structure also.

The loans require State Government guarantee. For management of the programme, HUDCO was required to set up a separate cell, and the regional offices of HUDCO were expected to render assistance to the State Governments in the formulation of proposals. The guidelines provide for the creation of a co-ordination committee at the Central level, as well as co-ordination committees at the state level. A recommendation has been made to create state-level cells or to nominate an existing institution for channelising the subsidy and HUDCO loans to the implementing agencies. The cell may be registered as a society. In the State of Madhya Pradesh, the Slum Clearance Board was nominated as the nodal agency.

According to an estimate prepared by a Committee constituted by Planning Commission, there were 400,000 scavengers and 5.4 million dry latrines in urban areas in 1989, and the practice of manual scavenging continues in 3117 towns. Seven states have declared themselves as scavenger free - Goa, Kerala, Gujarat, Manipur, Mizoram, Sikkim and Tripura. Six Union Territories - Andaman & Nicobar Islands, Pondicherry, Chandigarh, Dadra & Nagar Haveli, Daman & Diu, and Lakshadweep - have also declared themselves scavenger free.

The number of households without access to a proper system of removal of human excreta is bound to be much higher than the number of dry latrines estimated by the Committee, because the number of households in urban areas without even dry latrines, who use open places for defecation, is estimated to be 7.3 million. Therefore the number of households in need of low-cost sanitation or community toilet facilities may be as high as 15 million, if not more.

Importance of Low Cost Sanitation

Towns which do have sewerage do not often have

sewage treatment plants, with the result that water sources are getting polluted. It has been assessed that 80 per cent of pollution is caused by sewage alone. It is unfeasible to provide underground sewerage or septic tank latrines in all cities and for all residents. In the first place, highly urbanised, industrialised and densely-populated urban centres may be provided with sewerage, with priority being given to installing sewage treatment plants to prevent pollution of water sources. For the majority of the urban centres, low cost sanitation is the appropriate technology.

Low cost sanitation is not a programme solely for the urban poor or slum population. It has to be propagated as the appropriate solution wherever the costly option of underground drainage is not feasible. In this sense, there is need to offer more options to households that desire sanitation facilities which, while being based on the 'twin-pitpour-flush' model, is in keeping with their needs and capacity to invest. Low cost sanitation is best propagated as a part and parcel of the maintenance of environmental health. This includes the areas of water supply, protection of the environment and preservation of environmental cleanliness, and promotion of health among infants, expectant and nursing mothers, and children. Within a town or city, the proper approach would be to take up a coordinated programme covering sanitation in schools, individual households, and public places with special emphasis on the sanitation needs of the urban poor and slum-dwellers and pavement dwellers. The practice of focusing on water supply to the exclusion of sanitation and waste water treatment, should be given up in the Tenth Plan.

Programme Improvement Measures

Rejuvenating the Implementation Organization : States should set up a State Sanitation Council to be in overall charge of supervision of the programme. The Council should be headed by the Chief Minister or his nominee, and consist of experts, NGOs, representatives of PRIs and ULBs, HUDCO, other institutions in the field of environmental sanitation, health workers, and other concerned officials. The mandate of the Council shall be to carry out extensive propagation of the principles of sound practices in hygiene and sanitation, and supervise the programmes of individual and community toilets, school toilets, payand-use toilets, and water quality. The areas of solid waste management and waste water treatment including drainage, will also be within the ambit of the Council. The Council will implement measures to promote the concept of sanitary latrines while bringing home the indignity of open defecation as well as manual scavenging.

Sanitary latrines have to be promoted as part of an overall health, sanitation and environmental awareness programme, especially among the young. Adequate provision should be made to meet the cost of information, education, communication (IEC) activities under the programme, which seems to be lacking at present. The Task Force had recommended that upto 10 per cent of the budget allocation be earmarked for this component. Out of this, 5 per cent could be utilised for project management and NGO involvement. The cost of training of skilled workers should also be met out of this provision and training should be organised locally with the help of NGOs, Building Centres, and technical institutions. A part of the provision should be used for organising safai karmacharis (manual scavenging workers) to undertake construction of LCS units.

Use of sub-standard materials and construction by untrained workers, in order to cut costs, may result in units which do not fulfill the user expectations, and these may be discarded. There is a minimum water requirement without which the unit cannot be kept clean and may lead to bad odour. Similarly, the space requirements, and suitability of soil must be taken into account before starting work on installing the unit. The guidelines prescribe the distance to be maintained from a potable water source to avoid contamination, and this must be fulfilled. The users need to be trained to keep the units clean and free from odour, and regarding the resting period and removal of the contents of the pit. The superstructure must cater to the comfort of the users, for protection against rain, privacy, etc., and has to meet the minimum criteria of acceptability. These issues will have to be tackled to the satisfaction of the users before the programme can make headway. Strict standards for the construction of the LCS units need to be prescribed and followed in implementation.

The subsidy programme should, however, be based on the cost of the basic twin-pit pour flush model for a small household. Subsidy should be extended to cover the super-structure and substructure. The unit cost should be determined on the basis of local costs, and the loans and subsidy provided accordingly. The householder should have the option to design a unit that meets his requirement. It is suggested that the financing pattern of 50 per cent subsidy and 50 per cent loan, which existed prior to 1988-89 should be restored during the Tenth Plan with the further modification that it should be available to both the sub-structure and the super-structure.

There should be no distinction between the states that have scavengers and those that do not have, because the programme is intended to prevent both manual scavenging as well as open defecation. HUDCO should establish state-wise units for the management of the programme to provide technical and organisational back-up.

Ambedkar Awas Yojana

HUDCO is also involved in the implementation of the pay-and-use toilets programme under the Night-shelters schem, and has reported sanctioning 69 schemes for pay and use toilets, under which a subsidy of Rs 14,000 per seat is provided. This scheme has now been merged with the new scheme of Valmiki Ambedkar Awas Yojana (VAMBAY), as part of the sanitation component of the scheme for which 20 percent of the funds are earmarked. The stand-alone toilet complexes, as distinct from the units provided in slum housing colonies, will continue to be financed under the scheme as earlier.

Community toilets are needed for slum and pavement dwellers, rickshaw pullers and the floating population. However, the experience of maintenance and upkeep of these units by municipal authorities has been dismal, with the conditions turning so insanitary that people prefer open air defecation rather than use the public toilets. The maintenance of the units should, therefore, be handed over to an NGO or a community-based organisation. The beneficiary community should pay a small fixed monthly amount towards upkeep of the toilet and the money should be used for cleaning, water supply, and remuneration of a caretaker.

The construction and maintenance of pay-and-use toilets for the floating population or places such as bus-stands, markets, parks, and other places were people congregate, should be done by an NGO like Sulabh International. In some instances, such installations may even generate a surplus. Despite the possibility of commercial viability of some of the installations, it is premature, in the view of the Task Force, to base the programme on assumptions of viability. In the Tenth Plan, therefore, the construction of community toilets for the urban poor, and of payand-use toilets for the floating population should continue to be supported through subsidy from the Central Government.

Treatment of Urban Waste Water

Three-fourths of surface water resources are polluted and 80 per cent of the pollution is due to by sewage alone. On the other hand, in addition to organic matter sewage contains nitrogen, phosphate and potassium in sufficient quantities, which are essential nutrients for plant growth. Sewage is also viewed as an economic source of methane fuel. Thus it can be a valuable resource after with due treatment and processing.

Water supply has direct linkage with sewage generation. A survey of 345 towns with population between 50,000 and 100,000, revealed that over 95 per cent of them do not have any waste water treatment facilities, and disposal on land, and direct and indirect use for irrigation is the predominant mode of disposal.

Scheme to Provide Sewerage for River Bank

The problem of pollution of river waters is particularly acute in the case of densely populated cities located on river banks and which do not have adequate treatment facilities for sewage or safe disposal of solid waste. In such cases, urban waste - both solid and liquid - finds its w. y directly into the rivers, causing a serious pollution problem. The Ministry of Environment and Forests is implementing a massive programme of cleaning of rivers and lakes in the country. The programme, which was started with the Ganga Action Plan (GAP) in 1985, now extends to the polluted stretches of 27 major rivers with works spread over 149 towns in 16 states. The approved cost of these works is nearly Rs. 3,100 crore. This is in Addition to the Rs. 450 crore already spent on GAP

Phase-I. So far, an amount of Rs. 1,100 crore has been spent on the programmes.

Solid Waste Management

India produces about 42 million tons of urban solid waste annually. The per capita waste generation varies between 0.2 kg. to 0.6 kg. per day, and the current municipal solid waste generation is estimated to be approximately 0.4 kg per capita per day.

It has been estimated that because of the increasing per capita waste generation of about 1.3 per cent per year, and the growth of urban population of between 3 and 3.5 per cent per annum, the yearly increase in the overall quantity of solid waste in the cities is about 5 per cent. Urban waste management by the ULBs is already under stress because of poor resources and inadequacies of the system. Unless concerted efforts are made to improve the flow of resources to solid waste management and build up systems which incorporate the basic requirements of a proper waste management practice, the problem of urban waste will be further aggravated and cause environmental health problems. The composition of urban waste is another factor to consider, with increasing use of packaging material made of both paper as well as plastic

In October 2000, the Ministry of Environment and Forests notified the Municipal Solid Wastes (Management and Handling) Rules, 2000, which lay down the procedures/guidelines for collection, segregation, storage, transportation, processing, and disposal of municipal solid waste. The rules require that all cities should set up suitable waste treatment and disposal facilities by 31 December 2001. The rules also specify standards for compost quality, leachate control, and management and closure of landfill sites.

A comprehensive manual on Municipal Solid Waste Management has been brought out by CPHEEO for the guidance of ULBs. This manual was prepared by an expert group consisting of various bodies such as the CPHEEO, Central Pollution Control Board, National Environmental Engineering Research Institute, Ministry of Nonconventional Energy Sources, ULBs, academic institutions, etc. In pursuance of Supreme Court directions in 1996, a Technology Advisory Group for improving solid waste management in the country has also been set up by the Ministry of Urban Development, with three core groups to deal with appropriate technologies and R & D, financial resources and private sector participation, and on capacity building, human resource development and IEC.

Waste management in the cities is receiving attention from a number of departments relating to health, environment, agriculture, nonconventional energy, as well as urban development. Participants are not only government bodies but include NGOs, CBOs and the private sector as well as research organisations.

The problem of urban waste management is notable not only for the large quantities involved but also its spatial spread across over 5000 ULBs and the enormity and variety of problems faced by them in setting up and managing systems for collection, transportation, and disposal of waste. In fact, in the municipal budgets the staff salaries relating to solid waste management are normally among the largest items, accounting for up to half of the total municipal staff. It is estimated that the ULBs spend about Rs 500 to Rs 1500 per ton on waste collection, transportation, treatment and disposal, most of it on collection and transportation and very little on disposal and treatment, and 75 to 80 per cent of this expenditure is on staff salaries. In spite of this, collection efficiencies range from 50 to 90 per cent of the waste that is generated. Localities of the urban poor and slums are likely to be the ones most neglected, exposing the residents to extreme squalor, made unbearable especially when it rains.

While transportation arrangements are generally inadequate due to the unavailability of the right kind of vehicles, and low productivity of the personnel, the major problem is that of indiscriminate disposal in open spaces, road margins, tank beds, etc. A survey by the CPCB on the status of municipal solid waste management reported indiscriminate dumping of garbage in open lands. There have been studies of the public health impacts and pollution of surface and ground waters resulting from the liquid and solid waste disposal practices of the small and medium towns. Sanitary landfills designed and constructed so as to prevent contamination of ground water, creation of stench, and other forms of environmental hazards, are largely absent. Studies of the existing landfill sites and their environmental effect are yet to be taken up. The ULBs find it hard to raise resources to acquire suitable land, and lack the technical capability to design a proper sanitary landfill facility. There is need to prevent dumping in open spaces and introduce sanitary landfill.

Resources for solid waste management is generally met out of the overall property tax receipts of the ULB, though some states provide for a general purpose tax to which surcharges towards specific services such as sanitation, water supply, etc. are added on. Promotion of composting of urban solid waste was implemented by the Ministry of Food and Agriculture in the 1960s through soft loans to ULBs. Block grants and loans were given to State Governments in the Fourth Five Year Plan (1969-74) for setting up composting plants. The Surat plague epidemic in 1994 highlighted the inadequacies and risks inherent in poor solid waste management. The

Bajaj Committee in 1995 made a number of recommendations including waste segregation at source, primary collection, levy of user charges, use of appropriate equipment and vehicles, focus on sanitary land filling and composting, and encouraging private sector participation.

Post-Surat the country saw the emergence of more than 35 waste treatment projects between 1995 and 2000, with private sector participation, mostly for composting facilities. There has been increased awareness and people's participation in solid waste management. NGOs and CBOs have begun to participate in this movement and have found wide acceptance among municipal and State Government functionaries. Private sector participation has been encouraged with a view to economy in cost, efficiency, introduction of new technologies, and more effective service delivery. Municipal bodies have engaged private sector agencies for different activities such as street cleaning and collection of solid waste, its transportation, as well setting up composting plants. Experience in such cases has shown that with suitable agreement being reached on provision of land, supply of solid waste, and where appropriate, sharing of capital cost, the private sector and NGOs can assist in setting up compost plants.

Urban Transport

A good network of roads coupled with an efficient mass urban transport system play a catalytic role in urban economic growth, with a beneficial impact on the urban poor. However, there is a growing trend towards an increasing number of personalised vehicles, especially two-wheelers which account for 60- to 80 per cent of motor vehicles. This results in congestion on the roads, slowing down of traffic and atmospheric pollution.

Narrow carriageways and poor road surface add to the problems. Growing vehicular pollution in cities is a cause of great concern, as are noise levels and traffic accidents. Traffic and transport are emerging problems in many cities which are experiencing heightened economic activity and mobility of people.

Growth of cities leads to a sharp increase in the demand for urban transport facilities. However, the provision of public transport facilities has suffered because of a number of reasons. As population density in cities increases and cities expand in are, there is very little planning for this growth, especially for transport needs. Older areas suffered because of lack of resources for developing appropriate carriageways and public transport systems. Capacity constraints of the existing public transport systems grew worse with densification of the inner cities, and increase in land values and development in excess of the capacity of the existing infrastructure, made the provision of relief more difficult.

Seventeen of the 23 largest cities have organised bus services, with a combined fleet of about 25,000 buses including private buses. Use of urban rail services is extremely limited, with only three cities - Mumbai, Kolkata and Chennai - having suburban rail systems. Phase I of the Delhi Mass Rapid Transport System is under construction. Except for mega cities, modal split in favour of public transport is poor and generally less than 20 per cent.

In smaller cities and towns, circulation of people and vehicles is hampered by narrow roads. This is further constrained by the fact that the carriageway is occupied at the margins by vendors, unauthorised structures, solid and liquid waste, and parking of vehicles. Poor road construction and inadequate maintenance further hamper smooth traffic flows. Failure to provide for genuine requirements such as parking areas for lorries and buses, vehicles for hire as well as for private vehicles leads to haphazard use of road space and acts as an obstacle to the smooth movement of traffic. The solution to these problems is better design and construction of roads, provision of parking areas and bus-bays, provision of suitable areas for vendors, and enforcement of traffic regulations.

The transport situation can be improved by better planning and coordination among the various agencies involved, and augmenting the public transport system. A meaningful urban transport policy would need to address the following:

— Ensuring the fullest use of available transport infrastructure through low-cost optimisation measures (Transport System Management techniques).

— Development, as appropriate, of costeffective road-based, rail-based and waterbased (where applicable) forms of public systems and inter-modal integration.

— Reducing emissions from motor vehicles.

— Land use - Transport integration. Urban transport has to be recognised as a subsystem of the urban system, and transport planning has to be given highest priority in urban planning.

— Central and State Governments must provide higher levels of financial support for urban transport projects. Innovative sources of financing must be explored.

The road capacity of cities is seriously impaired due to wasteful use and neglect. Traffic management measures in most cities are inadequate. Traffic problems of different degrees are caused by:

— Poorly planned traffic circulation;

— poorly designed intersections;

— inadequate signalling/other traffic management measures;
— inadequate parking facilities and parking on the streets;
— on-street loading/unloading activities;
— heavy 'through' traffic in central areas;
— encroachment on footpaths/roads;
— general lack of regard for traffic regulations;
— inadequate enforcement of traffic rules and regulations.

As a complement to creating more physical capacity through major investments in urban transport infrastructure, there is a lot of potential for the effective use of existing road space by appropriate traffic engineering and management/ enforcement measures. During the Tenth Plan period, studies will be carried out in a number of the larger cities to develop integrated transport systems particularlyr to strengthen the modes of transport for the urban poor such as the urban public bus system, nonmotorised transports, and informal transport.

The objective will be to strengthen the public transport systems by increasing its capacity, while integrating all other modes of transport so as to optimise the options available in each city to reduce congestion and pollution, while improving access, speed and safety. Emphasis will be laid on urban planning, including development of satellite towns, creation of ring-roads and bye-passes, and decongestion of the cities by shifting non-essential activities to the outskirts. Measures to improve the viability of public transport projects, and innovations to attract greater investment into this sector, including strengthening the network of urban transport infrastructure consisting of roads, grade separators, pedestrian subways, etc., will also be undertaken.

Rail Based Urban Transport

In cities with a population of 3 million or more, there are several corridors of heavy - 20,000 or more - peak hour peak direction traffic. Provision of rail-based urban transport system on such corridors becomes inescapable, and institutional arrangements for introducing such systems in eligible cities are overdue. City-wise specific projects for rail-based urban transport systems together with funds required for them need to be identified.

8

Power

Power is one of the prime movers of economic development. The level of availability and accessibility of affordable and quality power is also one of the main determinants of the qualify of life. The Government has, since Independence, been giving priority to this sector while fixing the Plan outlays. As a result, the installed generation capacity has risen from a mere 1,300 megawatt (MW) at the time of Independence to more than 1,00,000 MW today. Along with the growth in installed generation capacity, there has also been a phenomenal increase in the transmission and distribution (T&D) capacity. However, despite these achievements, the power sector has not kept pace with the growth in demand with the result that the country has always faced energy and peaking shortages.

The state electricity boards (SEBs), have, in the past, played a significant role in the generation and supply of power. But the present financial health of the SEBs is not sound, to say the least,. This is mainly due to uneconomic tariffs for agriculture, lower slabs of domestic consumption and high T&D losses, which often disguise large-scale theft, and low billing and collection efficiency. This is the main roadblock to attracting the much-needed private investment and, in fact, has been one of the main reasons for the shortfall in capacity addition from private sector projects during the Ninth Plan. The actual capacity addition during the Ninth Plan was 19,015 MW against a target of 40,245 MW. The other major reasons for shortfall in the capacity addition were delay in land acquisition and environmental clearances, unresolved issues in fuel linkages, contractual problems, resettlement and rehabilitation (R&R) problems and law and order problems.

As far as the Tenth Plan is concerned, the Working Group Report on Power has envisaged a capacity addition requirement of 46,939 MW during the Plan period. However, keeping in view the status of the ongoing, sanctioned and new projects in the pipeline, the Planning Commission assessed that a capacity addition target of the order of 41,110 MW (comprising 18,659 MW from on-going, 9,193 MW from projects cleared by the Central Electricity Authority (CEA) and 13,258 MW from new schemes) would be more realistic.

The Government proposes to enhance public funding for the sector as well as encourage the public sector undertakings (PSUs) to take up projects in joint ventures with private investors and state governments during the Tenth Plan period. As part of these efforts, the Accelerated Generation and Supply Programme (AG&SP) is proposed to be extended during the Tenth Plan to provide funds to critical on-going schemes at subsidised interest rates. There is also a focus on initiating suitable policy measures to accelerate the pace of hydro power development as well as to make nuclear power generation as competitive as power generation from other fuels. The Government is making concerted efforts to channelise adequate investment to ensure the completion of the National Grid by the end of the Eleventh Plan. This would enhance the inter-regional transfer of power and facilitate the optimum utilisation of existing assets.

Power sector reforms were initiated in 1991 to encourage competition in each sub element of the sector, namely, generation, transmission and distribution under an independent and transparent regulatory regime. With this objective in mind a Central Electricity Regulatory Commission (CERC) has already been set up at the national level and State Electricity Regulatory Commissions (SERCs) set up in 19 states, 11 of which have issued tariff orders. Private sector participation has also been set in motion with the enactment of the Electricity Laws (Amendment) Act in 1998. The draft Electricity Bill, 2001 has been introduced in Parliament which will replace the existing three laws relating to electricity: the Indian Electricity Act, 1910 as amended from time to time; the Electricity (Supply) Act, 1948 as amended from time to time; and the Electricity Regulatory Commission Act, 1998.

The Electricity Bill recognises trading of power as a distinct activity and permits SERCs to allow open access in distribution of electricity in phases that would ultimately encourage efficiency and competition. These reforms have to be carried forward aggressively to improve the financial health of the SEBs. The issue of one-time settlement of dues payable by SEBs to central power utilities (CPUs) has been addressed by securitising the dues. It is likely to facilitate further reforms in the sector. Reforms in the distribution sector have been identified as the key area of reform.

The Accelerated Power Development Programme (APDP) was initiated in 2000-01 in order to give a fillip to the reform process in the power sector. One of the main strategies identified in this regard is the development of distribution plans/projects for all distribution circles as centres of excellence that can be replicated by the states in the later phase of distribution reforms. Sixty-three such circles have been taken up initially under APDP funding, which envisages metering of 11 KiloVolt (KV) feeders, improvement/strengthening of sub-transmission and distribution network, 100 per cent metering, establishment of a management information system (MIS) to improve billing, collection etc.

To ensure better utilisation of funds for reforms, an Accelerated Power Development and Reforms Programme (APDRP) has been formulated by making certain modifications in the APDP scheme. It is aimed at promoting investment for distribution reforms. The funding under APDRP is proposed to be 50 per cent on investment stream and 50 per cent on incentive stream. The focus is to ensure that investment must result in quantifiable physical and financial benefits in the selected circles.

Out of the estimated 80,000 villages yet to be electrified, the Tenth Plan proposes to electrify 62,000 villages through grid supply. The balance 18,000 remote villages are proposed to be electrified by 2011-12 through the use of decentralised nonconventional sources of energy. In order to facilitate the flow of funds, the rural electrification programme has been included as a component of the Pradhan Mantri Gramodaya Yojana (PMGY) and the states are being encouraged to pool resources from other schemes under the Minimum Need Programme (MNP) and Rural Infrastructure Development Fund (RIDF) to meet the objective of 100 per cent electrification.

A new scheme called Accelerated Rural Electrification Programme (AREP), with provision for interest subsidy, is being launched. The participation of decentralised power producers will be encouraged, especially for electrification of remote villages. Village-level organisations like panchayat raj institutions (PRIs), rural cooperatives and non-government organisations (NGOs) will play a crucial role in the rural electrification programme. Community participation is essential for success of the programme.

The restructuring of the existing renewable energy programmes towards gradual commercialisation as initiated during the Ninth Plan would be continued during the Tenth Plan period. In this context, a draft Renewable Energy Policy formulated by the Ministry of Non-Conventional Sources of Energy is under the consideration of the Cabinet. Private sector investments in renewable energy sources are to be encouraged by promoting a bidding process for available subsidies. The contracts should be awarded to private entrepreneurs who provide the maximum benefit with the lowest amount of subsidies.

Power Sector Reforms

Apart from envisaging the setting up of the CERC, the Common Minimum Plan formulated at the Chief Minister's conference in December 1996 also accepted the need for rationalisation of tariffs so that subsidised sectors like agriculture would pay at least 50 per cent of the average cost of supply within three years. The establishment of SERCs had been envisaged by the State Power Ministers' conference, also in December 1996.

Besides licensing and setting of performance norms, the CERC was expected to set tariffs for all generation and transmission utilities supplying power across several states. The SERCs were expected to discharge a similar function for state utilities. Most importantly, the regulatory bodies were expected to encourage competition, on a level playing field, in each sub sector, namely generation, transmission, distribution and supply. Such competition under an independent adequate and transparent regulatory regime was expected to yield the desired efficiency gains. Accordingly, the Electricity Regulatory Commissions Act, was passed in July 1998.

The Electricity Laws (Amendment) Act was passed in 1998 to enable private participation in the power transmission sector. The Indian Electricity Grid Code (IEGC) was established by the CERC in January 2000 to ensure grid discipline and set operation and governance parameters for individual players in the T&D sector. Trading of power has been recognised as a distinct activity that would encourage efficiency and competition. The Power Trading Corporation (PTC) was set up to facilitate inter-state trading in power. The Availability Based Tariff order notified by the CERC in January, 2000 is a step towards encouraging greater reliability and efficiency in generation.

Hundred per cent metering of 11 KV feeders have either been completed or is in the final stages of completion in Goa, Maharashtra, Gujarat, Andhra Pradesh, Karnataka, Tamil Nadu, Kerala, Lakshadweep, Haryana, Himachal Pradesh, Delhi, Uttar Pradesh, Madhya Pradesh, Rajasthan and Punjab. The Ministry of Power has signed memorandums of understanding (MoUs) with 20 states to undertake reforms in a timebound manner. These MoUs provide for timebound metering in two phases i.e. (i) metering of 11 KV feeders and (ii) all consumers. Monitoring is being done to ensure that the agreed milestones are achieved.

Measures initiated for reducing T&D losses have largely been unsatisfactory with only six states (Andhra Pradesh, Haryana, Rajasthan, Karnataka, Orissa and Uttar Pradesh) taking steps in the direction. None of the states, (except Haryana to some extent) have initiated any measures towards 100 per cent metering, billing and collection. Energy audit is also pending.

A Conference of Chief Ministers and Power Ministers was held on 3 March 2001 to discuss the challenges confronting the power sector. There was general consensus on the urgent need to depoliticise power sector reforms and speed up their implementation.

In addition to reforms in the sector, the Tenth Plan priorities include the achievement of a more optimal primary energy mix for the country. Hence the Tenth Plan proposes to raise the share of power sector investment in hydro, nuclear and renewable energy resources from the Ninth Plan levels.

Electricity Bill, 2001

The main features of the Electricity Bill, 2001 are:

— The central government is to prepare a National Electricity Policy in consultation with state governments.

— Thermal generation is to be delicensed and captive generation permitted freely. Hydro projects would, however, need the approval of the state governments and clearance from the CEA.

— The regulatory commissions may also permit open access to the distribution network in phases to promote competition and efficiency.

— Trading is recognised as a distinct activity.

The regulatory commissions are authorised to fix ceilings on trading margins, if necessary.

— Provision for payment of subsidy through budget.

— Consumer tariff should progressively reduce cross subsidies and move towards actual cost of supply.

— Thrust towards 100 per cent rural electrification, with provisions for the the management of rural distribution by panchayats, cooperative societies, NGOs, franchisees, etc.

— Provision for generation and distribution in the rural areas without licences.

— Non-conventional energy sources and stand alone systems to be freely permitted.

— SEBs to be corporatised within one year and unbundled into one or more companies through a statutory transfer of assets, liabilities and staff. However, the state governments would have the flexibility to continue with the SEBs through a notification.

— Metering to be made mandatory and 100 per cent metering of all supply is to be done within two years. Where necessary, the concerned regulatory commission may give additional time for completing the task of metering.

— Constituting of SERCs is a mandatory requirement.

— An appellate tribunal to hear appeals against the decision of the CERC and SERCs.

— Provisions relating to theft of electricity have been made more stringent.

Power Generation

The gross energy generation from power utilities at the beginning of the Ninth Plan was 394.5 billion units (BU). The Ninth Plan envisaged a gross energy generation target of 606.7 BU for the utilities in the terminal year of the Ninth Plan (2001-02). As against this, the actual energy generation has been 515.3 BU. This works out to a compound annual growth rate (CAGR) of about 5.5 per cent during the Ninth Plan period. The shortfall of 91.4

BU in 2001-02 is mainly due to the shortfall in generation capacity addition and hydro generation due to inadequate rainfall in the catchment areas of hydro power stations.

Capacity Addition

The all-India installed generating capacity of utilities at the beginning of the Ninth Plan was 84,893 MW (excluding wind capacity of 902 MW). This included 21,568 MW of hydro, 61,012 MW of thermal and 2,225 MW of nuclear power. The Ninth Plan programme envisaged a capacity addition of 40,245 MW. As against this, the actual capacity addition was 19,015 MW during the Ninth Plan. The capacity addition of 19,015 MW during the Ninth Plan represents 47 per cent of the targeted addition. In contrast, capacity addition during the Eighth Plan was 54 per cent of the target (16,422 MW against the target of 30,538 MW). The sector-wise shortfalls during the Ninth Plan were : central sector 62.2 per cent, state sector 12.1 per cent and private sector 71.2 per cent. The achievement of 19,015 MW represents an addition of 3,803 MW per annum, compared to the target of 8,049 MW per annum.

The main reasons for the shortfall in capacity addition are: inability to get private sector projects off the ground in the absence of adequate arrangements for ensuring payment security, delay in land acquisition and environmental clearances, unresolved issues relating to fuel linkages, contractual problems, resettlement and rehabilitation problems and law and order problems.

Thermal power plants

The performance of the country's thermal power plants registered an overall improvement during the Ninth Plan. The all-India average Plant Load Factor (PLF) of the thermal power plants was 64.4 per cent at the beginning of the Ninth Plan and had increased to at 69.9 per cent by the end of the Plan period. This is mainly due to a reduction in the weighted average of the generating stations, improvement in the design of the new units and better plant maintenance practices.

Power supply position

At the beginning of the Ninth Plan, it was estimated that the energy and peak deficits were 11.5 per cent and 18 per cent respectively. However, at the end of the Plan period, despite achieving only 47 per cent of the envisaged capacity addition, the energy and peak deficits were restricted to 7.5 per cent and 12.6 per cent respectively. This is mainly due to a marked improvement in PLF of the thermal plants and a lower than projected growth in demand during the Ninth Plan.

The central sector undertakings viz. the National Thermal Power Corporation (NTPC), the National Hydro Electric Power Corporation (NHPC), Nuclear Power Corporation India Ltd. (NPCIL) and North Eastern Electric Power Corporation (NEEPCO), continue to play an important role in adding new generation capacities in different parts of the country. The central sector share in the total installed generation capacity increased from 25.6 per cent at the end of the Seventh Plan to 31.52 per cent at the end of the Eighth Plan and stood at 30.1 per cent at the end of the Ninth Plan due to shortfalls in capacity addition.

Renovation, Modernisation and Life Extension

Since 1984, renovation & modernisation (R&M) has been considered the most cost-effective option to maximise generation from the existing capacity. Phase-I of the R&M programme, taken up in September 1984 for execution during the Seventh Plan, covered 163 thermal units with a total capacity of 13,570 MW at 34 selected power stations. The programme was successfully completed in 1991-92 at a total cost of Rs.1,066 crore. An average additional generation of 10,000 million units (MU)/year was achieved as against the targeted benefits of 7000 MU/year after completion of the programme.

Encouraged with the results of Phase-I of the R&M programme, Phase-II was taken up in 1990-91 for 44 thermal power stations comprising 198 units with a total capacity of 20,870 MW. The programme was estimated to cost Rs. 2,383 crore and was scheduled to be completed during the Eighth Plan. An additional generation of 7,864 MU/ year was expected on completion of the programme. However, many utilities could not implement their R&M schemes on schedule due to the non-availability of funds. As a result, by the end of the Eighth Plan, only around 50 per cent of the works could be completed, yielding an additional generation of 5,000 MU/year. The remaining R&M activities under Phase II, were taken up during the Ninth Plan period. The works for 153 thermal units are at various stages of completion.

By the end of the Ninth Plan, Life Extension Work on 28 units (with a total of 1,981 MW) is likely to be completed. The life of the units covered by the programme is likely to be extended by 12-15 years. The R&M and Life Extension Programmes face various constraints. These include:

— Non-availability of timely and adequate funds due to poor financial health of most SEBs/utilities.

— Delay in obtaining loans from the Power Finance Corporation (PFC) due to nonfulfilment of loan conditionalities.

— Procedural delays in the formulation of schemes and finalistion of orders by SEBs/ utilities.

— Reluctance on the part of the SEBs to undertake renovation and modernisation since this leads to the units going out of the system temporarily, thereby lowering generation.

R&M and Uprating of Hydro Power Stations

In the Ninth Plan, 36 hydro schemes (23 under Phase-I and 13 under Phase II), with an aggregate installed capacity of 9,001 MW, were identified for Renovation, Modernisation and Uprating (RM&U) work at an estimated cost of Rs. 917.30 crore. The RM&U programme was estimated to add 1,609 MW of capacity and enhance generation by 4,987 MU.

Of these 36 schemes, RM&U work has so far been completed on 18 hydro schemes with an aggregate installed capacity of 4,860 MW at an estimated cost of Rs. 554 crore and benefits expected to accrue are to the tune of 1,123 MW/3,350 MU. Of the remaining 18 RM&U schemes, five, with an aggregate installed capacity of 369 MW, have been declared 'closed' and work on four, with an aggregate installed capacity of 380 MW, is yet to commence. The balance nine schemes, with an aggregate installed capacity of 3,392 MW, are under various stages of implementation,

Transmission and Distribution Facilities

The major portion of the 400 KV transmission network planned to be set up during the Ninth Plan was in the central sector, while that of the 220 KV network was in the state sector. Most of the targeted additions under the transmission programme are likely to be achieved during the Ninth Plan. Capacity addition was adequate as neither the targeted generation nor the projected demand was realised.

Transmission and Distribution (T & D) Losses

T&D losses continued to remain high during the Ninth Plan. The reported all-India average T&D losses increased from 19.8 per cent in 1992-93 to 26.45 per cent in 1998-99 and is anticipated to increase to 27.8 per cent by the end of the Ninth Plan. There is a wide variation in losses reported by different states for 2000-01 (RE), ranging from 17 per cent to 56 per cent. Based on the experience of a few states that have unbundled their utilities, actual T&D losses for the country as a whole are estimated to be in the 35-45 per cent range. The high T&D losses are attributed to:-l Weak and inadequate sub-transmission and distribution systems due to haphazard growth of demand to meet the short-term objective of extension of power supply to new areas.

— Long transmission and distribution lines.

— Inappropriate size of conductors.

— Improper load management, resulting in overloading of systems.

— Pilferage and theft of energy.

— Unmetered supply.

— Financial constraints to undertake system improvement schemes.

In order to reduce T&D losses, it is necessary that various electricity supply organisations take up system studies and carry out energy audits for identification of the causes of excessive losses. Based on these studies, system improvement projects should be formulated for strengthening and revamping the distribution system, improving the MIS and addressing issues of governance.

Accelerated Generation and Supply Programme Scheme

The Accelerated Generation and Supply Programme (AG&SP) was launched in 1997-98 initially for one year and was later extended up to the end of Ninth Plan. The scheme covers the following activities:

1. R&M and life extension/rehabilitation.
2. Ongoing generation projects.
3. Missing transmission links and system improvement.
4. Grant for studies.

The Ministry of Power provides a grant from its budget to fund an interest subsidy of 4 per cent on normal lending rates of the PFC to SEBs/State Generation Corporations (SGCs). R&M schemes costing less than Rs. 100 crores are currently also being financed under APDP. It is proposed that in the Tenth Plan, all R&M schemes would be financed under AG&SP only and no financing would be made through APDP.

Programme for Central Assistance under APDP

Projects relating to the following areas are financed under the APDP, which was initiated in 2000-01 in order to give a fillip to power sector reforms:

i) R&M/life extension/uprating of old power plants (thermal and hydel).

ii) Upgradation of the sub-transmission and distribution network (below 33 KV or 66 KV) including energy accounting and metering.

One of the main strategies identified for distribution reforms is the development of distribution plans/projects for all distribution circles. Sixty-three such circles have been identified initially in which 11 KV feeders will be taken as profit centres. Improvement/strengthening of the subtransmission and distribution network, 100 per cent metering, establishing of an MIS to improve billing, collection etc. will be taken up in the selected circles. It has been decided to utilise APDP funds to develop the selected circles as centres of excellence that can be replicated by the states in the later phase of distribution reforms. Funds under APDP are released to state governments as additional Central Plan by the Ministry of Finance under advice from the Ministry Power.

An amount of Rs.1,000 crore and Rs.1,500 crore were provided under APDP during 2000-01 and 2001-02 respectively. An amount of Rs. 3,500 crore has been provided for the Annual Plan 2002-03, which is the first year of the Tenth Plan. There is a need to restructure the concept of APDP from being merely an investment window to a mechanism for supporting power sector reforms in the states, linked to the fulfilment of certain performance criteria by way of benchmarks. This is necessary to reduce the burden of transition and to ensure that the reform is sustainable and irreversible. The existing APDP may be revised to provide enhanced investment to cover all the distribution circles during the Tenth Plan and also provide for transition finance based on the financial performance of SEBs/utilities.

However, the funding and financing pattern for investment in distribution will be the same as APDP. Transition finance may be based on actual cash loss reductions effected by the SEBs/utilities, net of tariff increases given by the regulator, additional purchase of power and increase in fuel costs. In order to avail of transition assistance, states may have to conform to minimum eligibility conditions:

— The state should have set up a SERC.

— The SEB/utility should have filed its first tariff petition before the SERC.

— The SEB/utility should have achieved a minimum prescribed percentage reduction in cash losses compared to the previous year.

Financial performance of the SEBs

The financial health of the SEBs has deteriorated over the years mainly due to higher level of technical and commercial losses and subsidised sale of electricity to agricultural and domestic consumers. The net subsidy of Rs. 5,404 crore on agriculture and domestic sectors in 1991-92 was 46 per cent of Central Plan assistance flowing to states/Union Territories in that year. The same has increased substantially to Rs. 25,607 crore in 2000-01 and is likely to be 69 per cent of the funds flowing from Central Plan assistance. Further, the subsidy on account of the sale of electricity to the agricultural sector has come down from Rs. 29,461 crore in 2001-02 annual plan (AP) and is expected to come down to Rs. 26,959.30 crore for 2002-03 (AP). This may be partly due to the reform and restructuring process initiated by some of the states.

The March 2001 conference of Chief Ministers/ Power Ministers noted that the large amount of dues owed by the SEBs to central public sector undertakings (CPSUs) was a major impediment to power sector reforms. The conference resolved that an expert group should be set up to recommend a one time settlement of the past dues of SEBs to CPSUs and dues of the SEBs from CPSUs. The outstanding dues payable by SEBs to CPSUs as on September, 2001 was Rs. 41,852.63 crore including interest liability of about Rs. 16,000 crore.

The recommendations of the expert group headed by Shri. Montek Singh Ahluwalia for securitisation of dues through the issue of tax-free bonds by the respective state governments have been accepted by the Government with certain modifications. Under the arrangement, 60 per cent of the surcharge would be waived while securitising the dues. But the SEBs would have to pay the current dues in future, failing which certain steps like graded reduction in the supply of power from central power stations and in coal supplies would be taken. The SEBs should accept reform-based performance milestones such as setting up of SERCs, metering of distribution feeders and improvement in revenue realisation. The milestones should be specified in the MoU to be signed with the Ministry of Power.

Plan expenditure during the Ninth Plan

An analysis of the Plan expenditure on the basis of actuals for 1997-98, 1998-99 and 1999-2000 (for central/ state and Union Territories) and the actual/RE (2000-01) for central/state and revised estimates for 2001-02 for the central and state sector reveal the following:

Central Sector

The actual expenditure on power by the Central sector during the first four years of the Ninth Plan (1997-2001) and approved provision for 2001-02 accounted only for 83.30 per cent of the approved Ninth Plan outlay at current prices. Similarly, at constant prices, it accounts for only 69.4 per cent of the Plan outlay. The estimated domestic budgetary support (gross budgetary support minus external aid) during the Ninth Plan was Rs.14,381 crore which works out to about 98 per cent (at current price) of the approved amount of Rs. 14,380 crore. At constant prices, it works out to Rs.11,662 crore, at 81 per cent of the approved provision. The major shortfall in the central sector was due to the nonmobilisation of resources through internal resources and bonds and because four gasbased extension projects of the NTPC were not taken up.

State Sector

The Plan expenditure for the state sector during the first three years of the Ninth Plan was 53.4 per cent of outlay at current prices. The major shortfalls were in the states of Assam, Bihar, Haryana, Meghalaya, Orissa and Uttar Pradesh. The areas most affected by the shortfalls were transmission and distribution.

Approach to the Tenth Plan

According to the Sixteenth Electric Power Survey (EPS), the electricity requirement at the busbar (utilities only) in 2006-07 will be as follows: added by the private sector. Thus, the public sector will continue to play a dominant role during the Tenth Plan while progress along the reform path helps clear the roadblock for greater private participation in the medium to long term.

A major portion of this incremental capacity can materialise only during the later years of the Tenth Plan. This implies the likelihood of power shortages increasing beyond current levels during the first three years of the Tenth Plan. To overcome this, at least partially, it is imperative that all-out efforts are made to take up R&M work at existing plants aggressively and operate the power system efficiently.

The capacity addition will be contingent upon fuel linkages being firmed up and early start of work on new projects. For the new projects, particularly in the central sector, it is essential to simplify and streamline procedures for input linkages/techno-economic clearance/ investment clearance. Based on this, the cumulative generation capacity in the country by the end of 2006-07 will be as follows.

The Tenth Plan Working Group Report on Power has envisaged a capacity addition requirement of 46,939

MW during the Plan period, with 24,405 MW coming from the central sector, 12,033 MW from the state sector and 10,501 MW from the private sector. However, keeping in view the status of the ongoing, sanctioned and new projects in the pipeline, the Planning Commission felt that a target capacity addition of 41,110 MW - 18,659 MW from ongoing projects, 9,193 MW from projects cleared by the CEA and 13,258 MW from new schemes - would be more realistic. Even under this lower estimate for capacity addition, only 27,852 MW appears to be firmed up so far.

Power Supply Position

The energy and peaking shortages at the end of the Ninth Plan are 7.5 per cent and 12.6 per cent respectively. The Working Group on Power estimated that if capacity addition targets are met, the energy and peaking shortages would be 11.6 per cent and 9.5 per cent respectively by the end of the Tenth Plan. Lower capacity addition targets proposed above will raise these projected deficits unless there are significant improvements in management and plant operations.

Hydro Power Development

The share of hydel capacity in the total generating capacity of the country has declined from 34 per cent at the end of the Sixth Plan to 25 per cent at the end of the Ninth Plan. The share is likely to decline even further unless suitable corrective measures are initiated immediately. Hydel power projects, with storage facilities provide peak time support to the power system. Inadequate hydel support in some regions is adversely affecting the performance of the thermal power plants. In the western and eastern regions, peaking power is being provided by thermal plants. This is a costly and inefficient use of thermal capacity. It is proposed to add 14,393 MW capacity from hydro in the total capacity addition of 41,110 MW during the Tenth Plan period.

Geological uncertainty, contract management, resettlement & rehabilitation, delay in land acquisition and infrastructure development have been the main reasons for time and cost overruns in hydro projects. In order to avoid delays in project implementation, the following steps need to be taken before the zero date of the project implementation.

1. Bankable detailed project report (DPR), based on a detailed survey, should be prepared to avoid geological uncertainty.
2. Contract monitoring, as distinct from project monitoring, should be emphasised.
3. Land acquisition and infrastructure development should be settled and completed before the start of the project.

— Further, the following steps need to be taken in order to accelerate the pace of hydro development:

— Although the preliminary ranking study of the remaining hydro potential sites of all the basins in the country has been completed by the CEA, detailed ranking study and preparation of detailed feasibility report based on economic viability needs to be done.

— Adopt a national rehabilitation policy (supported by appropriate legislative changes and the apex court directives) and implement the policy uniformly.

— Streamline clearances for pursuing priority projects.

— Simplify approval procedures.

— Facilitate the early financial closure of projects through a concerted approach (comprising centre, states, Indian financial institutions, private sector promoters) towards multilateral agencies and other international funding sources.

Nuclear Power

Atomic energy is an important source of electric power which has environmental advantages and is also likely to be economical in the longer run. At present, nuclear energy accounts for only 2.4 per cent of total primary energy consumption, against the global average of 13 per cent. This is far too low. Nuclear power plants have shown progressive improvement in generating performance. The PLF of NPCIL stations has increased from 60 per cent in 1995-96 to 82 per cent in 2000-01. During the Ninth Plan, NPCIL completed the refurbishment and upgradation of Rajasthan Atomic Power Station(RAPS)-2 (200MWe), and commissioned Kaiga 1 & 2 (2x220MWe) and RAPS 3 and 4 (2x220 MWe). It is proposed to add 1,300 MWe of new capacity during the Tenth Plan period and 5,915 MWe during the Eleventh Plan so as to achieve about 10,000 MWe by 2011-12. The NPCIL has demonstrated the capability of setting up and operating nuclear energy power plants with high levels of technical efficiency and safety. It is desirable to plan for a significant expansion in nuclear power generation capacity. An expanded programme would also make it possible to reduce the costs of construction.

In the context of moderate uranium and vast thorium resources in India, a three-stage nuclear power programme is envisaged. This programme consists of setting up of Pressurised Heavy Water Reactors (PHWRs) in the first stage, Fast Breeder Reactors (FBRs) in the second stage and reactors based on the Uranium 233-Thorium 232 cycle in the third stage. It is also envisaged that in the first stage of the programme, capacity addition will be supplemented by electricity generation through Light Water Reactors (LWRs) initially through imports of technology with the longterm objective of indigenisation. PHWR technology was selected for the first stage, as these reactors are efficient users of natural uranium for yielding plutonium fuel required for the second stage FBR programme.

The FBRs will be fuelled by plutonium and will also recycle uranium for breeding more plutonium fuel for electricity generation. Thorium as blanket material in FBRs will produce Uranium 233 to start the third stage. An Advanced Heavy Water Reactor (AHWRs) is being developed by the Bhabha Atomic Research Centre (BARC) , Mumbai, for demonstration of technology to utilise thorium for electricity generation. AHWR will be a forerunner of reactors to be set up under the third stage of the nuclear power programme.

The first stage programme of PHWR has progressed well and the technology has reached a state of maturity. A beginning has been made in the introduction of LWRs with the intergovernmental agreement between India and the Russian Federation for co-operation in setting up of 2x1,000 MWe LWRs at Kudankulam, Tamil Nadu. A 40 MWe Fast Breeder Test Reactor (FBTR) has been set up at Kalpakkam to gain experience in the technology. This has been followed by progress in the development of technology for the first Prototype Fast Breeder Reactor (PFBR) of 500 MWe capacity, which has reached an advanced stage. Pre-project activities for commencing construction of the PFBR are in progress as is research and development on the utilisation of thorium.

Aggressive nuclear power development is essential in the context of energy security, environmental advantages and changing perceptions about nuclear power in developed countries such as the United States and the United Kingdom. Improvements in nuclear technology are likely to make nuclear power more economical and total life cycle costs more competitive in comparison to other fuels. Therefore, India needs to:

— Aggressively build capabilities and capacity in nuclear power to progressively raise its share in India's fuel mix.

— Actively promote research and development on FBRs and thorium-based technologies.

— The reactor/dome in nuclear power plant facilities is highly technical and sensitive. This should be implemented by NPCIL/ Department of Atomic Energy. Other components of nuclear power plant area like turbo generator (TG) facilities etc. should be permitted for private sector participation. The Department of Atomic Energy should decide on the components of the nuclear power plant which could be entrusted to the private sector.

— Encourage innovative financing mechanisms (infrastructure debt from financial institutions/banks, supplier credit/ equity, long term bonds, private sector equity in non-nuclear island).

— Measure NPCIL's investment and operational performance against international benchmarks.

Private Sector

The initial response of domestic and foreign investors to the policy of private participation in the power sector had been encouraging. However, many projects have encountered unforeseen delays in the finalisation of power purchase agreements, guarantees and counter-guarantees, environmental clearances, matching transmission networks and legally enforceable contracts for fuel supplies One of the most important impediments to private participation was the bankruptcy of the monopoly purchaser - the SEBs. That necessitated complex payment security mechanisms for achieving financial closure. Further, the high tariff of power from some of the commissioned independent power projects (IPPs) due to factors such as high cost of liquid fuels, risk factors involved and unrealistic forecast for future growth of demand etc. have prevented full utilisation of available capacities. With the power sector reforms already set in motion, these problems are expected to be sorted out in due course.

In addition, 18 private projects not requiring techno-economic clearance of the CEA, with a total capacity of about 2,340 MW, have been commissioned and two projects with total capacity of 36 MW are under construction.

Formation of National Grid

The National Powergrid will comprise a transmission system associated with the central generating projects and inter-regional lines. It is expected that the first phase of the National Powergrid will be completed with a 500 MW High Voltage Direct Current (HVDC) Transmission System back-to-back at Sasaram in Bihar coming up by December 2002 connecting the eastern and northern region. This will enhance the cumulative inter-regional power transfer capacity to a level of about 4,850 MW.

It is proposed that in the subsequent phase, a strong synchronous National Powergrid would be established, including schemes to evacuate the power from major generating resources, covering hydro projects in the northeastern region and large-sized thermal power plants in Bihar, Orissa and Madhya Pradesh. The transmission scheme for the ultimate National Powergrid would involve the development of a high capacity transmission corridor in the Chicken Neck area in the northeast and the establishment of a ring of 765 KV lines interconnecting the eastern, western and northern regions. With the completion of these links, the cumulative inter-regional power transfer capacity would increase to a level of about 30,000 MW by 2012.

Captive Power Generation

The industrial sector is the largest consumer of electricity. Besides purchasing power from the utilities, a number of industries, viz. aluminium, cement, fertiliser, iron, steel, paper, sugar etc. have their own captive power plants either to supplement the electricity supply from the utilities or for generating electricity as a by-product through co-generation. Captive power plants are being set up by industries to meet their own power requirements to enable them to tide over problems due to power shortages and poor quality of supply. The Electricity Bill, 2001 proposes to free captive generation and enable captive generators to sell directly to other consumers by wheeling power through the grid under an open access regime. However, the Tenth Plan capacity addition has been finalised based on the demand as per the Sixteenth Electric Power Survey that excludes the demand met by captive power plants.

In accordance with the guidelines issued by the Ministry of Power, the following categories would be eligible to install captive power plants:

(a) A consumer of electricity.

(b) A group comprising more than one consumer as a joint venture.

(c) An actual user of power but not a consumer.

(d) A group of actual users of power, but not consumers, as a joint venture.

(e) A group comprising both consumers and actual users of power as a joint venture but excluding 'Generating Company' as defined under Section 2(4A) of the Electricity (Supply) Act, 1948.

(f) If the captive plant falls under the category of hydro or co-generation plant, such plant may be permitted, irrespective of its size and the power supply position in the state.

(g) If the captive power plant is based on coal or liquid fuel or gas and if the state is deficit in power supply, the installation of the plant could normally be allowed and the plant can be permitted to have a capacity up to 200 per cent of the requirement of the host industry.

(h) If the captive power plant is based on coal, liquid fuel or gas and the state is surplus in power, the installation of such captive plants can still be considered in cases where the state/SEB cannot guarantee uninterrupted supply or stipulated quality of supply (within prescribed voltage and frequency variations) required by the industry or a particular process. Further, captive generation may also be permitted if it is found, after a review of costs and tariffs, to be more economical than grid supply.

(i) Banking facilities may also be provided to the captive plants so that available capacities are utilised to the extent possible and when required. The rates for banking may be determined on mutually agreed terms.

(j) Units in Special Economic Zones (SEZ) and industrial estates may be allowed to set up captive power plants liberally.

Rural Electrification

The rural electrification programme is one of the important components in rural development and as important as rural drinking water supply, health, nutrition, primary education, shelter and rural connectivity. The availability of power in rural areas will lead to economic development and its attendant spin-off benefits like food security, better health, literacy, etc. With this in view, the Government has been focussing on village electrification since the beginning of the planning process. While this has resulted in the electrification of around 86 per cent of the country's villages, the use of electricity in villages for productive and subsistence needs is still very limited.

About 70 per cent of the rural households are yet to get electric connections and power-based economic activities in the electrified villages are minimal. The actual benefits of the investments made in the rural electrification programme can only be realised if the people are in a position to use electricity for their day-to-day activities as well as for industrial and commercial activity. Therefore, the second phase of the rural electrification programme, apart from seeking 100 per cent electrification, must also ensure more widespread use of electricity by the rural people in a time-bound manner.

The existing definition of an electrified village has been found to be inadequate as it does not meet the requirements of the rural people. The existing definition states that 'A village will be deemed to be electrified if electricity is used in the inhabited locality within the revenue boundary of the village for any purpose whatsoever.' There is need to change this definition so as to declare a village as electrified only if a minimum number of households in that village are provided with electricity connections. According to the 1991 Census, there are 5,87,000 villages of which 5,00,000 (86 per cent) are declared to be electrified on the basis of the existing definition. Further, available data shows that only 31 per cent of the rural households are electrified. Finally, against the total estimated potential of 19.5 million electric pumpsets for irrigation, only 12 million pumpsets have been energised. The expansion of the programme of energising pumpsets needs to take into account issues like energy efficiency, water conservation, watershed management, rain water harvesting and other matters related to the optimum use of ground water and the danger of over exploiting this scarce resource.

Around 80,000 villages in the country are yet to be electrified even on the basis of the current definition of village electrification. Thirteen states have declared 100 per cent electrification of their villages. The villages yet to be electrified are mostly in Assam, Arunachal Pradesh, Bihar, Jharkhand, Madhya Pradesh, Meghalaya, Orissa, Rajasthan, Uttar Pradesh, Uttaranchal and West Bengal. Of these 80,000 villages, it may be feasible to electrify only around 62,000 through the conventional grid expansion. The balance 18,000 villages are located in remote areas, hilly terrains, islands, deserts etc. and are also thinly populated. Such villages can be electrified more economically through decentralised and non-conventional energy sources like solar, wind, small hydro and biomass. 8.2.80. The strategy and time-frame for rural electrification will be as follows:

— The Tenth Plan proposes to cover all 52,000 villages that can be electrified through grid extension. The balance 18,000 remote villages are to be electrified by 2011-12 through the use of nonconventional technologies. A survey to identify these villages is required.

— In order to facilitate the flow of funds, the Rural Electrification Programme was included as a component of the PMGY in 2001-02. Special category states are eligible to receive 90 per cent of the funds as grant and 10 per cent as loan. For other states, the funds will be made available in a grant-loan ratio of 30:70.

— In addition, the funds available under Minimum Need Programme for Rural Electrification will be pooled to meet the objective of 100 per cent electrification. 1 The funds available under Member of Parliament Local Area Development Scheme (MPLADS) and Jawahar Gram Siddhi Yojana (JGSY) should also be utilised for supplementing the funding of village electrification.

— Involvement of MPs through district-level committees in the selection and monitoring of village electrification may be made mandatory. The states would also be well advised to try and persuade MPs to provide funds under the MPLAD for extending village electrification. They could consider evolving arrangements where the provision of, say, 25 to 50 per cent of the cost of electrification of an area could ensure automatic provision of the remaining funds under PMGY.

— SEBs may receive an interest subsidy on debt raised for rural electrification through the proposed Accelerated Rural Electrification Programme. Interest subsidy would be provided for the loans to be taken by the state governments for the electrification of unelectrified villages including dalit bastis. Rural electrification could be done through conventional as well as non-conventional sources of energy.

— A suitable mechanism to disburse funds directly from the central government to states may be followed for which the states will be required to maintain a separate account so as to ensure that the funds are not diverted for purposes other than rural electrification.

— Given the positive impact of this programme on poverty alleviation it is a legitimate claimant for soft International Development Agency (IDA) funding. This should be pursued through the Department of Economic Affairs which may indicate to the World Bank the high priority that the Government gives to this programme. 1 Village electrification would also include the electrification of dalit/tribal bastis, wherever applicable.

— The Kutir Jyoti programme to extend single point light connections to rural households below the poverty line (BPL) will be revamped so that 100 per cent coverage of such households will be achieved by 2012. The norms of expenditure for rural BPL households has already been enhanced from the present Rs. 1,000 to Rs. 1,800 per household in special category states and Rs. 1,500 in other states.

— The Rural Electrification Corporation (REC) will continue to carry out system improvement and load intensification activities in electrified villages. It will finance these activities through the Rural Infrastructure Development Fund (RIDF) and issue of bonds under Section 54 EC of Income Tax Act that provides tax exemption on capital gains.

— The proposals of the states for rural electrification will be scrutinised and appraised by the REC and the present arrangement of monitoring by the REC and the CEA will be continued with the Ministry of Power acting as the central nodal ministry.

— The participation of decentralised power producers will be encouraged specially for electrification of remote villages. Villagelevel organisations like PRIs, rural cooperatives and NGOs will play a crucial role in the rural electrification programme. Community participation is essential for the success of the programme. The concept of barefoot solar engineers may be adopted.

— States which are to electrify the left-out villages are required to finalise a yearwise action plan for completing the electrification of all villages to be connected through grid during the Tenth Plan.

— Electrification of remote villages will be done through the Ministry of Non- Conventional Energy Sources in association with the Indian Renewable Energy Development Agency (IREDA), the financial institution under the Ministry.

— The Electricity Bill, 2001 contains an enabling provision in regard to decentralised generation so that cooperatives/PRIs and NGOs can also bid for and supply electricity to dispersed communities.

Sustainable Power Development

The utilisation rate of fly ash in India is of the order of 2 per cent as compared to 80 per cent in Germany followed by 20 per cent in the Netherlands. The poor rate of utilisation is attributed to the non- availability of proper machinery, ignorance regarding the potential of the use of fly ash in various applications and lack of clear policies to promote fly ash utilisation, among other things. The following steps are necessary to promote the use of fly ash:

1. Private entrepreneurs should be encouraged to set up facilities to utilise fly ash in building materials such as bricks, cement etc. To this end, state governments may exempt the end products of ash from sales tax, on the lines of the excise duty exemption given by the central

government to products having a minimum 25 per cent ash content.

2. Financial institutions may extend loans on a priority basis for the manufacture of ashbased industrial products.

3. In order to promote manufacture of flyash based Portland Pozzland Cement (FAPPC) government departments like the CPWD, DDA and power utilities should be advised to use FAPPC for a majority of applications.

4. All new thermal power stations should be advised to earmark land in the planning stage itself for ash-based industries.

Concerns relating to pollution and the disposal of the large amount of ash from coal-based power stations, which are the mainstay of India's power generation, are being addressed through strategies to promote environmentally sustainable power development. In order to undertake fruitful channelising of investment for afforestation works, the project authority should actively involve the state government and set up a specific cell with a forest officer on deputation, if need be, to monitor the implementation of afforestation work.

Energy Efficiency/Conservation

Energy efficiency and energy conservation involve all the sectors of the economy. Although energy efficiency and energy conservation have been discussed for nearly ten years now, the efforts on the ground have been fragmented and halfhearted. There has also been a lack of adequate focus on the institutional arrangements which will devise suitable incentives and disincentives appropriate to each sector, backed by adequate statutory power of enforcement.

During the Ninth Plan, it was realised that it is necessary to have an Energy Conservation Act. Accordingly, the Government has enacted the Energy Conservation Act, 2001 to meet the legal requirement needed to enforce energy efficiency and conservation measures. The Act provides for:

— The establishment of the Bureau of Energy Efficiency (BEE) in place of the existing Energy Management Centre (EMC). 1 Declaring a user or class of users of energy as a designated consumer.

— Laying down minimum energy consumption standards and labelling for identified appliances/ equipments and norms for industrial processes for energyintensive industries.

— Formulation of energy consumption codes. 1 Establishment of an Energy Conservation Fund both at the central and state levels. 1 Penalties and adjudication. No penalties would be effective during the first five years as the focus during this period would be on promotional activities and creating the infrastructure for implementing the Act.

— The BEE would facilitate the evolution of a self-regulatory system and organisations that will regulate on their own because saving energy also makes good commercial sense.

The central government has established the BEE with effect from 1 March 2002. Further, the provisions of Section 1 to 29 and Sections 46 to 62 of the Energy Conservation Act relating to this have come into force from the same date. In India, demand side management measures have a key role in eliminating power shortages to a considerable extent. Demand side management would ultimately result in saving of electricity, in keeping with the concept of energy conservation. It also has an important role in the context of safeguarding the electrical power industry. The demand for electricity fluctuates within a 24-hour cycle as well as between seasons. This has an important implication for planning generating capacities. In a developing country like India, where per capita availability of energy is very low, needbased demand for energy can be unlimited. But the supply side is limited by the lack of investible resources and the demand side is constrained by lack of purchasing power. In such a situation, it is clear that the capacity to provide additional energy is always likely to lag behind rising demand, unless the consumption of energy is also restrained.

The new approach to mitigating power shortages is based on demand side management. One of the basic reasons for energy inefficiency in India is energy pricing. Electricity rates, kept deliberately low for a large block of consumers, do not send correct price signals to consumers to alter consumption behaviour. There is, therefore, an urgent need to look into the issue of economic pricing that delivers the desired behaviour. Innovative pricing options which have proved successful in managing electricity demand in several developed and developing countries, such as time-of-day tariffs, interruptible tariffs and seasonal tariffs, should be taken up by the utilities.

Resettlement and Rehabilitation (R & R)

The setting up of large hydel and thermal plants often necessitates clearing of large tracts of land, affecting the lives of people, flora and fauna. Since displacement of people becomes unavoidable, the Government has already evolved certain compensation measures that need to be implemented rigorously. These include: (a) providing early financial compensation and settlement;

(b) resettlement of people including construction of dwellings in new areas; © providing subsidy for farming in the new areas; (d) starting special training programmes in poultry, breeding, handicrafts and cottage industries; (e) providing employment opportunities in the project; and (f) provision of education, medical and drinking water facilities.

Manpower Development

The additional manpower requirement for the power sector in the Tenth Plan has been projected to be to the tune of 1,25,000. The total manpower in the power sector is expected to reach around one million by the end of Tenth Plan. Different indices have been considered for thermal, hydro and nuclear capacity and power system to arrive at the above estimate.

The overall training load expected during the Tenth Plan is 4.37 lakh man-months per year against the available training infrastructure of only 74,000 man-months per year.

The major observations and recommendations of the Working Group on Manpower Development in 2001 are:

— The success of the process of power sector reforms requires human resource development (HRD) intervention to ensure its success. It is proposed that everybody be provided training of minimum one week per year. The level of training may be refresher/ advanced/managerial, depending on the actual need. Inductionlevel training should also be made compulsory for T&D personnel. The duration of the training could be three months for executives and one month for non-executives. Training must also be arranged for each individual on promotion/ transfer to assignments that call for performing new/different roles and working conditions.

— Backward integration of the power training programmes of National Power Training Institute (NPTI) with All India

Council of Technical Education (AICTE) approved degree/diploma courses providing relevant education should be gainfully utilised by the power sector. A full-fledged Hydro Power Training Institute, with necessary training tools including a simulator, needs to be established. Networking with the training/academic institutions like NPTI, Indian Institutes of Management (IIMs), Administrative Staff College of India (ASCI) and other reputed institutions for providing training to power sector personnel and other stakeholders is recommended. Central assistance should be provided for augmenting training facilities, procurement of simulators and diversification of existing recognised training institutes. At least 5 per cent of a power sector organisation's salary budget should be spent on training personnel.

Research and Development

Since the power sector is highly technology-intensive, technological upgradation and modernisation assume an important role, especially in realising economy in generation, T&D and efficient utilisation of electrical energy. The research and development programmes must necessarily provide inputs to future power programmes relating to both generation as well as T&D. Full advantage should be taken of the large base of existing research and development capabilities. Emphasis must be laid on solving field problems adversely affecting the production of power, creating bottlenecks in the operation of the power system and affecting the quality of power supplied.

Various areas of research and technology development in the field of hydro, thermal, nuclear and power system have been identified where R&D activities could be focused on achieving improved performance of existing facilities, optimum utilisation of resources and to keep pace with the state-of-art technologies suiting our environment and prevailing conditions. Thrust areas identified are: a) Development of Integrated Gasification

The following action points have been identified for research and development in the power sector: a) Creation of a Research and Technology Demonstration Fund for demonstration projects with the major portion as grant and the balance as long-term interest-free loan for research and demonstration of new technologies. b) Making technology transfer mandatory in the case of foreign direct investment.

The Government may consider liberalising the import of technology at par with the import of materials and capital goods. c) Encouraging the commercialisation of indigenous technology leading to their fullscale development. d) Enhancing bilateral / multilateral cooperation with developed countries for state-of-the-art technological transfer and exchange of technical experts. e) Enabling the CEA to oversee the progress and status of research and development facilities in the country. f) Networking and mapping the research and development resources, including intellectual capital.

The power sector outlay as a proportion of the total outlay by the central and state governments has been declining, the central power sector outlay as a proportion of total power sector outlay has remained in the range of 38-43 per cent in the 1991-2001 period. The share of the state sector has shown a declining trend, coming down from 27 per cent in 1991-92 to 17 per cent in 2000-01. This has been mainly on account of the drive to enhance private sector investment in the power sector since 1991-92. The states have practically stopped investing in new generation projects. The share of the central power sector in the total central sector outlay has also declined from 13 per cent to 10 per cent during the same period . Keeping in view the low level of investment by the private sector, it would be desirable, in the short term, to step up public sector investment even as efforts continue to put the SEBs back on the rails in order to attract private sector investment. The schemewise break-up for the Tenth Plan outlay in respect of Ministry of Power & Deptt. of Atomic Energy (Power) is given in the Appendix.

The roadmap for the Tenth Plan will have the following reform objectives:-l Rationalising power tariffs and making the tariff setting process transparent.

— Reflecting cost of service in the tariffs and transferring all subsidies explicitly to state budgets.

— Improving efficiency in all the three segments viz. generation, transmission and distribution, either by creating separate profit centres with full accountability within the vertically integrated structure, or unbundling SEBs into generation, transmission and distribution entities or through other models of reform depending on the choice of the state government.

— Encouraging competition and private parti cipation in each element of the electricity value chain.

— Instituting open access by separating the carriage (transmission & distribution network) from the content (power and energy) thereby enabling customers to source their requirements from the most efficient source.

— Strengthening the T&D system to reduce losses, improve metering, instituting energy audits and improving billing & collection.

— Redesigning APDP as APDRP with provision for release of funds linked to the achievement of certain parameters and benchmarks.

— Integrating captive generation (especially co-generation) into the power system. l Stepping up public funding for the sector even as steps are taken to attract private investment.

— Encouraging NTPC to take up projects through joint ventures with private promoters and the state governments.

Revenue Sources of Energy

The development model followed so far, with an excessive reliance on fossil fuel resources like coal, oil and natural gas to meet the energy requirement of the country, is not only unsustainable in the long-run, but also has an adverse impact on the environment and ecology. The increase in land, water and air pollution levels during the energy conversion process in this model has become an area of serious concern. The depleting nature of these fossil fuel resources compels the search for other alternatives. It is in this backdrop that nonconventional or renewable sources of energy have attracted global attention as a viable option to achieve the goal of sustainable development. While it may not be possible, at this stage, to substitute conventional energy sources with renewable energy sources, the latter would help in supplementing energy supply efforts.

The different renewable sources of energy include hydel power, wind power, solar power, biomass power and ocean energy etc. In addition, there is a significant potential to recycle the industrial, urban and agriculture waste to extract the energy content for useful application. This method leads to environment-friendly waste disposal and also helps to recover the energy contained in these wastes to supplement different energy supply options. Since the transport sector consumes huge quantities of hydro-carbons, alternate environment-friendly fuels such as electricity (stored in batteries), compressed natural gas (CNG) and fuel cells can be used.

The economics and other constraints faced in development of the renewable energy programmes are:

Hydel power

India is endowed with a vast and viable hydro potential for power generation of which only 17 per cent has been harnessed so far. The share of hydro power or hydro-electricity (hydel) in the country has been steadily declining from over 50 per cent in 1963 to 25 per cent in 2001-02. Based on a systematic survey carried out during the Seventh Plan, the hydro-electric potential in the country is estimated at 600 Bkwh per year as against 472.15 Bkwh per year assessed earlier. Out of the total potential available, about 30 per cent has either been developed or is being developed. Greater emphasis on hydro-electricity is important, particularly to meet the peak loads. Hydro-electricity is also a clean and renewable source of energy.

The long gestation of the hydro projects due to delays in forest and environment clearances, rehabilitation of the project-affected people, interstate disputes, construction delays in civil works etc. come in the way of accelerating hydro projects. Large hydro projects involving significant pondage have serious environmental impacts of their own that need to be evaluated and mitigated. Small hydro projects, therefore, assume importance since they do not require large pondage and have the potential to provide energy in remote and hilly areas where extension of grid systems is either not possible or is uneconomical. Small hydro projects, especially run-of-the-river projects are economically viable, environmentally benign and have relatively short gestation periods. Hydro projects with up to 25 MW station capacity are classified as small hydro projects and are being implemented by the Ministry of Non-Conventional Energy Sources.

Wind Power

The harnessing of wind power for electricity generation in recent years has been quite impressive. The country has achieved an installed capacity of 1,507 MW for electricity generation through wind power. The estimated potential in the country has been revised upwards to 45,000 MW from the 20,000 MW estimated earlier in view of the technological advances and the availability of more modern equipment. Works are in progress to assess the wind resource potential at different locations and India is fifth in the world after Germany, the United States, Denmark and Spain in terms of wind power. The participation of the private sector in this area is highly encouraging. The economic viability of wind power projects depends a great deal on the capacity factor and, therefore, very careful site selection is called for.

The unit size of wind turbine generators is also being enlarged. The unit size of machines has gone up from 55-100 KW in the first few projects to 750-1000 KW in recent projects. The productivity of the larger machines is higher than that of the smaller machines. The present capital cost of wind power projects ranges between about Rs. 4 crore to Rs. 5 crore per MW including local civil, electrical works and erection. This takes into consideration various central/state fiscal incentives available for wind power projects, which help to offset the low capacity utilisation. The life of a wind power project is estimated at about 20 years. Levelised costs over the life of the project compare quite favourably with those for new thermal power projects located away from coal mining areas, as there is no recurring cost on fuel. If environment and social benefits offered by the wind power projects are also considered, these projects would favourably compare with conventional power projects.

Solar Power

There is abundant potential of solar radiation available during most part of the year for a tropical country like India. It has been estimated that a potential of 20 MW/sq.km is available through the Solar Photo-Voltaic (SPV) route and another 35 MW/sq.km through the Solar Thermal route. There are ongoing programmes to tap this potential both for stand-alone applications and for grid connected power systems. The stand-alone applications include the installation of solar-powered street lights, domestic lights, portable solar lanterns, solar-powered water pumps and solar power packs all based on the principle of conversion of solar energy directly into electricity through SPV cells. The cost of crystalline photo-voltaic (PV) modules at the international level is in the range of $ 3-4 per watt. Despite extensive efforts, the cost of these cells and modules has not come down to commercially viable levels of below $ 1 per watt.

Other types of solar cells using amorphous silicon technology were developed with a view to bringing down the cost. However, the performance of amorphous silicon-based solar cells suffers over time. Elemental silicon continues to be the best material for PV and cost cutting is only possible with newer concepts and thin film materials. With the large scale production, the thin film PV technology could produce per watt cells at 5 per cent at 10 per cent efficiency. The future of PV technology for application as a decentralised energy source mainly depends upon the cost reduction of the PV modules. The utilisation of the SPV technology to meet the energy requirement of people living in far-flung areas for applications like lighting etc. is becoming attractive since extending conventional electricity grid to these areas is not cost effective.

The other route is to convert the heat energy contained in solar radiation to useful applications. Various types of solar thermal devices are now available in the country which include solar water heaters for industrial, commercial and domestic applications, solar cookers (both domestic and community type), solar stills, solar dryers etc. Besides, solar energy is also being used for space heating by including solar passive features in buildings and for agriculture through solar greenhouses. Work is in progress to set up solar thermal power plants by utilising the heat from the sun to produce high temperature/pressure steam to generate electricity. An integrated solar combined cycle thermal plant is being set up in Rajasthan with a capacity of 140 MW. This type of plant would make it possible to generate electricity even during nonsunshine periods with the support of a combined cycle gas plant. However, the economic viability of such plants for commercial applications is yet to be established. It is expected that these plants may become economically viable in the future on lifecycle cost basis and also on the basis of indigenous technology development. In any case, the environment-friendly nature of solar plants and the renewable fuel source would justify the setting up of such plants in the future.

Biomass power

Bio resources, such as firewood, agroresidues and animal wastes form an important component of the energy mix of a developing country like India, and account for nearly 30 per cent of the primary energy supply. These resources will continue to be used in order to meet the increasing demand for energy, though with higher end-use efficiencies. With a view to promoting efficient methods of using these energy resources the Ministry of Non-Conventional Energy Sources is implementing the National Project on Biogas Development (NPBD), National Programme on Improved Chulhas (NPIC), National Biomass Gasification Programme and Biomass Power/Co-generation Programme.

It has been estimated that the country has the potential to set up 12 million biogas plants and install 120 million improved chulhas. However, only around one-fourth of the potential has been tapped so far. It has been estimated that there is a potential to install 19,500 MW capacity through biomass conversion technologies viz. combustion, gasification, incineration, pyrolisis and also bagasse-based co-generation in sugar mills. So far only around 381 MW of this potential has been tapped. There is scope for expanding the size of these programmes as they directly benefit the majority of the rural population and help them meet their basic energy needs.

During the Tenth Plan, biomass production will assume an increasing and crucial role. Strategies for encouraging energy plantations on waste/degraded/marginal lands to feed biomassbased power projects need to be evolved. In addition, the technologies and projects for feed preparation relating to various agro residues also need to be encouraged.

Biomass offers an ideal option for rural electrification in remote areas and has been getting priority in certain areas in hilly states, islands etc. These schemes for decentralised power plants have particular relevance in the north-eastern states, Jammu and Kashmir and Sikkim.

9

Internet and Public Policy

In Internet research to date it has often been the heavy user to the light user, or those who have access compared to those who do not. For a variety of reasons, it has not often been the Internet in the United Kingdom compared to the Internet in Russia. Indeed it has not often been in matters of law and policy-matters where nation-states like Russia are important-where these research comparisons take place. Implications for policy have often ended at calls for public policy intervention (or occasionally, withdrawal), implying that the Internet is currently largely unregulated and the important decision for the state is whether or not to intervene. The task for researchers is now to understand the finer mechanisms of policy action, and this necessitates greater attention to internationally comparative research.

Internet, Social Problems and Opportunities

Even if we conceptualize law and policy related to the Internet using a more forgiving phrase such as an "area of research," a summary of this area is very difficult to imagine: much of what has been investigated has some implication for law and policy, but for this area to be considered as a whole the research needs a commonality of assumption that we have no right to ask of it. That is, to be a whole it must share central problems and theoretical foundations-even a world-view. Internet research consists of many strands. From research about the mechanics of policymaking to critiques that force a reconsideration of all existing structure, policy-relevant research is important in modern society.

Need for Policy-relevant Internet Research

While ARPANET, the famous Internet precursor, was first operational in 1969, the word "Internet" was not coined as a proper name until 1982. Social research relevant to the Internet is still in an early stage, as is our exposure to the network. Comparative research on matters of law and policy is presently underdeveloped, even in this context of newness. While it is true that social scientists stereotypically shy away from making bold conclusions, our point is more than the ritualistic call of, "further research is needed," appended to the conclusion of so many research articles. Policy-relevant research is needed now because state action in a given sector is not equally receptive to change at all times-communication policy, for example, has often been characterized by periods of intense struggle at the introduction of a new communication technology, such as the debate over the institutional structures and regulations that would govern broadcasting in the US, eventually leading to the Communications Act of 1934. These initial struggles often end in long periods of stability-it would be 62 years before majoı changes to the US 1934 act, and even then the institutional structure of broadcasting was little changed.

In telecommunications policy, by contrast, change has been much more common, but major change is rarely possible-policymaking proceeds by what Weare terms "disjointed incrementalism". Is the lesson for one who would influence policy action then: "act quickly!" That is, act during the infancy of a new communication technology? A relatively early flowering of "media effects" research in the UK and the USoccurred in the 1950s and 60s, focusing on the consequences of violent television programming for children. Some findings linked televised violence and aggression: the reports of groups like the Media Action Group of US President Johnson's National Commission on the Causes and Prevention of Violence and the later Surgeon General's Scientific Advisory Committee on Television and Social Behavior were controversial because of this suggestion, but still it was unlikely that they would have effected major policy changes in broadcasting regulation.

"Early" research in the academic community was some thirty years too late: even if the findings of these committees had been uncontroversial, this would not have changed the fact that the economic structures driving the production of television content were cemented in both industrial organization and law as early as the late 1920s. Similarly, a historical turn in academic work on broadcasting in the US in the late 1980s to mid-90s has produced a number of damning critiques of the industry's structure that are extremely relevant to public policy toward the industry. This is our paradox: the best hope for understanding communication systems may require decades of research and a historical perspective, yet it seems irresponsible to wait sixty years when this so greatly reduces the chance to contribute meaningfully to policymaking.

Past media's moral for the Internet may be that it is just when the least is known about a new communication technology that knowledge is most needed, and most influential. The early years of this century may be for the Internet structurally equivalent to the 1920s for US radio broadcasting: these are the formative years that will produce a lasting structure.

Research are Relevant

In the context of law and policy, there are two forms of research are relevant, those where public policy is present either as the object of or in the implications of a study: the first is research on policy and law itself, while the second is social scientific research on some other topic that can usefully inform public policy. Any reference to "policy research," tends to invoke the former, which sometimes goes by the name of "policy analysis" or "policy evaluation." Policy analysis is often conceptualized using the impoverished definition of evaluation; it is associated with hypotheses that take the form, "Is a particular law or policy effective?" Effectiveness is then measured by achievement of a law or regulatory program's stated goals, or an outcome's adherence to a literal reading of a statute.

Due to the assumptions hidden within the concept of effectiveness, hypotheses of this form have a tendency to beget the conclusion that, unsurprisingly, the policy in question does not function in the manner that the rhetoric surrounding it suggested that it would, or that actual experience will not fit a literal reading of the law without interpretation. In the worst examples of this tradition, researchers prove these general points over again with each study, never realizing their generality or articulating the underlying structures of rhetoric, symbolism, and interpretation. Policy analysis of this form is not our aim.

A second, richer type of research which treats policy as object rather than product is research concerning the mechanisms and processes of policymaking-for example what has been framed as the public policy specialization within political science and economics, political sociology, as well as the perhaps the very broad area claimed by many disciplines under the banner of political economy. The analytic tools developed in these traditions can be valuable to understanding law and policy about the Internet: Consider, for a moment, planning a research project in one of these traditions to study the control of the Internet's domain name system-the system that maps the name of an Internet host to an Internet Protocol address for that host.

ICANN

The 1997-1998 design of a non-profit private corporation to administer the Internet domain name system (eventually, the Internet Corporation for Assigned Names and Numbers, or ICANN) might be explained by conceptualizing Ira Magaziner, a senior policy advisor to the Clinton administration in the US, in the role of a "policy entrepreneur" who capitalized upon a "window". The policy window was the temporary prominence of unforeseen and politically unacceptable profit making by Network Solutions, Inc.-a company earlier granted a monopoly on providing this service by government contract. Magaziner took the opportunity to implement a privatization agenda. A researcher might also consider the US Department of Commerce or ICANN as "subgovernments," and the relations between actors as a subject for policy network analysis.

ICANN's results with the domain name system might be compared to an ideal model of "perfect administration". Alternately, the decisions of institutional actors in the system could be analyzed using rational choice theory or as an ecology of games. ICANN's procedures using objectivist concepts like institutional competence or we can take quite the opposite approach and critique ICANN as a ramshackle compromise, a small extension of thematic commitments to property rights and power relations made by other elements of the legal system.

There is a broad theoretical toolkit available for reasoning about policymaking within sub-disciplines that have been concerned with how public policy works. Considerable research to date can be classified solidly in the "policy as object" approach, but research on Internet-related policy has often lacked a grounding in any relevant theoretical framework. It is striking that despite the over-prominence of ICANN and Internet governance in the research to date, the above hypothetical gloss on possible research designs pays more attention to these theoretical models than most. Let us next consider policy suggestions arising from the implications of research, and then reflect on the practical effect of these two forms of research.

Policy from the Implications of Research

By "from the implications of," research ostensibly about something other than policy (technology, human behavior, market structure) that leads to conclusions-or inferences drawn from these conclusions-that have the potential to influence policy. This describes a great deal of work that never mentions the word policy. While in social research the claim is still heard that the research enterprise is essentially disinterested, creating knowledge for knowledge's sake, this position does not bear much reflection. Research is essentially a positive project-not in the sense Comte might mean but in Dewey's: knowledge is made to be used, and shaping the course of public affairs is one of the most important uses on offer. If research findings bear on matters of public policy and the researcher does not act as a policy advocate, one suspects naïveté at best.

Governments are now acting to control the Internet on a number of fronts, from the mundane to the sinister-from fiscal goals for infrastructure investment to secret political surveillance and censorship. Yet in most cases this has not happened; public debates often proceed without reference to scholarly Internet research. This may be a case of willful ignorance on the part of governments, but it may also indicate a lack in the research scholar's practical skill at engaging with political processes that are foreign to the research enterprise. Of course, situations like these arise whenever academic research intersects with matters of public concern; they are specific to Internet-related research only so far as the nascent Internet is more susceptible public interventions into its structure, as discussed above. The hope for research to facilitate positive regulatory action (or retreat) that might have long-lasting consequences makes Parker's observations, if not specific to the case of Internet-related research, at least more salient for it.

Policy as both Object and Implication

This division have been discussing involves an unfortunate separation into separate spheres of "social science" (where policy is often thought to derive from the implications of research) and "policy research" (where policy is often thought the object), which is counterproductive and explains some of the difficulty in integrating public policy into academic research. It appears to be inspired by the strange idea that people who know something about law should not be allowed to think about anything else, and by the related feeling that a social scientist who is found grubbing about with the legal and political practicalities of the present day is tarnishing a noble purity of purpose.

While it is said that policymakers and academics are notoriously prone to speak past each other (or not to speak), the marginalization of the academy in "Internet policy" in most countries is far from inevitable. It is mainly a repetition of socialized role relationships for "academics" and "policymakers." It is not just that social science holds lessons that are ignored, but also that the production of theoretically-informed research on areas relevant to the practical needs of policy requires an engagement that is often missing from Internet research.

Research Agendas

One way of formulating a research agenda for the study of the Internet is to seize the Internet as a case study for the application of problems, models and methods that are already well known. It is true that useful questions from the past deserve to be asked again in an Internet context if there is a substantive reason for asking. That is, if there is some chance of an unexpected answer, a socially problematic answer, or a hope of broadening our existing understandings of the world. It may be possible, for instance, that there are systematic biases in content available on the Internet, and that this cultivates a distorted worldview among heavy users, as has been argued in the case of television. Many of the Internet-related research projects to date are direct applications of earlier questions in this manner.

In some studies this awareness is explicit: Turkle's Life on the Screen is often cited as a landmark work in the scholarly study of the Internet; it used the Internet's emerging culture of simulation to re-approach and elaborate psychoanalytic theories of a decentered self. For example, beginning in the late 1990s a number of researchers examined the global diffusion of the Internet. There is a substantial base of existing knowledge about the diffusion of innovations and the diffusion of interactive technologies that much work in Internet diffusion made little to no attempt to build upon.

Law and Public Policy Relevant to Research

Just what public policy should Internet-related research aim to understand and affect? When one thinks of media policy-or more commonly, media regulation-the most significant legal and institutional structures that come to mind are those inherited from television, radio, and telecommunications. This idea of regulation is often ex ante: what is prohibited and what is allowed to be said on the television, how the communications regulatory agency controls participation in the market. The Internet turns this upside down, and it is this inversion that is often mistaken by the casual observer for a lack of regulation. One way of interpreting the situation at the opening of the 21st century would be to say that governments are awakening to the need to apply regulation to the Internet.

While this is commonly held to be true, it is wrong; it is a misreading of history that is overly focused on content regulation. It is not that the Internet has traditionally been less regulated than other systems of communication, but that it was regulated by different agencies in a different manner. As it is in some ways quite a different technology, this is entirely predictable. It is not the ex ante action of the broadcast license or the telephone tariff price control that is the policy instrument of note in Internet space, but the post hoc antitrust action and merger approval. Regulation has been quietly establishing the framework and structure for the Internet as a communication system, but this has escaped popular attention (with some notable exceptions like decency and cyberporn) because regulation of the Internet has not looked like the definition of "regulation" we expect, and it often occurs in obscure settings that may not even appear relevant to the Internet.

We hardly need to point out that nominally different policy sectors influence each other: even though categories like "city planning" and "environmental policy" are mostly useful formulations, they do not really represent separate boxes with no overlap between. A box for "Internet policy" is still more confusing: The Internet is a creature of communication policy, while it simultaneously is provoking a reconsideration of policy in many policy sectors ostensibly unrelated to communication. Just consideration of the Internet in terms of policy must then encompass both the Internet as a creature of law (that is, law about the Internet) but also the Internet as a force for reordering in other areas of law. When the barbed-wire fence was invented, it had dramatic consequences for both society and the law-the new fencing forced a fundamental reconsideration of property rights on the prairies of the American west, among other places.

This example is relevant because a small debate in legal circles has concerned itself with whether or not the Internet can be said to have its own law-is the Internet a technology to which one merely applies existing law, or is there in fact a new "law of the Internet,". The Internet as a technology might challenge the law and realms of social action regulated by law even setting aside laws meant to deal with the Internet. For our purposes, it does not matter if there is a discrete "cyberlaw:" the domain of inquiry deserves attention even if it is a fractured one, whether it is explicitly about the Internet or not.

Considering the Internet as a regulated creature of public policy is a multi-layered position. There are at least four broad domains in which the state is now deeply committed to Internet regulation: the state as customer, conduit regulator, content regulator, and agent of development. The state as customer. Perhaps the most obvious sense in which the network is controlled by policy is the Internet's often-cited origins in the ARPANET, a product of US defense policy during the cold war. At first blush, it is not unrealistic to consider the idea that the original design goals of a system designed for the US Pentagon might influence its subsequent development. It is tempting to see the Internet as springing directly from the 1966 US Government request for quotations for the ARPANET, but unlike the massive SAGE and Atlas defense projects that were its contemporaries, with the ARPANET, while "military needs can be discerned in the background," the network was more a research tool for advances in computing and communication than a close fit to military need.

This is not to say that early design decisions were not significant, just that they may not have been consciously military. That the workings of the Internet are published and the protocols are non-proprietary is essentially an effect of ARPAs interpretation of its obligation as a state agency dispersing public funds-that is, it required subcontractor Bolt, Beranek & Newman to release the source code for the first Internet switch. More recently, governments of the world are again acting as purchasers of new Internet technologies by mandating the Internet's use in public enterprises: education, socalled electronic government, and so forth. This role of the state retains potential to shape the development of the network in normatively significant ways; the governments are an important market (e.g., the US government is the world's largest purchaser).

The state as conduit regulator. Beyond the idea of the government as procurer of the Internet, the network is also what Hughes has termed a "second-order" system. Significant parts of it were (and are) built upon what has already been built-as an experiment in wide area networking, the ARPANET would have been prohibitively expensive unless the Internet took advantage of the existing infrastructure of the telephone system. At first this was through leased lines connecting universities and military facilities, but when with the advent of commercial dialup Internet access and then the current varieties of broadband, almost every existing electronic communication network (cable, satellite, radio, television) now forms part of the Internet. Communication policy (specifically telecommunications policy) heavily regulates the Internet whether this is explicit or not, because much of the Internet lives on top of regulated networks.

Indeed, the emergence and structure of Internet service providers (ISPs) in the different countries of the world have been almost entirely dependent on telecommunications policy action-most notably the rules for settlement. For instance, in the UK the "free ISP" model of zero-cost Internet service exists because of the telephone charges transferred to the ISP as a terminating operator, while the emergence of the ISP as a commercial entity in the US may have depended upon the Federal Communications Commission's Enhanced Service Provider (ESP) exemption which absolved ISPs of common carrier obligations. In many developing countries, the rush to telecommunications privatization during the last twenty years precisely legislated the shape of the Internet provision market by government grant-e.g., when Peru sought increased foreign direct investment into its ailing national telecom operator, the government offered the incentive of a limited-term monopoly ISP franchise to multinational investors from the developed world.

Praising the Internet as unregulated or a triumph of "unregulation" is simply dissembling. The state as content regulator. A third sense of the policy construction of the Internet involves content. It is this sense in which the popular sentiment that the Internet is unregulated (or just recently regulated) is most accurate, as until fairly recently there were no laws about what could be said on the Internet as such. Again, however, this does not mean the Internet was truly unregulated-any communication content is subject to a variety of legal obligations, and the medium of communication is not always relevant to obligation at hand. Today no law expressly prohibits making death threats by chiseling them on stone tablets; the prohibition of death threats is sufficient. The point is that while in some legal contexts the form of communication matters a great deal, this does not mean that the form always matters.

Though enforcement and jurisdiction have been seen as problematic (and they remain so), there has been no reasoned expectation that the Internet would be free from law. So far this has not been a conjectural typology: the conduit/content distinction is an old one in media regulation, and is here borrowed from Pool. Benkler conducted a survey of all public laws passed in the US that contain the word "Internet." He categorizes these laws into three types that roughly match our categories above. We can find one additional category:

The state as an agent of development. After Melody's conclusion, a fourth and important sense in which the government is invested in policy action to regulate the Internet is as an agent of development. By development, domestic and international, social and economic-usually this translates to development of the Internet itself where the stated aim is developing the network as a critical economic input or instrumental step necessary for broader economic or social development plans. Not just the state acting as procurer to provide Internet technology in the educational system, but rather the government mandating public Internet access centers or global aid projects to encourage international development via communication technologies.

While it might be said that this category is really a subset of the state acting as conduit regulator, policies involving the Internet in a development context tend to have different goals and methods than what is usually conceived as conduit regulation. It is this form of policy which sees the state as funder of the Internet infrastructure to others (such as "digital divide" policies for access to the Internet among the poor) and promoter of the Internet at home and abroad. The state is not alone in its involvement, however.

Notion of Regulation

The entire notion of "regulation" is most simply described by the phrase: delegated legislation-that is, regulatory power occurs when some part of a state's authority is granted to a subsidiary body such as a rulemaking commission. While the four categories above have dealt explicitly with state action, applying the case of the Internet to traditional understandings of regulation has been, in a way, like subjecting them to a powerful centrifuge. Authority usually vested in the state has been flung to an alphabet soup of non-state actors such as nonprofit organizations and standards bodies, some of which effectively hold plenipotentiary powers that they were never explicitly delegated to them. A few of these global bodies have captivated the attention of public policy scholars, the typology above asserts the continuing importance of state action in the context of public policy affecting the Internet.

The excitement about global governance of the network has unduly reduced consideration of government action, and inaction by some governments has been mistaken for impotence. In the four categories above, the state is far from impotent, and some states have been active. It is true that much of what is effectively regulation occurs beyond the boundaries of the state as it has traditionally been described. Recently the case of the Internet has forced legal scholars to grapple with non-legal sources of authority-perhaps more than they are used to. Still, modern legal consideration of "soft law and the Internet" or technology "as" law might be seen as an unwitting popularization of ideas developed a decade earlier in the sociology of technology, or as a continuation of the philosophical debate about the importance of technology, which has an even longer history.

Whatever the origins of this awareness, nevertheless we must be aware that substitutes for state power are now important to consider. In the case of the Internet, this awareness implies a need for greater attention to technological standards development, international nongovernmental or quasigovernmental organizations, and other "regulators" such as norms. Rather than focusing exclusively on unusual Internet-related groups, some understanding of the overall system using an integrated approach is called for.

Digital Divide

A potential social problem related to the Internet that had been addressed in this book is the *"digital divide,"* or unequal access to the Internet and information technology along several dimensions. A variety of inequalities are worrying: these include both dimensions of inequality based on race, gender, income, geography, and national citizenship, and dimensions of access, including access to equipment, connectivity, software, training, content, and facilities for content production. If unequal access to information technology tends to exacerbate existing patterns of inequality (creating a new barrier to economic opportunity for those with low incomes, for instance), some collective action to alleviate this problem seems called for.

While the academic research in this area is preliminary, there has been a rare consensus among policymakers in many nations that access to the Internet and related technology is necessary for economic growth (lately, this has been described by the phrase "digital opportunity") and that unequal access is a problem deserving of state attention. Indeed, the term "digital divide" was coined by a government agency, not university researchers . Even with a loose agreement in goals across many nations (roughly: to promote Internet penetration and use) each state has crafted a very different policy response. To mention a few of these for contrast, the US has established subsidies for telecommunications carriers to provide reduced-rate service for schools, libraries, and rural health care providers (the "e-rate").

The Brazilian government is subsidizing the development of an Internet-ready low-cost computer system called the "volkscomputer" targeted at those who cannot afford computer equipment at market prices. In South Korea, a large government training program provides a few hours of free training on how to use the Internet to populations that are thought unlikely to seek out such training on their own: housewives, the elderly, farmers, and prison inmates. In Greece, government price regulation authority has been used to mandate tariff reductions for portions of the telecommunications system thought to be the most directly related to growth in Internet infrastructure, such as leased lines. Portugal has introduced a certification program for second-hand computers to encourage the re-use of less-expensive machines. Germany has developed an Internet-skills certificate program explicitly designed for and offered free to the unemployed.

A few of the strategies mentioned here have been adopted by many countries, others are more unique. It is fairer to say that many countries have implemented a package of policy efforts in the last eight years to address a perceived "digital divide" or "digital opportunity," and while some strategies and policy mechanisms are found across many packages, no two countries have responded with the same package. In the face of this diversity of policy mechanism, the role for academic research is emphatically not to stop at a simple call for policy action. Very little is known about these mechanics of policy, about the value of particular strategies in particular contexts. Policy engagement in academic research is often understood as knowing when to advocate for or against regulation. An essential tool to investigate this question is comparative research across nations.

Policy Choice

The late political scientist Ithiel de Sola Pool wrote in 1974 that communication policy research could be best understood as "normative research about alternative ways of organizing and structuring society's communication system" . Pool thoughtfully observed that the increasing pace of innovation in the technology of communication created the research need now call "communication policy." To anthropomorphize: countries "choose" between policy options as new technologies emerge. Following Pool's view of communication policy research as the task of imagining and investigating alternative structures (or choices), where is the researcher to find these alternatives?

Admittedly, our simple framing of the problem as "policy choice" masks a great deal of complexity; in Gourevitch's words, "[t]he notion of choice implies consciousness, and the notion of policy implies coherence. Frequently in decision making we find neither". Even at the risk of gross reductionism, these policy choices-unconscious and incoherent as they may be-by examining other public policies in history and in other nations. It is not that there are no new ideas in communication law and policy, but that will interpret the plausibility of any new path by comparing and contrasting it with paths already taken. This is the task of comparative research.

A large group of law and media scholars stand firmly in the belief that conducting comparative research across countries is no different from any other kind of research. Other scholars pursue their comparisons without ever giving a thought to the possibility that crossing borders adds to the complexity of interpreting the results of the study. But some researchers are only too well aware of the many problems of doing comparative research in a world of complex interdependencies. Without becoming paralyzed by these challenges, they go ahead, opting for compromises and trying to make existing tools provide new insights. These positions but argue that in order to advance our knowledge about comparative media law research it is necessary to raise questions about distinctive characteristics of comparative studies. One can distinguish two broad methods of comparative research. The exponent of "microcomparison" analyzes law or policy belonging to the same legal family. By observing their differences, the "comparatist" will decide whether they are justified and whether an innovation made in one country would have value if introduced elsewhere.

The researcher pledged to "macrocomparison," on the other hand, investigates those systems differing most widely from each other in order to gain insight into institutions and thought processes that are foreign to him. For the "pure jurist," concerned mainly with legal technicalities, microcomparison holds the greater attraction; whereas macrocomparison is the realm of the political scientist or legal philosopher, who sees law as a social science and is interested in its role in government and the organization of a given society. Microcomparison demands no particular preparation. The specialist in one national system is usually qualified to study those of various other countries of the same general family-the chief need for this is access to bibliographical material. The situation differs greatly in consideration of macrocomparison. Here no comparison is possible without previously identifying and thoroughly mastering the fundamentals of the appropriate legal systems as they differ from place to place.

The scholar must, as it were, forget his own background and begin to reason according to new criteria. Within comparative research, both types are often present. In analyzing, for instance, regulatory responses to the changing media, both micro and macrocomparison can be used simultaneously. Microcomparison then takes first priority when a range of regulatory challenges and problems, such as data protection, competition, content control and others are examined within a specific nation and described by a country expert. Macrocomparison follows when the selected jurisdictions and their detailed descriptions are compared by the research project managers. The route to the comparison seems in general to be approached in two ways, which can roughly be defined as vertical and horizontal. Vertical comparison concerns social and legal contexts showing a very different level of economic and technological development, such as Internet penetration or take-up of digital television.

Horizontal comparison is concerned with contexts sharing a relatively similar level of economic and technological development, but largely differing in their organization of production, their political and legal regime and/or other relevant characteristics. Many comparative media law and policy research projects combine both approaches. For instance, the European Commission launched a research project in 1997 called the European Survey of Information Society. Its objective was to compare data concerning new regulatory developments in the field of telecommunications and the Information Society as well as to present a mapping of the actors building infrastructure, services and applications. In the ESIS, regions were compared from a vertical perspective, and within the regions it was obvious that for example Albania and Poland differed substantially in macrocomparative perspective. Tunisia and Morocco however were compared horizontally and using microcomparison.

North American research focuses mainly around "the Internet" or "cyberspace" for a variety of reasons (e.g., connotation, tradition, and possibly an emphasis on technologically deterministic explanation). Within Europe and internationally the term "information and communications technologies" (or "ICTs") is often used, and yet the precise meaning varies by country. Both Japan and Europe have embraced the "Information" or "Knowledge Society" as a term of substance, while in the US this connotes pretensions to grandeur. The scope and method of scholarship also differs. Research themes may largely correspond across regions, yet the approach differs widely.

The digital divide is for instance examined universally, yet in the US (where the term was coined) it has been overwhelmingly framed as "the haves vs. the have-nots" and concerns the spread of computers and Internet access through society while European research is more likely to consider a multidimensional view centered on concepts like "social exclusion". The relative weight and involvement of academic disciplines also too differs from state to state, as in the social sciences an academic discipline of the same name cannot be said to be the exactly the same animal once a national border is crossed. Within Europe the societal implications of the Internet have been more broadly analyzed within the field of Communication Studies and Computer Science, where in the US, Law and Political Science have had a major stake in Internet research so far.

The societal utility and format of Internet research also differs dramatically between nations, even when considering only fairly pragmatic Internet-related research with clear implications. In the US, Internet research is more purely a scholarly activity with a tendency to fragmentation and cyber-hype, while in contrast Europe has seen a large amount of consultancy papers preoccupied with the policy agenda of the European Union and grounded in a certain real-politik. Some of these differences can be explained by another difference: sources of funding for Internet-related work. Internet research in the United Kingdom is a function, in large part, of strategies and methodologies evolved by the Economic and Social Research Council (ESRC).

In the US, while early development of the Internet and antecedent technology was significantly funded by the federal government, today private foundations are at the forefront of understanding the social consequences of the Internet and Internet governance. As in other research areas, comparatively well-endowed US universities are also able to sponsor their scholars to take a lead in defining academic directions globally, both by providing greater time for research and by underwriting conferences.

Scholarly attention to the Internet in a country is likely to positively correlate with Internet penetration, so that the most developed countries also have an advantage in defining the academic agenda. Complicating these questions are issues relating to comparative research: research undertaken by several scholars or institutions based in different countries (as opposed to comparative research in the sense of efforts by a single scholar or group at one institution) to study the operation of Internet in a variety of national contexts. One may legitimately ask how the location of the coordinator or initiator of the research changes the focus and method of the work.

10

Rationale of Public Policy

Policymakers and the public have credited basic research with longer and healthier human lives; huge increases in agricultural production; and immense improvements in transportation, energy production, and communications. During this time, a rationale for public support of basic research became firmly established and elaborated. First, basic research is, according to the rationale, the foundation for technological development, which provides military and economic advantages to countries that are technologically advanced. Second, government support of science is necessary because the private sector, being unable to realize individual competitive advantages from basic research, has insufficient motivation to undertake it. Consequently, the government's investment in basic research is a "public good," providing the basis for national competitiveness in politics and in markets, expansion of knowledge, and continuing improvement in the quality of life.

At the same time, a different function of scientific research has emerged - science as a base of knowledge upon which to build policy. Policy's need for science has generated whole subspecialties of science, e g., toxic waste disposal. Policies on health, education, energy, the environment, etc., now require scientific findings and "risk-based decision-making." Sometimes characterized as "speaking truth to power," this function of scientific research has brought it more explicitly into the political arena. When research results can be attached to a particular political philosophy, the area of research that produced the results, and the organizations that sponsor it, can be labeled as partisan rather than objective.

Managers of publicly funded science need to understand the historical bases for government support and the root issues underlying the current debates. Science policy and trends in public funding for science have been shaped by debate about the function of science in society and the appropriate division of responsibility between the public and private sectors for directing and supporting scientific research and development. Beyond the immediate arguments about what gets funded and at what level are questions about the nature of science, the justification for government funding, and evaluating such a long-term and inherently uncertain activity.

During the Scientific Revolution in the sixteenth and seventeenth centuries, science was conceptualized as the highest intellectual calling of a scholar, with scientist-scholars taking on questions of philosophical and religious importance, trying to understand the fundamental laws of nature and society with the aim of improving people and their world. Science was defended for its intrinsic value and reflection of human intellect and spirit of inquiry, one justification that is still used. Scientists were largely self-funded, independent of government support.

Governments quickly came to see advantages in scientific advances and allied themselves with investigations that seemed influential and/or likely to result in tangible advantages of improvements in war making, political control, or market domination. "From the eighteenth century, most scientists believed not only that knowledge would increase through the support of political power, but that political power itself is tied to contributions from science". The Enlightenment fostered a close relationship between science and government, with the belief that progress in science would ensure the progress of humanity. This relationship continues today.

States have become nearly everywhere the main patrons of basic research- particularly where private benefits are low and public benefits are high. States, further, have exercised considerable control over detailed public allocations for science; defined topical research boundaries; steered private investment in science, to some extent or another; and regulated degrees of scientific interdependence with the outside world. States have relied on science and technology to secure their political, economic, and strategic viability.

In Europe, the science-government alliance was established well before the twentieth century, but in the United States laissez-faire, extending the theme of the free market, was an article of faith. Even in the latter half of the twentieth century, science-government institutions in each location differed in three important ways:

(1) U.S. bodies such as the Department of Energy's Office of Science and Technology Policy are informational and advisory only, while European institutions responsible for science policy have funds for launching research programs;

(2) the members of advisory committees in Europe are much more likely to include social scientists than are committees in the United States, reflecting a broader view of what constitutes science in Europe; and

(3) the U.S. agenda focuses on national security problems and military research, while the European agenda focuses

on civilian interests such as education, basic research, and industrial matters.

Since World War II, science policy and the principal justifications for public sponsorship of science in the United States have reflected a utilitarian definition of science, as articulated by Vannevar Bush in his enormously influential report, *Science, the Endless Frontier*. The first justification has been that science is important to national defense: excellent science before and during the war directly led to the weapon that won the war, and excellent science will keep the country in the forefront of military technology. The second justification has been that science plays a critical role in national economic growth and competitiveness: basic scientific research provides the fuel for U.S. industry to continue to grow and dominate world markets through innovation.

The original view of science as an intrinsically valuable activity and of scientists as independent intellectuals did not disappear. Vannevar Bush affirmed the need for scientific independence by writing, "Support of basic research in the public and private colleges, universities, and research institutes must leave the internal control of policy, personnel, and the method and scope of the research to the institutions themselves. This is of the utmost importance." The formulation of science that has dominated U.S. policy since World War II has been increasingly challenged by changes in the nature of science, post-Cold War globalization, the patterns of funding for research and development, and the conceptualizations of science and society held by both academics and the public.

The growth rate of support for research and development (R&D) in the United States (public and private) increased in the mid- to late 1990s, in contrast to earlier years in the decade, when increases in R&D

spending did not keep pace with inflation. However, federal R&D funding has fallen almost continuously in real terms for decades. From a high of 75 percent of all R&D funding in the United States in 1963, the federal share fell to 59 percent in 1998 (Figure 1). Funding by industry accounted for all growth in each of the three R&D categories: basic research, applied research, and development. The non-manufacturing sector led the way, driven principally by increases in funding for R&D in information technology and biotechnology.

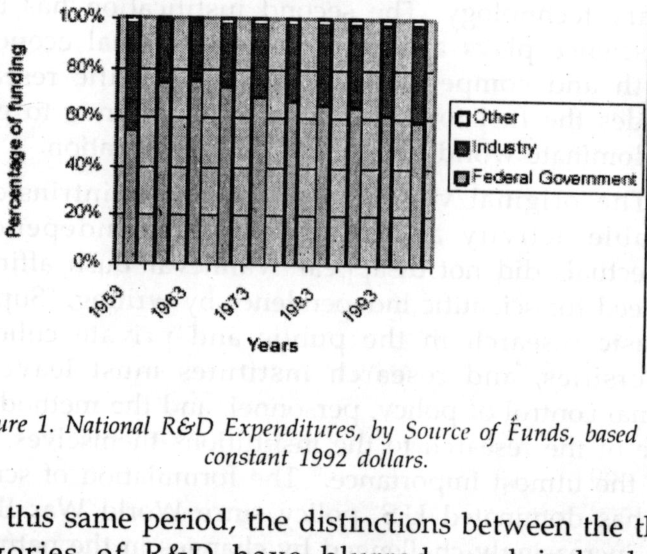

Figure 1. National R&D Expenditures, by Source of Funds, based on constant 1992 dollars.

Over this same period, the distinctions between the three categories of R&D have blurred—and indeed the distinction between research and development has faded as well. Traditionally this categorization has been based on whether the results of a particular kind of research are appropriable by individual firms. Basic research, driven by a need to understand fundamental processes, is generally classified as a "public good," that is, its results cannot be patented or otherwise used for private gain. Therefore, it has been considered appropriate for the federal government to sponsor such research. Applied research and development, from which firms can reap the competitive benefits of new products and processes, has traditionally been considered the appropriate province of industry.

Science and its Social Value

How is value, and hence "excellence," understood regarding science? Theoretical texts about the sociology of science explore alternative conceptualizations of science and its value, as well as alternative standards of excellence for science. These conceptualizations are revealed in the justifications given for the funding of scientific research and for the seeking of such funds. As mentioned above, Bush's report to the President invoked at least two conceptualizations of science and its value: (a) heroic activity and (b) the engine of military security and of progress. An examination of the following differing conceptualizations of what science is, the justifications for funding science, and the bases for evaluating science as excellent (or less than excellent) provides insight into science policy and public support issues that are affecting both science funding and science implementing organizations.

Science is often thought of as uncovering (or discovering) the general laws of the universe, the ultimate Truths about how the Earth was made and continues to function, how plants and animals live and interact, and how humans came to have a place in Earth. The fact that so many "ultimate truths" and "general laws" have been "discovered" and then discarded is, first, evidence that science has not yet discovered the Truth and laws (which, nevertheless, exist) and, second, that science is making progress toward this goal (i.e., each candidate truth or law is a successive approximation).

Many physicists and those who think of physicists when they think of scientists hold this view.

In exploring the quantum world and what happened during the first few seconds of the Big Bang, scientists think of themselves as unlocking the secrets of how the universe works. Those who hold this view think of science like religion, a highly moral quest with devoted practitioners (hierophantic or heroic scientists) who are held in some awe by nonscientists who lack the requisite training and knowledge. In this view, if scientists do "discover" how the universe works, then they are engaged in excellent science.

Since, of course, the lay persons outside science cannot judge what is a valid general law of the universe and what is not, they can either unquestioningly accept what scientists tell them (and many do) or try to judge how convincing scientific claims to truth are. The justification for providing public funding for science is a kind of faith in the heroic quest, a confidence that scientists will make discoveries as they have in the past.

Technological Progress and Economic Prosperity

Another common view is that science has made technological progress possible. For example, in this view the principles of Newtonian mechanics lie behind all the technological marvels of the Industrial Revolution. Certainly in the twentieth century, science and technology have been linked. The clear example is the tight link between advances in nuclear science, atomic weapons, and nuclear generation of electric power. Bush (and many others after him) conceived of "basic" science as a vast reservoir upon which creators of technology can draw for ideas and knowledge. Today the initialism S&T (for science and technology) is common in policy papers and journal articles; the two are thought of as a continuum.

Michael Porter believes that part of government's role in stimulating innovation is to invest in basic research as well as in educational systems and infrastructure, although he clearly states that such investment must be consciously advanced and specialized. In many cases, first the technology works, then scientific research is undertaken to find out why-or why it fails over time. Technology, then, has been a source of empirical knowledge that provides a stimulus to scientific research, which in turn may make major breakthroughs that allow technology to advance or be transformed.

The mid-1960s had seen a vociferous critique of the social consequences of unfettered technological development, ranging from the environmental damage caused by the side effects of modern science-based production processes to the use of sophisticated electronics in the war in Vietnam. There was a backlash against even the peacetime uses of science, which was equated to its destructive products: DDT, Agent Orange, nuclear weapons and radioactive materials, and other deleterious and deadly things spawned by scientists who are characterized as black magicians. This view is represented today by the Living Simply movement and by many environmentalists, who see many of the products of science as inhuman, destructive, and unnecessary.

A less absolutist variant of this definition characterizes science as neither good nor evil in itself, but needing to be under the control of moral persons and open to scrutiny by citizens or their accountable representatives. Science, is not necessarily good for us. Medical cures may seem wonderful, but treatments themselves can cause severe problems, including the prolongation of life. Products may be at the same time convenient and the cause of toxic wastes.

Moreover, scientific inputs into policy often clash with government's attempts to manage scientific activities, with the result that scientific endeavors are fragmented; resulting policy is also fragmented or unclear. In such a situation, policy fails to guide science with, perhaps, the "unforeseen and incalculable consequences of technical failure". In both these views, science must be environmentally and socially responsible as well as reflexive and self-limiting. To be excellent, science would have a moral dimension.

Another conceptualization of science revolves around the actual practice of science, from the craftwork of scientists in laboratories to the scientific communities in which scientists debate and form a consensus about what should be recognized as scientific knowledge and theory. Two elements are necessary for scientific craftwork, (1) a community of scholars with common standards and commitment and (2) individuals with high personal integrity. The process of developing truth in a scientific inquiry depends in the highest degree on specialized training and knowledge, with judgment a critical component.

The objects of inquiry are intellectual constructs (not natural things), studied as problems for which the questions may change during the course of the investigation - or even prove to be unanswerable. Furthermore, scientific methods are mostly informal and tacit, and the craft knowledge of the scientist must guide the selection and transformation of the research result through the publication process. The standards of the craft (e.g., how an experiment is set up or a research study is designed), how well scientist-researchers adhere to them, the ethical conduct of scientists in collaboration and peer review, and the judgment of peers all determine the excellence of the science. In this sense, excellence is a name for science that other scientists judge to be highly original and significant to advancing research within that scientific community. This reflects an emphasis on the methods of knowledge creation (laboratory work, instrumentation, peer review, usefulness by other scientists) rather than a focus on the ends of science (discoveries and technology), although the judgment is still significantly based on the "significance" of the discovery or development (theory, method, empirical evidence).

The construction and maintenance of science as a social category depends upon scientists' abilities to convince public and policymakers that science is a unique endeavor that is somehow useful to them. Excellent science might then be noted by metaphorical explanations that are most persuasive to scientists within scientific communities and their patrons in funding organizations and the public.

Especially for its champions, science is often presented unproblematically in terms of one conceptualization or another - or as two or more at once. In U.S. politics, the idea of science as the engine of technological dominance - military and industrial - has been invoked again and again to justify both no-strings funding for scientific research and the need to provide scientific advice to the President and Congress. The conceptualization of science as the fount of technological progress has often been joined to that of science as the search for disinterested truth. Science, the Endless Frontier links these two concepts. The first is evident in the statement that "without scientific progress no amount of achievement in other directions can insure [sic] our health, prosperity, and security as a nation in the modern world".

Vannevar Bush cites the products of science: radar, penicillin, full employment from new products and industries, and agricultural advances. Far from controlling or planning science, Bush recommends that scientists be enlisted to advise the government and that laws and regulations be revised to encourage industry to increase R&D activities. In fact, men of science form, as it were, an organized army labouring on behalf of the whole nation, and generally under its direction and at its expense, to augment the stock of such knowledge as may serve to promote industrial enterprise, to adorn life, to improve political and social relations, and to further the moral development of individual citizens.

In other words, science should be supported for the sake of increasing the human store of knowledge in the most general way - but the government, by pathways that cannot be foreseen, may expect to reap some very practical benefits also. The influence of Bush's report to the President has been enormous, not only in defining science as the source from which technology can be drawn, but also in setting up a linear model of how science leads to technology. The linear model starts with the concept of science as the quest for truth. This is "basic" research, which "is performed without thought of practical ends. It results in general knowledge and an understanding of nature and its laws".

Basic science seeks truth, "new knowledge" developed in "the purest realms of science". The linear model proceeds with government support of basic research, which will strengthen industrial research, which in turn will produce technologies. The distinction between basic and applied science and the development of many technologies from scientific results suggests a linear model of technological change. This model is a more detailed stage representation of the life cycle typology invention, innovation, and diffusion discussed previously. The states of this model are as follows:

— Basic research produces new scientific knowledge (discoveries)

— Applied research leads to proposed applications (patents)

— Further applied research and development refines this knowledge sufficiently to justify substantial investments in new technology (development)

— Investments are made in new production facilities, equipment, and specific products (innovation)

— Experience leads to improvements and adaptation in early applications (early commercialization)

— Widespread commercialization leads to new levels of technical standards, economic performance, and productivity.

Such impacts lead to scientific research and new information on causes of and possible solutions to adverse impacts. Following these steps in the order just presented represents and science or technology "push" view of technological change. Were we to follow essentially the same steps but in reverse order, we would have a "demand pull" view of technological change. Both are extreme perspectives. The first views technology development as driven exclusively by opportunities; the second views it as driven exclusively by needs.

Both linear models have been largely dismissed in the literature in favor of models with multiple feedbacks and various factors driving different phases of a technology's life cycle. In early phases science/technology push factors may dominate, whereas in later phases demand pull factors may be more important. There is a subtle tension underlying the dual quest-for-truth and engine-of-progress justifications. Scientists should be intellectually free to pursue the research that they judge to be needed (using scientific criteria), while at the same time funders should trust that the scientific results that emerge from scientist-directed research will strengthen the nation's defense capability and economic dominance.

The counter position, also underpinned by a conceptualization of science, is that excellent science could improve the health and well-being of mankind, but that scientists cannot be trusted to make the right decisions about the ends (or the means) of their science, and that defense capability and economic growth are not self-evident goods. All of these issues revolve around the relationship of science to government and of both to the rest of American citizens.

However, the reality is that scientists, like other people, do things for their own purposes: professional development, status, and competition, as well as the excitement of discovery. In contrast, sociological theories of science demonstrate that the practice and knowledge of science are inherently social and rhetorical. The largely tacit and informal social processes by which scientists formulate hypotheses and theories, design methods and specialized instrumentation, and maintain a rich social matrix of mentoring and evaluating other scientists and their work.

Universities provided research and teaching of scientists; in return, they received public funding and institutional autonomy. Industry developed applications of science in its laboratories so that the United States would remain dominant; in return, the government filled the gaps between university and industry research in such areas as defense, energy, public health, and standards.

Today the boundaries and roles of these institutions are becoming unclear. Government is becoming more like industry with the shift from defense to competitiveness and quality of life issues and with privatization of public utilities. Universities, too, are becoming more industrial, performing objective-driven research and becoming more accountable for its "products". These changes in the parties to the old social contract signal the need to radically revise the old contract.

So there is a shift from valorizing "reliable" knowledge to valuing "socially robust" knowledge. Society is now speaking back to science, transforming it by demanding that the boundaries of review, formerly limited to disciplinary peers be extended to other stakeholders. Gibbons calls this process "contextualization." Scientific knowledge must be validated by both scientific and lay experts. For example, various groups, including ordinary consumers, are demanding voices in the debates about genetically modified organisms.

As a consequence, the sites of problem formulation and negotiation have moved from funding and research institutions to the "agora," the public space where science and scientists interact with government and industry funders, consumers, interest groups, and the media. In short, the new contract between science and society "will be based upon the joint production of knowledge by society and science.

Bibliography

Birkland, Thomas A. *An Introduction to the Policy Process: Theories, Concepts, and Models of Public Policy Making*. Armonk, NY: M.E. Sharpe, 2001.

Braun, Dietmar, ed. *Public Policy and Federalism*. Aldershot, England: Ashgate, 2000. JC355 .P835 2000

Cooper, Terry L. *Handbook of Administrative Ethics*. New York: Marcel Dekker, Inc., 2001. JK468.E7 H36 2001

Dresany, Dennis L. *Public Policy Management and Public Policy*. New York: Longman, 1999. JF1601 .D7 1999

Gargan, John J. *Handbook of Local Government Administration*. New York: Marcel Dekker, 1997. REF JS11141 .H35 1997

Golembiewski, Robert T. *Practical Public Management*. New York: Marcel Dekker, 1995. REF JF1351 .G623 1995

Henry, Nicholas. *Public Administration and Public Affairs*. Upper Saddle River, NJ: Prentice Hall, 1999. JF1351 .H45 1999

Ho, Lok Sang. *Principles of Public Policy Practice*. Boston: Kluwer Academic Publishers, 2001. JF1351 .H59 2001

Klingner, Donald E. and John Nalbandian. *Public Personnel Management: Contexts and Strategies*. Upper Saddle River, NJ: Prentice Hall, 1998.

Miller, Gerald J. and Marcia L. Whicker. *Handbook of Research Methods in Public Administration*. New York: Marcel Dekker, 1999. JF1338.A2 H34 1999

Rabin, Jack and James S. Bowman, eds. *Politics and Administration*: Woodrow Wilson and American Public Administration. New York: Marcel Dekker, 1984. REF JK411 .P83 1984

Rosenbloom, David H. and Richard D. Swartz, eds. *Handbook of Regulation and Administrative Law*. New York: Marcel Dekker, Inc. 1994.

Van Horn, Carl E., Donald C. Baumer, William T. Gormley Jr. *Politics and Public Policy*. Washington DC: CQ Press, 2001. JK468.P64 V35 2001

Index